THE ESCORIAL

HENRY KAMEN

THE ESCORIAL
Art and Power in the Renaissance

YALE UNIVERSITY PRESS
NEW HAVEN AND LONDON

For information about this and other Yale University Press publications, please contact:
U.S. Office: sales.press@yale.edu   www.yalebooks.com
Europe Office: sales@yaleup.co.uk   www.yaleup.co.uk

Set in Janson Text by IDSUK (DataConnection) Ltd.
Printed in Great Britain by TJ International Ltd, Padstow, Cornwall

Library of Congress Cataloging-in-Publication Data

Kamen, Henry.
   The Escorial: art and power in the Renaissance/Henry Kamen.
      p. cm.
   Includes bibliographical references.
   ISBN 978-0-300-16244-8 (cloth: alk. paper)
   1.   San Lorenzo del Escorial (Spain)—History—16th century.
2.   Renaissance—Spain—San Lorenzo del Escorial. 3.   Philip II, King of Spain, 1527–1598. 4.   Monasteries—Spain—San Lorenzo del Escorial—History—16th century. 5.   Palaces—Spain—San Lorenzo del Escorial—History—16th century. 6.   Historic buildings—Spain—San Lorenzo del Escorial. 7.   San Lorenzo del Escorial (Spain)—Buildings, structures, etc. 8.   Art and society—Spain—San Lorenzo del Escorial—History—16th century. 9.   Architecture and society—Spain—San Lorenzo del Escorial—History—16th century. 10.   Power (Social sciences)—Spain—San Lorenzo del Escorial—History—16th century. I. Title.
   DP402.E8K36 2010
   946'.41—dc22
                                                                      2009039201

A catalogue record for this book is available from the British Library.

10 9 8 7 6 5 4 3 2 1

Published with assistance from the foundation established in memory of Oliver Baty Cunningham of the Class of 1917, Yale College.

By this mighty monument it may be inferred that Philip the Second, though he was a little man, yet he had vast gigantic thoughts in him, to leave such a huge pile for posterity to gaze upon and admire in his memory.

James Howell (1623)

CONTENTS

ILLUSTRATIONS

Unless otherwise acknowledged pictures are from the picture archive of Espasa Libros, S.L.U. in Madrid.

CHRONOLOGY

1561	Philip II and Jeronimites agree on founding of monastery
1562	Plan for Escorial by Juan Bautista; clearing of terrain begins
1563	Juan de Herrera appointed assistant to Juan Bautista
23 Apr. 1563	Foundation stone of monastery laid
Dec. 1563	Closing session of Council of Trent
Apr. 1567	Philip II issues Letter of Foundation of monastery
May 1567	Juan Bautista dies, Juan de Herrera takes over
1573	Beginning of translation to the basilica of the royal dead
1576	Philip II names Arias Montano first librarian of the Escorial
1584	Italian painters contracted to decorate Hall of Battles
13 Sept. 1584	Formal laying of last stone of the monastery of the Escorial
1586	Consecration of the basilica
1595	Dedication of the basilica
13 Sept. 1598	Philip II dies in the Escorial
1605	Death of José de Sigüenza, historian of the Escorial
1617–54	Philip III and Philip IV construct the Pantheon
1671	Fire, caused by lightning, destroys part of Escorial and library
1684	Consecration of altar of Sagrada Forma donated by Charles II
1692–4	Luca Giordano paints staircase of monastery
Mar. 1836	Suppression of monasteries in Spain, including the Escorial
Dec. 1936	Massacre of the monks of the Escorial by Republican authorities

PREFACE

Few buildings have played so central a role in Spain's history as the monastery-palace of San Lorenzo del Escorial. Constructed in the era of Spain's imperial greatness, from the very beginning it challenged and provoked. Protests were raised against its excessive cost, its isolation, its privileges. The king who built it also received a considerable share of the invective. Commentators of a later generation considered his creation to be a symbol of superstition and oppression. The critics dominated public opinion, and their voices drowned out the few who claimed the monument was a 'wonder of the world'. The argument has continued into our own times. For some, the building encapsulates the faith and power of an historic past. By contrast, some decades ago *Time* magazine rated the Escorial a 'symbol of the change-resisting spirit of Spain', 'a bulwark impregnable to the new doctrines, in which Throne and Religion can take shelter confident that not one single idea of those which are stirring up the world will penetrate within'.[1] The looming vastness of the great monastery-palace led the magazine to dub it a 'dogma shaped in stone'.

Perhaps uniquely among the buildings of early modern Europe, the Escorial seems to challenge us with its Sphinx-like immobility. It raises questions to which there appear to be no simple answers. Why was it built? Was there something mysterious behind its construction? What was it meant to express? What did it wish to achieve? The answers offered are always grounds for disagreement, though there is no disagreement about the magnificence of the achievement. The theme continues to be inexhaustible, with many claiming that the building guards hidden secrets waiting to be revealed. A scholar has affirmed that the Escorial is 'a message waiting to be decoded'.[2] That may be true, but what is the likely message, and where is the code?[3] Thousands of words have been published on how the building should be explained and interpreted; yet no such controversy arises over how we should visualise Hampton Court, Versailles or Sanssouci, palaces built in the same pre-industrial epoch of history. Why, of all the royal monuments created in Europe in early modern times, does the Escorial alone seem to need 'explaining'?

Nearly all queries about the Escorial bring our attention back to the motives and intentions of the man who created it, Philip II. The building, a historian of today suggests, 'effectively epitomized the man and his times'. This echoes the view of a nineteenth-century monk from the monastery, José de Quevedo, who stated: 'it is a faithful reflection of the Spanish nation and of the monarch who ruled over it'. But can we really read in the imposing lines of the Escorial the reality of the king and the period in which he lived? The present book questions this assumption. Identifying a man with a building and a building with a man is not necessarily a reliable procedure and does not always make sense of the basic facts. One has to agree with the opinion of the writer Unamuno (incidentally, no admirer of the king), who felt that 'nearly all who visit the Escorial go with blinkers, and political and religious prejudices. They go in search of the shadow of Philip II, a man little known and even less understood, and if they do not find it they invent it.'[4]

In English, there are some masterly studies of the art and architecture of the Escorial, but few surveys of how it came into being. These pages attempt to penetrate some aspects of the enigma of the building by examining the role of its creator. At almost every point, the visitor today tends to be presented with an Escorial that is interpreted in a sense bearing little relation to the intentions of its founder. Studies have claimed that in building the palace Philip II intended to vaunt his military victories, construct a pantheon for his family, raise a monument to his own power, proclaim the triumphs of the faith, imitate the Temple of Jerusalem, and shut himself up in a gloomy anchorite's cell. In reality, as we shall argue by looking closely at the available evidence, little of this is true. Nor did the king's efforts necessarily reflect the soul of Spain alone. The Escorial was a building in which peninsular rock and timber were worked by the sweat of Spanish labourers, but it was also inspired by European experiences, constructed and decorated by men of international vision; it is a hillside eyrie where the sounds of the chase and of folk music mingled with the chants of friars, where the gallop of Arabian horses was complemented by the trumpeting of Indian elephants.

For the relatively brief attention given here to art and architecture, I am inevitably enormously indebted to the many scholars who, particularly in the past fifty years, have explored the nooks and crannies of the ever-intriguing monastery-palace; my book could not have taken shape without my reliance on their assiduous researches. However, art history is in my account secondary to an examination of the role of Philip II. As I pointed out in my 1997 biography of the king, Philip spent fully eight years of his early life in northern Europe (principally in Germany, the Netherlands and England), an extended Rhodes Scholarship from which no other monarch of his time benefited. They were eight years that formed him as a statesman and aesthete, and are the fundamental basis of any attempt to understand his cultural activity in Spain. This work, then, is neither an artistic profile of the Escorial nor a tourist's guide to its rooms and corridors, but something rather different, an essay on the relationship between the building, its creator and the time in which they existed. Some themes are omitted, others touched on only briefly, and I have attempted not to repeat excessively information that is easily found elsewhere. If I have escaped errors in my presentation, the credit is in part due to the excellent revision of my text by Yale's copy-editor, Lucy Isenberg.

At several points, I have drawn substantially on relevant material presented in my 1997 biography, so that this book is in some sense a continuation of that one. Readers should note that I use the form 'San Lorenzo' generally to refer to the monastery building (which Philip II and other of his contemporaries referred to as 'San Lorenzo del Escorial'),[5] in order to distinguish it from the village of El Escorial.

Lake Oconee, Georgia, 2009

CHAPTER 1

GENESIS

The Fortunate Journey; An interlude in Germany; The young king of England

In the entire history of Spain, nothing like it had ever before been attempted.[1] The great and magnificent cathedrals that towered over the cities had been raised up slowly, generation after generation and with stubborn fortitude, by clergy and believers who had the patience to wait and hope. Clergy likewise had helped painstakingly to construct the ambitious religious houses secluded in the countryside, as at Guadalupe in Extremadura, or seated defiantly on peaks as at Montserrat in Catalonia. These edifices were the fulfilment of the dreams of medieval religious orders, the militant arm of the Catholic Church in western Europe. After that age of building, there came a time of repose. The nobility, whose ambitions were restricted to the ambit of their local territories, and whose vision did not encompass the building of enduring structures to the glory of God, managed occasionally to construct substantial castles, but they were intended to exclude enemies rather than to attract visitors. Outside Spain, from the fourteenth century newer ideas about how to build were beginning to develop, but they bore no fruit in the peninsula. Even at the end of the fifteenth century, when an ambitious union of peninsular monarchies took place, the new rulers – Ferdinand of Aragon and Isabella of Castile – took no interest in constructing either cathedrals or palaces.[2]

The appearance of the Escorial in the middle of the sixteenth century was therefore, for Spain, an event without precedent. Moreover, it was unique because it was inspired neither by the aspirations of the clergy nor by the ambitions of the nobility. Unlike other great historic buildings in Europe it was conceived in the mind of one man, with whom it would remain imperishably associated. Every detail of its construction can be traced back to the lifetime of his accumulated experience.

Born in 1527, prince Philip was sixteen years old when his father the emperor Charles V left for Germany and appointed him regent of Spain.[3] With effective power in nearly all areas of decision-making, Philip was now the real ruler. Thirty years later he had no doubts in dating the fact: 'I began to govern in the year 1543.'[4] By that date, he had travelled around a good part of the country, and seen much of its art and architecture. He was obviously acquainted with the royal residences, particularly the hunting estates of central Castile, and knew most of the principal towns in the centre of the peninsula. A fresh dimension was added to his experience when from May to December 1542 he made the first lengthy journey of his political career, a royal visit (in the company of his father) through Navarre, Aragon, Catalonia and Valencia to swear fidelity to the constitutions of those realms. By the time he took over power in 1543, he had a close personal knowledge of most of his kingdom apart from the southern – Islamic – part, which had been conquered from its Muslim rulers barely a half century before. The absence of contact with the south, which he eventually visited only in 1570, undoubtedly had an important effect on his subsequent cultural tastes.

Those tastes, as it turned out, were destined to be European rather than derived from the south of the peninsula. Over the next twenty years, his preferences came to be based in great measure on what he learned during his travels through the continent. European critics in later generations would write him off as a typical Spaniard (they cultivated a special, inevitably unfavourable, vision of what a Spaniard was like).[5] Philip may have evolved into one, but ironically in the peninsula he was continually criticised – right down to today – for not being enough of a Spaniard.[6] Charles V, who feared the prince was in danger of being too limited in his upbringing, made an effort to instil into his son a European perception of things. Four years after the prince had assumed power in Spain, in the spring of 1547, he was summoned north by the emperor at a time when great changes had taken place in European politics. In 1546 the German Protestant leader Martin Luther died. Then early in 1547 Henry VIII of England passed away, to be followed a month later by Francis I of France. It became urgent to prepare Philip for the new scenario in European politics. Fortunately, the times had become more peaceful.[7] Charles's victory over the German Lutheran princes at the battle of Mühlberg in April 1547 restored some tranquillity to central Europe and it was now safe for the prince to travel abroad. Plans were made to bring him to visit Germany, and in Augsburg Charles gave instructions to the duke of Alba to return to Spain and accompany the prince back to the north.

In February 1548, Philip summoned the Cortes of Castile to Valladolid and informed them of his impending departure, but they did not welcome his message. Castilians had already lived nearly six years without their king; now they were losing their prince as well. They petitioned Philip not to leave the realm, and sent a letter of protest to Charles. Preparations went ahead regardless. In September Charles' nephew the archduke Maximilian,[8] who was due to exercise the regency during Philip's absence, arrived from Vienna with his retinue. A marriage negotiated some time previously between him and Philip's sister María took place two days after his arrival. The wedding duly celebrated, at daybreak on 2 October Philip's party set out from Valladolid for Barcelona.

The royal party was a large and distinguished group which included the chief nobles (among them Alba) as well as clergy, administrators and Philip's personal staff, among them Gonzalo Pérez as secretary, Honorat Juan as tutor and Cristóbal Calvete de Estrella as chronicler.[9] Foreigners in the entourage included the German cardinal of Trent, who accompanied Philip during the entire journey. The prince was also accompanied by his musicians, among them his guitar teacher Luis Narváez and the blind composer Antonio de Cabezón. The prince's steward, Vicente Alvarez, went along to supervise food arrangements, and in his spare time kept a journal of the whole trip. The group left Barcelona on 18 October and headed north for the port of Rosas, from which they eventually set sail aboard a fleet of fifty-eight galleys commanded by the great Genoese admiral, Prince Andrea Doria, on 2 November.[10]

THE FORTUNATE JOURNEY

The prince's trip – termed in Calvete's revealing chronicle a 'Felicísimo Viaje' or 'Fortunate Journey' – would turn out to last three years, and had a more profound impact on him and on Spain's subsequent history than anyone could have imagined. Some writers have tended to downplay its relevance in their accounts of Philip's reign because it interferes with the standard image of a narrow-minded Spaniard who, they suggest, refused to learn from other peoples, maintained a closed mind in both politics and religion, hated women and entertainment and, above all, detested travelling abroad. Happily, not a single aspect of this image proves to be true. Philip's character emerges clearly from the available sources, because the journey of 1548–51 was closely documented by the prince's own companions, and by Philip himself in his letters. The royal personage who went abroad in 1548 turns out, the sources confirm, to be an open-minded young man eager to learn. And among the information he picked up were the first clear influences that would play a part in the building of the Escorial. Instead of putting together a travelogue of his movements, we would be better served to try and pinpoint episodes that contributed to the genesis of the monastery.

The first such episodes centre on northern Italy. Philip's excitement at his first sea voyage shines through in his letters.[11] Landfall was made at Savona (northern Italy), where he participated whole-heartedly in festivities – dancing and tournaments put on for him by the wealthy Spinola family, powerful allies of Spain. The voyage ended on 25 November, when the entire fleet sailed into the harbour at Genoa. Philip was for sixteen days the guest of Prince Andrea Doria at his palace outside the city. The party left Genoa on 11 December, a day of cold and snow. They took the route through Alessandria and Pavia, and in each town did a bit of sight seeing and admired the fortifications. During these weeks, Philip's attention seems to have been concentrated on military architecture and on the landscaped gardens which Italian princes were beginning to construct. In Genoa the new Palazzo Doria-Principe, where he was lodged, reflected the style, splendour and ornamentation on which European nobles were lavishing their money. The development of gardens, in particular, was a Renaissance innovation as yet unknown in Spain, and the terraced orchards of the Granarolo hill to the north of the palace would have excited the curiosity of the prince.

A few days later, on 19 December, the royal group approached Milan, where they were met by the duke of Savoy, Carlo III, who accompanied them into the city. Philip himself had the title of duke of Milan (by gift of his father)[12] and was therefore ruler of the territory. He entered to a suitably triumphant welcome. The stay, which lasted nearly three weeks, was taken up with tours, feasts, banquets, tourneys, theatre visits and balls. Philip took part personally, as always, in the jousts. On New Year's Day the governor, Ferrante Gonzaga, put on a great feast followed by dancing. However, the stay was not all gallantry. Philip visited the principal buildings of the city and took time off to have his first meeting with his father's preferred painter, the great artist Titian, from whom he commissioned several portraits.[13] He also made contact for the first time with the sculptor Leone Leoni, who joined the royal party and travelled with the prince to the Netherlands.[14] It was the beginning of one of the most fruitful artistic collaborations, and one that proved to be of crucial significance for the Escorial. Among the colleagues of Leoni who attached themselves to the young prince was the sculptor and medallist Jacopo da Trezzo, who also went to the Netherlands in Philip's service.

The next relevant episodes concern the prince's first contact with the international Catholic Church. The travellers resumed their journey from Milan in the first week of January, on a route that took them through Cremona and then Mantua (a four-day stop, as guests of the duke of Ferrara). From here, they began an ascent up the mountainous valley of the River Adige. They then crossed out of Italy proper, into the territory of the Holy Roman Empire, and on the 24th of the month they arrived at the city of Trent where Philip was welcomed by the cardinals of Trent and Augsburg, and by Charles V's ally the young Protestant elector of Saxony, Maurice.[15] Triumphal arches decked the streets. Trent was a centre of world attention because of the church council which should have been in session there. In 1547, however, the prelates convening for the council had been instructed by the pope to move temporarily to Bologna, because of an outbreak of plague in Trent. Only those prelates dependent on Charles V – the Germans and Spaniards – disobeyed the pope and stayed on at Trent. It was this small group which now took part in welcoming the prince of Spain.

Philip had talks with his bishops on the theme of reform, which was one of his policy concerns (see Chapter 8). He also had time for leisure. Every night there was a banquet. On the first night, 'the dinner was joyous and very German because everyone drank a lot; it ended at ten and then the celebrations began'.[16] The next two nights, a Friday and a Saturday, the prince dined alone. It was a self-discipline which the prince had practised for many years, and which he continued for the rest of his life. From our perspective, it can be seen as a highly significant habit, for it showed that Philip had for some time cultivated austerity, contemplation and solitude, but was capable of combining the virtues with decidedly vigorous social activity. Twenty years later an ambassador reported that he was still following the practice of two nights of retreat per week.[17] The apparent solitude that would eventually mark his existence in the Escorial was evidently something he practised all his adult life, but it was never deemed to exclude normal social obligations. In those early years, he successfully combined in his character the roles of monk and gallant. The last of the five nights which the party spent in Trent took the form of a masked ball that lasted almost till, dawn. The prince, Elector Maurice and the other nobles wore masks. So general was the gaiety that the cardinals of Trent and Augsburg also danced with the ladies.[18]

The journey to northern Europe lasted a full six months, an extended pleasure tour that also aimed to be educative. As the party went north, they were preparing for the cold and snows of the Alps. Philip's companions noted the well-being of the people in the Tyrol, the wayside crucifixes, the beauty of the women, the gradual disappearance of vineyards. On 3 February they made their way up to the Brenner Pass, and then descended towards Innsbruck, which they entered on the 4th. From this point, the cardinal of Trent acted as Philip's translator into German (the prince normally used Latin if Spanish did not serve). After a rest at Innsbruck, where Philip spent a whole day hunting in the woods, the entire group embarked in boats and sailed down the River Inn as far as Rosenheim. It was a relaxing journey, which they broke every night in order to sleep ashore. From Rosenheim they pressed on overland, spending the night at the abbey of Ebersberg. On 13 February the party arrived at Munich, where they were greeted by duke Albrecht V of Bavaria and his family. The beauty of the town, its little houses and clean streets, immediately impressed the Spaniards. There were banquets nearly every night. On the second day, they went hunting in the woods round Munich and enjoyed a lavish picnic in the country. Bavaria was the German territory of which Philip always retained the most pleasant memories. The months he eventually spent there were vitally important to the formation of his ideas.

Philip came from a part of Europe where neither the kings nor the great lords and prelates had dedicated themselves to constructing massive palaces or laying out opulent gardens. Apart from a few fortresses built long ago for defence against the Moors, sixteenth-century Spain was singularly lacking in princely architecture.[19] As Philip travelled through southern Germany and the Rhineland, his keen eye and photographic memory would certainly have preserved images of the impressive castles, monasteries and gardens he visited. The trip opened his eyes and imagination, preparing him for the wonders he was yet to discover in the Netherlands.

Two days after leaving Munich the party, which since Trent also included Maurice of Saxony, entered Augsburg. It was 21 February. Now, for the first time, Philip learned what it was like to live among 'heretics', since the area was largely Lutheran. It did not affect his conduct. His father had for decades given support, though reluctantly, to a policy of coexistence with Lutherans, and had just approved an imperial decree of toleration (the Interim of 1548). Philip accepted it without protest, and at least for the next ten years continued to allow that toleration for political reasons might be acceptable if it could not be avoided. Those who tend to view him as a religious zealot would certainly be puzzled by his conduct in Germany, above all because Maurice of Saxony, his close companion during the journey, was an active Lutheran and leading ally of the emperor. Moreover, Augsburg, in which Philip now spent four days, was a partly Protestant city. The prince took the opportunity to visit the sumptuous palace of the Fugger family, financiers who had enriched themselves by lending money to his father. One day after their departure from Augsburg, Elector Maurice took his leave in order to return to Saxony. The next important stop for the travellers was Ulm. Philip was now travelling through the solidly Lutheran territory of Württemberg. They made their way north, towards the Rhine. At Vaihingen they were met by the Grand Master of the Teutonic Knights, the Lutheran duke Albert of Hohenzollern, with a military escort that accompanied them as far as Speyer. It was not yet in Europe a period when religious differences between princes could provoke conflict. Indeed, Philip's ability to coexist with the German Lutheran princes was certainly the reason why many Europeans – among them Cardinal Pole of England (see Chapter 3) – looked upon him as a possible successor to his father's peace-seeking policies.

The royal party reached Heidelberg, capital of the Rhine Palatinate, on 7 March. The beautiful city, set on a hill overlooking the woods of the River Neckar, was at this time a Catholic area surrounded by Lutheran states. Philip spent four days here, in the magnificent castle surrounded by some of the most impressive gardens of any palace in Europe.[20] On the second day, he went out hunting in the mountains and picnicked in the woods. On the third, there was jousting in the castle courtyard, followed that night by a ball and a banquet. As at the other feasts along the route, the prince took pains to follow German drinking habits. There was a series of toasts, and each time he dutifully raised his glass and drank the wine, but 'that was hazardous, for His Highness was not used to these practices'.[21] Philip could not have been happier. He wrote from Heidelberg to Ferrante Gonzaga, governor of Milan, that 'I have been very well received by all these princes and cities of Germany, with great demonstrations of affection'.[22] He made no reference to matters of religious affiliation. The group left on the 11th and arrived in the evening at Speyer, on the Rhine. Here they were met by a Netherlands military escort under the command of the duke of Aerschot, and by the archbishop of Mainz, who came downriver to greet the prince. They then struck out westwards, instead of going down the valley of the Rhine. Passing through Kaiserslautern and Saarbrücken, they arrived in Luxembourg late on 21 March. Philip spent only one day in the town, his time taken up with inspecting the walls and defences. The prince was passionately interested in military fortifications and had inspected the defences of every city through which they passed. He was now on home ground, in the states of the Netherlands over which his father ruled. The party spent the last three days of March in Namur.

Towards nightfall on 1 April, the prince made a formal entrance into Brussels. The streets were brilliantly decked and illuminated; there were arches everywhere and torches in the windows. Over fifty thousand people, a witness estimated with evident exaggeration, were gathered in the city centre to greet him.[23] Philip made his way to the royal palace, where he was duly received by Mary of Hungary, sister of the emperor and regent of the Netherlands, and by her sister Leonor, the queen of France.[24] The queens accompanied him to a room where the emperor was waiting to receive him. The two embraced. Philip had not seen his father for six years.

For the first three and a half months of his stay, Philip remained in Brussels, in part because of the emperor's health. In February 1549 the French ambassador had reported from Brussels that Charles had 'tired eyes, a pale mouth, face more dead than alive, his speech weak, his breath short, his back bowed'.[25] All the same, he managed to make his son's visit agreeable: 'During all this period there were fine celebrations, banquets, dances, elegant masked balls, hunting parties and tournaments.'[26] But Philip could not avoid work. The emperor made him come 'every day for two or three hours to his study to instruct him person to person'.[27] On 12 July Charles set out with his son on a state tour, which had as its purpose the swearing-in of the prince of Spain as heir to each province. Charles intended that Philip should get to know his future northern subjects. For the next few months the cities vied with each other in the sumptuousness of their triumphal arches and celebrations, feting the royal party which included the households of the emperor, the prince, Mary of Hungary and the leading nobility. The journey was undertaken in two phases. In July and August 1549 the party toured the southern provinces and returned afterwards to Brussels. Then in September and October they went round the northern provinces. As on the trip through Germany, there was much to wonder at and admire.

The crucial core of visual memories was provided by the castles and gardens Philip visited. The highlight of the first part of the tour was the entertainment put on by Mary of Hungary for her guests in the last week of August 1549 at her palace in Binche. Mary had converted the old chateau into one of the most spectacular Renaissance palaces of northern Europe, and his stay there left an indelible impression on Philip. His suite of rooms was richly furnished and decorated in a way that he was later to imitate in his palaces in Spain. The little chapel contained a painting, *The Descent from the Cross*, by Roger van der Weyden which the prince so admired that he later (in 1574) acquired it for the Escorial; prior to that, in 1569, he commissioned a copy from the Flemish artist Michel Coxcie. On 24 August a great tourney was mounted in the palace courtyard, with the prince participating. Over the next two days the queen staged a superb feast based on the popular book of chivalry, the *Amadis of Gaul*. The knights, one of whom was Philip, had to overcome several obstacles in order to gain entrance to the Dark Tower, liberate its prisoners and afterwards make it safely to the Fortunate Isles. On the 29th the guests went out for celebrations and a tournament to Mary's nearby chateau at Mariemont. The next day at Binche there was another tourney, at which sixty knights took part. Years later, at his residences in Valsaín and the Escorial, Philip was unfailing in his adherence to the rites of chivalry which he had first encountered in the Netherlands at Mary of Hungary's castle. After nine days at Binche, Philip continued his tour, this time northwards.[28]

On 11 September, the prince made a formal entry into Antwerp, the commercial metropolis of northern Europe, where he was accorded the privilege of a magnificent Joyous Entry, as the ceremonial was called. Unfortunately, a heavy downpour dampened the occasion.[29] The visitors were particularly impressed by the opulence of the city, 'which could with good reason be called the market-place of the world'. The Spaniards also paid special attention to Rotterdam, which they visited on 27 September. It was the birthplace of the humanist Erasmus, doyen of Europe's intellectuals. Philip, who had studied the works of Erasmus with his tutor at a time when the thinker enjoyed a particularly high standing in Spain, specially went to mass at the church near Erasmus's family home, and 'the leading lords and gentlemen of the court' went inside the house to pay homage.[30]

The long and tiring tour ended with Philip's return to Brussels on 26 October. He had seen every corner of the seventeen provinces, and been sworn in as heir in every principal city. He now took a rest from travel, and turned to other matters. He consulted with the emperor over plans for a reunion of members of the Habsburg family; he wrote to Spain to congratulate his sister María on the birth of her first child, and in passing urged Maximilian to come to Germany for the reunion.[31] The feasts, the hunts, the tourneys, the balls, would start again.

AN INTERLUDE IN GERMANY

On 31 May Philip left with the emperor for Augsburg, where they were due to assist at the Imperial Diet. They passed through Maastricht and arrived on 8 June at Aachen, where the prince admired the quantity of saints' relics in the cathedral and visited the tomb of the emperor Charlemagne. On the 10th they reached Cologne, where they stayed four days. The Spaniards were dazzled by the large, beautiful and prosperous city, 'the splendid country-side along the Rhine',[32] and by the green cornfields stretching into the distance.[33] The visitors eagerly snapped up samples of the vast quantity of religious relics offered for sale in the city.

So greatly was the prince impressed by the quality of the relics that thereafter he always had recourse to the German market when seeking to augment his collections. 'Tomorrow,' he wrote to Maximilian on 12 June, 'I shall be at the German hunts which are the best anywhere. I would very much like Your Highness's company in them.'[34] The travellers left Cologne and arrived at Bonn the same day, the 14th. At this point they changed their mode of transport. In Bonn a small fleet of riverboats awaited them and the emperor and Philip were allotted a large, spacious vessel. The convoy, which left Bonn on the 15th, spent the next four days sailing in summer sunshine up through the spectacular gorges of the River Rhine. The emperor relaxed on deck, enjoying the breeze and dictating his memoirs (in French) to his secretaries.[35] Each night they slept on land, enjoying the hospitality and festivities. In this way they reached Mainz, where the emperor and Philip stayed as guests of the archbishop.

The rest of the journey was overland. Leaving Mainz on 21 June, they headed south towards Worms and Speyer. After three days in Speyer, they retraced the route Philip knew well from his previous trip. On 8 July 1550 they finally entered their objective, the imperial city of Augsburg. The Imperial Diet (the parliament of German princes and cities) had been summoned there by the emperor, and delegates were already assembling, though sessions did not commence until the last week of the month. The emperor was concerned to obtain the Diet's help against a threatened invasion by the Turks up the Danube, but for their part, most delegates were more interested in clarifying the religious situation in Germany. Philip was able to observe at first hand the comings and goings among Protestant and Catholic princes. It was an atmosphere that benefited from the freedom of religion laid down by Charles's Interim of 1548.

Philip spent an entire year in southern Germany. It was one of the most formative periods in his life, but curiously in later years he referred to it only in passing, and never at length. He attempted to get on with the young German nobles, whose manners he found brutish. 'Our prince is doing his best,' it was reported of him. 'He often goes out to join in their sports, and is to take part in a tourney next Thursday.'[36] Philip seems to have found living in his host country for an extended period rather different from the casual festive pleasures he had got used to during his travels. If his views coincided in any way with those of his steward, Vicente Álvarez, he probably found the Germans excessively restless, given to violence, drink and new-fangled ideas. In contrast to the constant conflicts in Germany, Spain seemed an oasis of tranquillity.[37] Apart from social pleasures the prince busied himself with art. In September, he was writing to the Spanish ambassador in Venice to make sure that Titian was coming to Augsburg: the artist should come 'as soon as possible'.[38] When Titian arrived, Philip gave him one of his most important commissions, for a series of mythological paintings known as the 'Poésies'. In Augsburg the artist completed what became Philip's favourite portrait of himself (he kept it in his study in Castile), in armour with his hand resting on a helmet. The portrait is now in the Prado. He had time also for architecture. In the same weeks he went over plans, drawn up by an Italian engineer sent by Ferrante Gonzaga, to rebuild the fortress in the Italian city of Siena,[39] then the centre of a bitter political dispute.

It is difficult to exaggerate the importance in the formation of the young prince of those peaceful months of the summer and autumn of 1550. The long stay in Germany, about which we regrettably have little information, had a direct bearing on Philip's subsequent plans for the Escorial, since it was in Augsburg that he discovered the riches of the famous Fugger library, the largest private collection of its time, housed in the Fugger mansion. During his visit, the head of the family and patron of the library was Johann Jakob Fugger, owner of a rich collection of some 10,000 manuscripts and books, 'primarily of intellectual and aesthetic interest, with precious manuscripts, a remarkably complete set of works of the Greeks, the Romans, Patristic texts, and works of humanist scholarship'.[40] In Augsburg also, the prince allowed himself the luxury of ordering a suit of armour of the finest workmanship. As an enthusiast of medieval tourneys, which had been his main pastime in Castile from at least the year 1544, he benefited in the Empire from the services of some of the most famous armourers in Europe (see Chapter 6).

Philip's ideas on politics and religion indubitably had a part in the way he eventually conceived the Escorial, and it is relevant to consider how his attitude in these matters developed in Germany. For Charles the next most pressing item on the agenda after the Diet was a reunion of the Habsburg family. It was a key moment in the experience of the prince, who perhaps for the first time came to understand the enormous international political relevance of his family connections. Charles hoped eventually to leave his inheritance entire to Philip, but to do so he needed the support of the other members of his family. This, he found, was extremely difficult – indeed impossible – to obtain. The chief members of the Habsburg clan gathered in the city, where for six long months they debate the issues. Charles had over the years consolidated control of the hereditary Habsburg lands – mainly Austria and Bohemia – in the hands of his brother Ferdinand. Strongly supported by most German opinion, Ferdinand wished the succession, and the imperial crown, to pass to his eldest son Maximilian, king of Bohemia and currently standing in as ruler of Spain during Philip's absence. Only a German, the cardinal of Augsburg declared in November, could rule Germany. The princes would prefer the Turk to Philip, reported an ambassador.[41] Ferdinand insisted to his brother that Maximilian be brought from Spain to express his views. Mary of

Hungary came especially from Brussels in September to lend support to Charles. The discussions (conducted in French, with only Philip using Spanish) seemed for a while to calm down, and Mary returned to the Netherlands after a fortnight. But Maximilian arrived from Spain in early December, and insisted firmly on his rights. The Diet closed in mid-February 1551, but the family dispute went on.

When it became clear that full agreement was impossible, Charles decided to impose a settlement. A diktat was drafted for him on 9 March 1551 by Antoine Perrenot, bishop of Arras,[42] and signed by all parties. The documents[43] declared that the imperial crown would pass to Philip after going first to Ferdinand; after Philip it would pass to Maximilian. The family accepted this, but as time would tell Ferdinand had little intention of honouring the agreement. Maximilian, who had long disagreed with Charles over many matters, was even less inclined to cooperate. Philip with the passage of time (see Chapter 6) decided that it was not advisable for him to insist on his father's wishes, and he informally abandoned all claims to the imperial dignity. It was not the least of the many issues on which his views came to diverge from those of Charles. The most notable divergence, which also took several years to mature, was over religion.

During the months in Augsburg, the prince accompanied the emperor to sessions of the Diet, and gave his support to Charles's religious policies. At the conclusion of the Diet, Charles guaranteed respect for the Lutheran faith in Germany, and referred outstanding religious disputes to the judgment of the council of Trent. Neither then nor later did Philip express disagreement with this decision. Indeed, the close accord on the matter with his father gave many people at the time the impression that Philip supported unhesitatingly the policy of compromise as a method of accommodating the differing views among Christians. When the Spaniard Felipe de la Torre (Chapter 4, below) dedicated a book to Philip in 1556, he specifically saluted him as the continuer of his father's irenic policies. It is indeed likely that Philip accepted the possibility of religious coexistence, so long as dissidents in the Diet could guarantee their political loyalty. His entire demeanour proves it. During more than two years in the Empire, he had spent much time in the intimate company of Lutherans; he had attended dinners and balls with them, jousted shoulder to shoulder with them and gone on excursions in their company. The religious difference had never bothered him, nor should it have. In this early period of the Reformation, the nobles in Germany, the Netherlands, France and England continued to treat each other with respect even if they differed in belief. All the Lutherans of his acquaintance were, at the time, allies of the emperor. If their political loyalty could be preserved, the religious question could in time be resolved. Religious war and rebellion were not as yet, in European politics, the order of the day. Well into the 1560s, at precisely the time that he was mulling over plans for the Escorial, Philip was still no supporter of intransigence in matters of religion.

In May 1551 the prince prepared to leave Germany for Spain. On the afternoon of the 25th, Charles left Augsburg for a brief visit to Munich. That same evening, Philip too left the city with a small escort that included the duke of Savoy.[44] Among the entourage was a Flemish violinist, Frans Massi, who had in his care (on the orders of the emperor) a five-year-old child who was kept in anonymity as a mere court page but was destined later to play an important role in the career of the unsuspecting Philip, as Don Juan of Austria. A separate group, which included Maximilian, went by a different route. Philip's party made leisurely progress through the beautiful mountain valleys of southern Bavaria, following the traditional route that has today evolved into a main road for vehicular traffic. That first night the group slept in the town of Landsberg; on the 26th they found lodgings in Schongau; on the 27th they were put up in the villages of Ammergau (the upper village, Oberammergau, has since become famous for its annual theatre performance of the Passion of Holy Week). Since the next day, the 28th, was 'the feast of God'[45] – more familiar to us as Corpus Christi – the prince decided to make a stop and celebrate the religious holiday tranquilly.

No document appears to be available to confirm it, but on Corpus Christi Philip would certainly have attended mass at the nearby Benedictine abbey of Ettal, three miles down the road. It was the principal religious house of the region, and the logical place for the royal party to visit for worship. Constructed in Late Gothic style by duke Ludwig IV of Bavaria (who was also at the time Holy Roman Emperor) and completed in 1370, the abbey went through various subsequent changes of appearance. In 1744 both the abbey and its church were damaged by fire, and later rebuilt in the Italian Baroque style they currently display. The impressive dome, similar to the type of structure that later became common during the Italian Renaissance, remains the most remarkable feature of the building, and probably existed in a comparable version when Philip passed through the region. Domes were known in late medieval church buildings in Germany, and increased in popularity during the Baroque period.[46]

Unfortunately, there seem to be no surviving images of what exactly Ettal looked like in the mid-sixteenth century, shortly before it passed from the Benedictine order to the Jesuits. There were similarly imposing houses in Castile, most notably the monastery, tended by friars of the Jeronimite order, at Guadalupe in Extremadura. But Ettal was different. The astonishing extant visual evidence leaves little room for doubt. Cradled in the slope of the hills, surrounded by green woods that set off to perfection the glistening dome enclosed within a huge patio marked on three sides by storeys of continuous windows stretching into the background, Ettal was spectacular. In the bright spring sunshine, set amid the green grass of the valley and framed against the magnificent background of the Alps, the abbey could hardly have failed to impress the travellers. Four years later, when Philip first made the conscious decision to construct a monastery of his own, his mind's eye must have conjured up the unforgettable image he first saw that day in the forested mountains of Bavaria. After mass at Ettal, the group returned to spend the night at Ammergau, then resumed their journey southwards, reaching Mittenwald on 29 May and Innsbruck very late on the following day.[47]

The next stage of his journey was no less decisive for Philip and for our understanding of the Escorial. He wrote from Innsbruck, where he spent three days, to tell his father that he was well. Shortly after, in the evening of 6 June, the travellers arrived at Trent. With the pope's encouragement, the famous council had now overcome its previous internal differences. A new, second, session had just begun, on 1 May, with a full complement of delegates. The council entered on its most significant phase, with the full backing of both the prince and the emperor. There were surprising developments, most notably permission for Protestant delegates to be present, some of them sponsored by Maurice of Saxony. The right of Protestants to attend the council was firmly defended by the emperor's officials, most notably by the Spaniards Francisco de Vargas and Francisco de Toledo.[48] When Catholic historians of a later day wrote about the council, most of them managed carefully to avoid referring to the role of Vargas and Toledo, which seemed to them to be shameful. However, even at the time there were many Christians, both Catholic and Protestant, who felt that the differences were less important than what both groups had in common. Philip, it is fair to note, was not one of them. Whilst he was always courteous to Protestants, as he had been throughout his months in Germany and as he would continue during his stay in England four years later, he never favoured concessions to them.

The meetings of the council received the close attention of the prince, who exchanged views with archbishop Guerrero of Granada, leader of the Spanish delegation. During the sessions, Philip got to know the theologian Fray Alfonso de Castro, whom he appointed a few years later as his confessor. He also met the Dominican priest Bartolomé Carranza, whom he appointed as a court chaplain when the latter returned to Valladolid in 1553. At dawn on 9 June Philip left Trent. In subsequent months, he continued to maintain an active interest in the Spanish contribution to the council, though overall policy towards it was decided directly by his father. His two visits to Trent made a profound impression on him. They were certainly unique, for he stood out as the only ruler of Spain ever to attend a council of the universal Church, and the only European prince ever to honour Trent with his presence. The visits help to explain why throughout his long reign he retained a deeply personal identification with Trent (see Chapter 8) and with the cause of religious reform.

Philip's party made its way across Lombardy, spent a couple of days in Mantua, then arrived in Milan. The governor, Ferrante Gonzaga, welcomed them and took Philip on yet another guided tour of the military fortifications. 'The prince', reported his chronicler, 'stayed in Milan four days, during which he visited the castle and the city fortifications.'[49] Perhaps also during this stay, if he had not done so earlier, the prince went to see the Ospedale Maggiore, an imposing work of architecture that had been constructed a century earlier and seems to have played an important part in the ideas he would eventually have about the Escorial (see Chapter 2). From here, the royal group passed through Padua and arrived on 1 July at Genoa, where Maximilian and his party joined them. On 6 July the entire royal party set sail in a huge fleet under the command of Andrea Doria. The complement of thirty-eight galleys included Doria's vessels as well as the galleys of Naples under García de Toledo and those of Spain under Bernardino de Mendoza. They put ashore briefly at Nice, then sailed for the port of Barcelona, which they entered on 12 July 1551. Philip wrote off to the duke of Savoy to say that he had had 'the most perfect voyage that one could wish for'.[50]

Some time later a Venetian ambassador dismissed Philip's entire tour as a disaster. The prince's demeanour, he suggested, was 'little liked by the Italians, disliked by the Flemings and hated by the Germans'.[51] The anti-Spanish stance of the ambassador was later taken up enthusiastically by Protestant historians anxious to demonstrate that Philip had always been a failure, but it does not coincide with what really happened. Within the limits of what the prince might have expected from the long trip, there is no reason to take a pessimistic view. He and his Spanish courtiers undoubtedly looked on it as a success. Philip may have made errors, but he learnt an enormous amount and expanded his horizons in every direction. The experience he gained cannot be exaggerated. Indeed, modern scholars are in no doubt that 'the future Philip II shaped his artistic tastes during the years that he travelled through Italy, Flanders and

Germany'.[52] When we begin to focus on the multiplicity of ideas that eventually came to fruition in the building of the Escorial, it becomes clear that the prince's first great journey abroad played a crucial part in their development. His travels were the genesis of his creativity as a king.

THE YOUNG KING OF ENGLAND

Philip's second great journey lay only three years ahead, making it possible for us to assume a real continuity between the two periods of travel. On his return to Valladolid in the autumn of 1551, he gave immediate attention to family matters. These normally took precedence over all other concerns, played a profound role in his career as ruler and turned out to be fundamental to his decision to build the Escorial. The week after his arrival, he went to Tordesillas to pay the customary visit to his grandmother, Queen Juana the Mad. The visits were a painful duty. Juana did not always recognise those who came to see her. For years she had refused to attend mass, or go to confession or communion. She identified all her attendants as devils. Her conversation seemed normal until, suddenly, she would say something that showed she was not in her right mind.[53] After the visit, he went on to stay with his sister Juana at her palace in Toro, 'where I think I shall relax for a week or ten days before going to work in Madrid'.[54] In fact he remained most of the month at Toro. During his stay he put on a tourney at Torrelobatón, in which two groups, each with sixty knights, jousted against each other.[55] The entertainment went on for two whole weeks in late September[56] and he would repeat the exercise from time to time in later years. The Renaissance cult of chivalry, which was virtually unknown in Spain but which Philip did his best to cultivate, was one of his most passionate interests. It was reflected in his collections of weapons and armour, and above all in his reading. Despite the excitement of the jousting, Philip felt drained. He had returned home only to be immediately separated from his sister María, to whom he had always felt particularly close but who of necessity accompanied her husband Maximilian, the king of Bohemia, back to

Prague. After the tourney, Philip wrote to Maximilian from Medina del Campo, 'I felt so depressed that I left at once. . . . Today I left Toro, feeling absolutely alone.'[57]

The rest of the year was spent alternating between Madrid and Aranjuez. Philip passed the Christmas of 1551 at Toro. The day after New Year he wrote to Maximilian: 'I came here for the feasts and after them I shall return to Madrid. Before that, my sister will be married.'[58] His youngest sister Juana, sixteen years old and strikingly attractive, was due to marry prince João of Portugal. About to lose her as well, Philip made sure he could spend the maximum amount of time in her company. 'At Easter I'm going to Toro', he wrote in April.[59] The prince's correspondence in these months confirms the intimacy among members of the royal family. All his life, Philip yearned for the closeness of family relationships, but political reality dictated otherwise and insuperable distances habitually separated him from his loved ones.

By 1553 the desperately poor health of the emperor took priority over other business. Charles was determined to abdicate, and wished the act to take place in his home country of the Netherlands. It now became more important than ever to resolve the marriage issue. Philip had been married in 1543 to the princess of Portugal, Maria, who, in giving birth to a son, Carlos, on 8 July 1545 suffered a serious haemorrhage that led to her death four days later. She was just over seventeen. A proposal that Philip marry again, to another princess of Portugal, fell through in favour of a far more tempting possibility. In July 1553 the young king Edward VI of England died and the succession to the still largely Catholic country fell on his elder sister Mary. Here was a heaven-sent opportunity to create an Anglo-imperial alliance against France. Many years earlier Charles himself had been briefly betrothed to Mary, and now proposed that she marry Philip.

The prince accepted the marriage with Mary as a purely political move. He was not enthusiastic about it, but deferred to his father's wish absolutely. His consent was given even before he received a portrait of her (now in the Prado), executed by the Flemish artist Antonis Mor. In 1553 Philip was twenty-six years old, eleven years her junior, and had been unmarried for eight years. The marriage contract, dated 12 January 1554, attempted to allay English fears. Philip would share responsibilities and titles with Mary, conform to all English laws and customs, admit no foreigners to office in England, and not involve England in the wars of his other realms. If Mary predeceased him, he would relinquish his powers. Eventually, on 2 April, Parliament approved the marriage. Arrangements were made to leave as regent in Spain Philip's younger sister Juana, whose husband the prince of Portugal had died on 2 January, three weeks after she gave birth to a son, Sebastian. The Cortes of Castile assembled in Valladolid under her presidency, while Philip and his entourage left the city on 16 May.

The royal fleet sailed from Coruña in the afternoon of 13 July, and a week later was met off the Isle of Wight by armed vessels from England, under Lord Howard of Effingham. They entered Southampton in the afternoon of 20 July, where the prince rested a couple of days before proceeding to Winchester. He entered the city on the 23rd with a numerous company, and 'riding on a faire white horse in a rich coate embroidered with gold, with a white fether in his hat'.[60] He was received at the cathedral by the bishop, Stephen Gardiner, and escorted to meet Mary. He spoke in Spanish to her, she spoke French (the daughter of a Spaniard, Mary understood Spanish but did not speak it well).[61] The marriage took place, with appropriate splendour, in Winchester Cathedral on 25 July, feast-day of St James, patron saint of Spain.[62] The day after the wedding, Philip was up at 7 a.m. and despatched business (for Flanders and Italy) until 11 a.m. In a personal letter to Juana, Philip reported that some days after the marriage 'we came to London where I was received with demonstrations of affection and general contentment'. The royal pair took ship down the Thames and made their entrance by water on 18 August, sailing under Westminster Bridge and disembarking in the heart of the city. 'After staying in London six or seven days,' Philip's personal account continues, 'we came to pass what remains of summer in this house' of Hampton Court.[63] The most recent and emblematic of Tudor royal palaces, Hampton Court combined the grace of a royal seat with the charm of a riverside retreat graced with an elegant park with gardens. Philip also came to know other English royal seats. In London he was lodged in Whitehall Palace, easily the most impressive of the royal residences in the city.

In the months after the wedding, Philip abstained scrupulously from interfering in English domestic affairs[64] and devoted himself closely to the politics of Spain, Italy and America. In few of these areas did his views coincide with those of his father. Philip had obediently accepted Charles' proposal of the English marriage. However, in matters of government, which had effectively been in his hands now for ten years, his perspective was consistently different and independent. When it came to the matter of the new religious trends in England – what later came to be called the Reformation – Philip's attitude still echoed that of his father. Charles had no sympathy for the Reformation, but managed, as in Germany, to make compromises in order to avoid greater problems, a policy which Philip followed closely. At the end of 1554 a number of English bishops' courts – the Reformation of Edward VI's reign had now been reversed and all the bishops were once again formally Catholic – began proceedings for heresy against selected persons. On 1 February 1555, the first victim of the persecution was sent to the stake. Many European observers in London, who felt from their experience that burning was no solution, were appalled. The king, however, had no power to intervene in the church courts so he approached the problem another way. On the following Sunday, 10 February, his confessor Fray Alfonso de Castro preached before the court a sermon in which he 'did earnestly inveigh against the bishops for burning of men, saying plainly that they learned it not in scripture to burn any for conscience sake; but the contrary, that they should live and be converted'.[65] There were no further burnings that month, possibly as a result of the sermon. Philip's first direct response to the issue of religious persecution was evidently one of moderation. He obviously did not disagree with Castro's sermon, for shortly afterwards he appointed him to Spain's second most important see, that of Santiago.[66] The king and his advisers wished to assuage rather than aggravate the problem of religion.

Philip's stay in England lasted just over a year, long enough for him to do some touring and get to know the English. But the urgent business of the emperor made it necessary for him to leave the country and his queen. On 4 September 1555, he and his entourage took ship at Dover and made the crossing in three hours to Calais. In the afternoon of 25 October, the momentous ceremony of abdication took place in the great hall of the royal palace in Brussels.[67] The hall was packed. The emperor made his entrance, walking slowly. He supported himself with his left hand on a stick, his right hand leaning on the shoulder of the prince of Orange. Behind them came Philip, Mary of Hungary, the duke of Savoy, the knights of the Fleece and the high officials of Burgundy. The emperor went up to the dais and sat down. Philip sat down on his right, Mary on his left. A courtier began by explaining briefly to the assembled dignitaries the purpose of the session. Then the emperor, seated because of his infirmities, put on his spectacles and glanced rapidly at some notes in his hand. He raised his head and began to speak. While he spoke, the English envoy observed, there was 'not one man in the whole assemblie that poured not oute abundantly teares'. The wave of emotion overtook Charles, who also began to weep. The emperor bade his son kneel before him, asked for his hand and embraced him. He placed his hands on Philip's head and blessed him. The prince then rose to accept the duties entrusted to him. He limited his intervention to apologising, in a few halting words of French, for the fact that he could not speak the language, the official one of the States General.[68] The bishop of Arras, he said, would speak for him. Then Mary said a few words. At the end of the ceremony Charles formally invested his son as the new sovereign of the Netherlands. The remaining acts of abdication were made in subsequent months.

In September 1556, Charles V sailed from Vlissingen for Spain accompanied by his two sisters, Mary of Hungary and Leonor of France. High winds drove the ships back, so Philip went aboard on 19 September to say a second farewell. It was to be the last time he saw his father. On the 28th the little fleet arrived at Laredo and the imperial party made their way slowly south, ending up at the monastery of Yuste (Extremadura) in late November. A small palace was being constructed for Charles next to the monastery. He moved into his apartments in February 1557, and died there in the early hours of 21 September 1558.

For the notables in the Netherlands, the crucial event of the year 1557 was the battle of St Quentin (see Chapter 2). Peace negotiations took place after the military campaign. In the moments of leisure available to him during those weeks, Philip went hunting. He was further detained in the Netherlands not only by political matters but also by the need to put his affairs in order following the deaths in 1558 of both the emperor and of his own wife Mary Tudor. In 1559, after making final arrangements to leave for Spain, he set himself a departure date of 8 August, 'expressing, whenever he spoke of it, a singular warmth for and desire to be in the land of his birth'.[69]

For Philip it had been a successful absence, perhaps much more so than the visit ten years before. Philip's anxiety to leave did not of course arise from any disdain for the Netherlands. In the north he may have been ill at ease in many respects, but he also came to know and cherish the culture, which played a fundamental part in his eventual plans for the Escorial. He valued the humanist environment, and specifically selected as tutor for his son the Spanish philosopher Sebastián Fox Morcillo, then a professor at Louvain. Above all, he was captivated by the artistic creativity of the north. His first journey had been decisive in determining his tastes; the second confirmed his preference for things Flemish.[70]

Flemish art had long been in vogue in the peninsula. It was influential during the reign of Ferdinand and Isabella, and Charles V inevitably confirmed the fashion for things northern.[71] Philip now brought his personal enthusiasm to bear, arranging for paintings and artisans to be brought to Spain. He was the first to introduce into Spain the landscaped gardens of Flanders whilst his experience of buildings in the north had given him further ideas on what could be done in his country. During the years of his absence, he sent a continual stream of instructions and suggestions to Spain for the reconstruction of the palaces. In August 1559 he signed in Ghent a letter to Juan Bautista de Toledo, of Spanish origin but resident in Naples, inviting him to Madrid to become his principal architect. In childhood he had come to know the Netherlands music that his father had made standard at the Spanish court. Philip went further by taking back with him to Castile his Flemish choristers. From then on, he always had two separate chapels, one Flemish and one Spanish. His contact with the north was for him a positive experience which he fully appreciated and about which he never uttered a single word of criticism. 'Without doubt,' Jonathan Brown observes, 'Philip's travels – the sights he saw and the people he met – transformed his taste and understanding of the visual arts and launched him on his career as a great patron. . . . The effects of his journey were nothing less than overwhelming. With the time of a few years and the space of a few countries, the prince's taste became internationalized.'[72]

Philip's anxiety to leave for Spain, however, is easy to understand. He was keen to return to a land whose climate, language and people he knew; 'desiring, above all, to obtain some rest and ease in his native land'.[73] All too often, we have failed to appreciate the fact that spending eight solid years in northern Europe must have had a profound impact on the formation and attitudes of a cultured young man who was always willing to learn. Of the sixteen years since 1543 during which he had been controlling Spanish affairs, Philip had spent eight out of the country, visiting northern Italy, the Alps, southern Germany, the Rhineland, the Netherlands, parts of France, and southern England. For him, Augsburg, Milan, London, Cologne, Antwerp, Munich and Trent were not faraway places but towns whose streets he himself had trodden. Excepting only his father, no other European ruler of the time had travelled so widely and seen so much, or accumulated so much practical experience of international relations. He had lived at close quarters with the Protestant problem in Germany, seen heresy punished in England and been present in person on the battlefield against France. He had met face to face, both in peace and in war, most of the prominent personalities of his day. In later years all this accumulated experience filtered through into his letters and influenced his decision-making. During the years abroad, his inability to speak any languages other than Castilian and Latin (in contrast with his father, who spoke all the principal European languages fluently) may well have limited his contact with others and reinforced the impression of a tight-lipped king.[74] But his keen and sensitive eye took in everything, eagerly devoured what evidently pleased him and rejected what did not suit his temperament. Though brought up in Castile, he was never limited to the horizon of Castilians. The new king of Spain who came home in 1559 was very much a European, with sophisticated European tastes.

His return by no means signified that he was cutting himself off from Europe. For generations, Spain's elite had been cultivating contact with foreign countries, and Philip could not fail to follow the trend. The fact that the Netherlands and many Italian states were now ruled by a monarch in Spain confirmed the development. Italian art, music, theatre, poetry, architecture and religion were percolating through to Spaniards. The Netherlands had been a primary source of art, music and religious and mystical thought; the king's enthusiasm contributed yet more to the process.[75] He took care to bring his northern personnel with him. For music, he came back with his new Flemish musicians of the chapel; for art, he brought back Antonis Mor, who stayed with the king for a year before returning to Utrecht.[76] To adorn his palaces he brought back tapestries and paintings. Nor did he omit to bring northern advisers, returning with Charles de Tisnacq and Josse de Courtewille, officials of the Council of State of the Netherlands.[77] In respect of the Escorial, he also had his plans, his vision, his ideas and his entire working team in place.

The royal party arrived at the port of Vlissingen on 11 August. Philip had been away for over five years – 'so many years that I have been absent', he had written to his father while he waited for a fair wind in Vlissingen.[78] After supper on Wednesday the 23rd, he moved into his cabin. Early on the 25th the formal leave-taking commenced and by mid-afternoon the English envoy in the Netherlands reported, 'the king embarked with his whole fleet towards Spain, with an easterly wind, very small, next to a calm. . . . The number of his ships was twenty Spanish, thirty Hollanders, and forty of others of less sort.'[79] The journey home was uneventful. They put in at Laredo on the evening of 8 September and the king disembarked. A day later, before everything from the ships could be unloaded, a storm hit the coast. Some of the ships capsized, with the loss of men, property (including expensive tapestries) and papers. After a rest, Philip set off directly for Valladolid. He entered the city, which was decked out with triumphal arches, on 14 September.

CHAPTER 2

THE BATTLE

The campaign of St Quentin; St Quentin, Titian and the Holy Shroud of Turin

THE CAMPAIGN OF ST QUENTIN

In his Letter of Foundation for the Escorial, issued by Philip II on 22 April 1567, four years after work on it had commenced, the king stated that the building would be dedicated to St Lawrence (in Spanish, San Lorenzo), on whose feast day, 10 August 1557, his forces had won a famous victory.[1] The church of the Escorial was accordingly dedicated to San Lorenzo, and the first important relic deposited inside the altar was a limb of the saint. The military event in question deserves attention for at least three compelling reasons. First, it took place far from Spain, in a war that did not directly involve the country's interests or security. That in itself was remarkable enough. Second, and even more noteworthy for a feat repeatedly claimed to be among Spain's greatest, is the fact that few Spanish troops or officers actually fought. Finally, the battle campaign is memorable because Philip, who took part in its final stages, was the last king of Spain ever to participate personally in a military action. The facts give unique significance to the event, its consequences and the role it played in the subsequent history of the monarchy.

There were two, quite distinct, events associating St Quentin and Philip II: a battle, and the capture of a town. About the famous battle we know very little. Although it has repeatedly been acclaimed one of the great military victories of Spain, curiously not a single historian of that nation has found time to study it.[2] Apart from the description given in the biography of Philip II by Cabrera de Córdoba in 1609,[3] written over a decade after the king's death and not published in full until the nineteenth century, the battle has been relegated to oblivion as a historical event and is invoked only to underscore political ideology. Cabrera, as we shall note below, had personal reasons for his interest; historians who lacked such reasons passed the event by. Many centuries later, in 1966, a Spanish general who decided to devote a few pages to the subject did so with the sole and specific purpose of eulogising 'Philip II and his glorious army'.[4] The king's armies, he claimed with a burst of nationalistic pride, were 'almost always victorious'. Yet he was unable to give much information about the battle and for what he did, he drew exclusively on a French life of the king published in 1880 and an English general history of warfare published in 1937.[5] Mere mention of the battle as an event served, obviously, to back up the fictitious image of a nation that had dominated Europe with its armies. Unfortunately, the famous battle continues to suffer oblivion in Spain. A recent scholarly conference in Madrid dedicated to Spanish warfare during the sixteenth century published its proceedings in two massive volumes. In the two thousand pages of printed discourses, there is not a single indexed reference to the victory of St Quentin.[6] Non-Spaniards, logically, did not contribute much to the subject. The best summary of events in English continues to be the one published by the American historian Prescott as long ago as 1855.[7] The only authoritative and detailed analysis of St Quentin was not published until 1896, in French,[8] but is sadly little known even to scholars.

The military campaign that led to St Quentin was inherited by Philip from his father the emperor. As we have seen, at the end of 1555 Charles V announced in Brussels his intention to abdicate from his realms. In January 1556 and over the subsequent weeks, Spain and other territories were formally transferred to Philip II. From the spring of 1556, Philip was ruler of the most extensive empire in the world, comprising Spain, England, America, the Netherlands with Franche Comté, and half of Italy. Excepting only America, these states did not 'belong' to Spain but happened to share the same king. The inheritance, however, brought conflicts that had been created in the days of Charles V. In December 1555 the king of France, Henry II, signed a military alliance with the pope, Paul IV. A short-lived peace accord was made with France in February 1556, but the problem remained Italy, where the duke of Alba was viceroy of Naples and headed an Italian-Spanish military force that attempted to resolve the differences with the papacy. Early in 1557 the anti-Spanish pope Paul IV invited French troops led by the duke of Guise into his states to defend him. Alba was unhappy about engaging the papal troops in battle, but adopted a strategy of retreat that succeeded in wearing down the invading French, who were far from their supply bases. In June, he also managed to scatter a small papal force. By the early summer of 1557, the duke was in a favourable position to enter the Papal States and march on Rome, where in September he was able to secure an agreement on peace terms from the discomfited pope.

Although the Italian campaign was drawing to an end, Philip was faced with a renewed French threat to the Netherlands. In February 1557, he sent his adviser Ruy Gómez back to Spain to see what money was available for the impending war. It was also now important to get some military aid from the English. In March he sailed for England from Calais, and on St George's Day held a ceremony of the order of the Garter. In June the privy council was finally persuaded to declare war on France. Philip hoped with the help of the English to bring about a final push that would end in peace. He had no claims on France, and even less on the papacy. 'He knows very well,' his ambassador in England declared, 'that war in Italy is contrary to his interest, for if he loses his states are lost, and if he is victorious he conquers nothing', since the papacy could not be touched.[9] Agreement was reached on the military assistance to be given by the English. His objective achieved, Philip took his leave again in the first week of July. Mary accompanied him as far as Sittingbourne, where they spent the night. On 6 July, just before dawn, he sailed from Dover. It was to be his last sight of England and of the queen.

In Brussels, he was plunged directly into the war. Charles V had made sure that his son would be brought up as a soldier. Philip's entire training, his long familiarity with tourneys and games of war, his skill at hunting, meant that he could adapt easily to a military role. He had, for all that, never been in action. The emperor gloried in war as a dimension of personal prowess, participating personally in campaigns, sieges and voyages. In this (as in many other respects), Philip differed from his father. He preferred the model of his great-grandfather Ferdinand the Catholic, who commanded armies but did not commit his own person.[10] That at least was his opinion in 1555. It may be that he forgot it during the enthusiasm of the summer of 1557. The young nobles who gathered in Brussels were eager for action. Philip was exactly thirty years old. The regent of the Netherlands and commander of its forces, Emanuele Filiberto, duke of Savoy and first cousin to Philip, was twenty-eight and had recently (in 1553) succeeded his father to the title. Slim, austere and excitable, with a commanding presence,[11] Savoy was an exile from his homeland, which was occupied by the French. He was eager to strike at the enemy, and the opportunity came soon enough.

The French chose to launch an unannounced assault upon the border towns of the Netherlands with a huge army that included the most illustrious of France's aristocracy. The forces were commanded by the Constable of France, Anne de Montmorency, with the support of the Admiral of France, Gaspard de Coligny, and the Marshal Saint-André. In the ranks served dukes and princes such as Montpensier and Nevers, Enghien and Condé. By mid-July, Philip had assembled a counter-force of 35,000 under the orders of the duke of Savoy, seconded by the prince of Orange and all the nobles of the Netherlands. The cavalry were entrusted to Lamoral, earl of Egmont. Among his other commanders were the Germans: Ernst, duke of Brunswick (a Protestant) and Hilmar von Münchhausen.

In Brussels, Philip combined the roles of commander-in-chief and paymaster general. He coordinated the movement of all the troops and their supplies, planned strategy with a council of war and scrupulously doled out the little money available for the campaign. His correspondence in those weeks (much of it still undiscovered by other scholars) shows an impressive command of all aspects of the situation, including the geographical distribution of the troops. The fact is that the participation of Charles V's troops was made possible only through Philip's remarkably astute and direct coordination of the available men and resources. After a few days of indecisive campaigning in the borderlands of France and the Netherlands, it was decided to make a stand against the invaders. Philip and his advisers had at first thought of doing this at the nearby town of Rocroi, but Savoy dissuaded them. 'Taking into account all opinions', the king wrote to Savoy, 'and the difficulties that you say exist over Rocroi, and the debates that we have had here, it was decided that the most convenient and suitable move is to invest St Quentin.'[12] The small French border town was defended by troops under Coligny. By a strange twist of fate, Rocroi nearly a century later was to be the scene of a historic French victory over the army of Spain.

The capture of St Quentin was seen to be crucial both in order to block the French advance and also to clear the way for a march on Paris. The king threw himself with energy into the campaign.[13] In the last week of July he was busily arranging for the scattered Italian and German troops under his command to rendezvous before St Quentin. Meanwhile, he informed the duke of Savoy, 'by the accompanying letter you will see how the earl of Pembroke remains in Calais with part of the troops, and the rest will come tomorrow'.[14] As for the duke, the best solution for now would be to wait in camp, 'until the rest of the troops who are on their way arrive, and I am urging all possible speed on them'.[15] Philip also made scrupulous arrangements for supplies of munitions and food. By the first week of August, it became urgent to counter-attack. Philip cancelled all other plans and decided: 'I shall go immediately to Cambrai, where I expect to be on Saturday. I shall be without fail at Cambrai on Saturday, in order to speed up everything, and my hope is that on Monday all the men will be where they should be, and you as well.'[16] He sent further instructions to the duke:

> Our decision is that you should set out on Thursday and position yourselves before St Quentin, which we believe you will be able to do by Monday. It would be most important that the new troops arrive with you on the same day, so that you can deploy them on all sides. We have written to the commanders of the German cavalry and to the infantry colonels, and have sent them persons who will help to speed them up.

Philip had already been one week in Cambrai, as he informed Savoy on 6 August in his own hand, and was still waiting for the English troops under the earl of Pembroke to join him. After his efforts to obtain English help, courtesy required that he not engage the enemy without them. Unfortunately, he had just received news that they would not arrive until 10 August, which he considered too late. Therefore, he wished to come to the front immediately 'without the English'; but, he added, 'I thought to delay that by just one day, hoping that the regiment will arrive'. Philip made use of the delay to arrange for further cavalry and cannon to be sent, and for field-kitchens to be set up in order to make bread for the troops. All this, he calculated, would regrettably take a couple of days. 'It greatly distresses me', he wrote in his own hand at the end of the despatch, 'not to be able to come today as I intended. But in order not to hold up these men I am sending them without me, and shall await the others and bring with me the rest of the artillery.'[17]

The next day, Saturday the 7th, found him deeply worried. In moments of personal anxiety, he always wrote his letters in his own hand. He did so now to Savoy. For a young man who had never been in a military action Philip's campaign letters, most of them still unpublished, reveal an astonishing command of the situation. 'I am extremely displeased at not being able to come nor is it possible to come soon, for the English have written that they will not arrive

here until Tuesday, although I have urged them to hurry up.' And
there were other troops, Germans, who could not arrive before the
10th. 'I am quite desperate.'[18] In any case, if Savoy could spare them
he wished the duke to have waiting for him in Honcourt on
Monday

> a regiment of Germans and a *tercio* of Spaniards and two more
> units of a thousand horse so that the same evening I can go and
> spend the night in Honcourt. And the next day very early I shall
> be there with you. However, it may not turn out this way, for I
> greatly fear that the troops I am awaiting will arrive only on
> Tuesday, so tired that they will wish to spend Wednesday resting,
> and if this happens I shall not arrive there until Friday, since the
> artillery will slow me down and I shall not make it in one day. I
> came here yesterday, Thursday, with the intention of leaving to
> meet you yesterday.

According to this calculation of delays, the king would not be able
to join up with Savoy's forces until 13 August.

It is obvious that Philip was making the maximum effort to arrive
at the front but was being delayed by the tardiness of his allies. On
Sunday the 8th he wrote to Savoy: 'on Wednesday evening you will
send to Beaurevoir the escort force that you deem suitable, as long
as it is not smaller than 1,500 Walloon horse and five or six hundred
Walloon archers. These with the English and with Münchhausen's
regiment, who are arriving on Tuesday, will make it possible for me
to join you.'[19] On Monday the 9th he received news at last that the
English were arriving, but would need one day to rest. 'I shall leave
on Wednesday', with the English, the Germans, and the Walloon
archers. 'You will make sure that on Thursday morning 1,500 more
cavalry come to meet me half-way.'

Philip knew, however, that a French relief force sent to the
town might provoke Savoy into a military action. He therefore
adjured the duke: 'Under no circumstances must you come here
or move from where you are. Touching your point about engaging
in battle in the event that they provoke it, what I can say is that
the first concern must be to take care that they do not relieve the
town. Unless absolutely necessary to prevent them relieving it,

you must avoid engaging in battle until I arrive, when we will decide what to do.' If, however, there was no option, Savoy must decide as seemed best. The haunting fear that there might be a battle without him made him add in his own hand: 'If there is no way to avoid an engagement before I arrive, I cannot enjoin you too strongly to inform me post haste, so as to give me the means and opportunity to arrive in time. Since I know that you desire my company in such an eventuality, I do not wish to press you further, but I beg you to have spare horses waiting day and night to be able to inform me.'[20]

'Seeing that the late arrival of Münchhausen with his regiment', Savoy wrote back on the 8th, 'has forced Your Majesty to delay coming until the English arrive, I can only say that it is infinitely important that Your Majesty cut the delay as short as possible.'[21] 'Make all possible haste', he also wrote to the king's secretary Eraso, 'so that His Majesty comes immediately.'[22]

Events turned out as the king feared. In the afternoon of the 9th, he learnt that Montmorency had set out with a large force to relieve St Quentin. Without knowing the precise location of the French troops, Philip dared not move. He sent an urgent message to Savoy, saying – in case Savoy did not know – that he had learnt from a French prisoner that the Constable had 18,000 men. On Tuesday, 10 August, the feast of St Lawrence, the Constable with some twenty-two thousand infantry and cavalry advanced upon Savoy's positions before St Quentin. In a short but bloody action, the army of Flanders under Savoy and Egmont routed and destroyed the Constable's forces. A contemporary estimate put the number of French dead at 5,200, with possibly seven thousand prisoners. By contrast, it appears that no more than five hundred of Savoy's army lost their lives. The French physician Ambroise Paré, who was sent to the scene by the king of France to attend to the wounded, witnessed the unusual number of French dead:

> We saw more than half a league round us the earth all covered with the dead; and hardly stopped there, because of the stench of the dead men and their horses; and so many blue and green flies rose from them, bred of the moisture of the bodies and the heat

of the sun, that when they were up in the air they hid the sun. It was wonderful to hear them buzzing; and where they settled, there they infected the air, and brought the plague with them.[23]

It took some time to appreciate the scale of the victory. Philip first heard of it at 11 p.m. that same night. Since first reports could be unreliable, he remained awake until around three in the morning, receiving further despatches. Early on the 11th, encamped at the village of Beaurevoir, he finally wrote to the emperor to confirm the news. In one of the most important letters of his career, Philip exceptionally wrote in his own hand to his father to express his elation and his hopes. His perfectly legible script[24] conveyed his deep emotion:

At 11 p.m. a messenger came from the camp to say that the enemy were defeated and the Constable a prisoner, at 1 a.m. another came to report the defeat but not the detail about the Constable, at 2 a.m. the marquis of Berghes who had been in the battle came and reported what Your Majesty will see in the report I am sending. He had no news however about the Constable. Today I arrived here at daylight in the camp and found a message from my cousin [Savoy] who states that he has seen the Constable and that all the others whom Your Majesty will see mentioned in the accompanying memorandum have been made prisoner. Your Majesty can understand how much it grieves me not to have been present there, or be able to give you a first-hand report of what happened. However, Your Majesty can imagine, if we take St Quentin as I hope we will, and if the king of France has no army left, what might possibly be achieved in France if we have the money. Since matters are in such a good state, I beg Your Majesty as humbly as I can, to see whether it is possible for money to be sent to me.[25]

The meaning of the last two sentences (which we shall comment upon shortly) is clear enough: if St Quentin were to fall, the way into France would lie completely open, since the king of France would have no army with which to defend himself; and with adequate money the advantage could be pressed.

The victors were unsure who had been captured. When they received details, they could hardly believe it: the prisoners included

Montmorency and three of his sons, together with the Marshal Saint-André, the duke of Montpensier, the prince of Condé and the duke of Longueville. Among the French dead were the duke d'Enghien and viscount Turenne. Philip, accompanied by the English troops, 3,000 Belgians and 500 Spaniards,[26] arrived at the camp on the 13th, but with no signs of disappointment. He had been handed one of the most brilliant military victories of the age. On the battlefield before St Quentin, 'accompanied by the princes and commanders of his army in full military regalia' (according to a witness) and flanked by the captured French standards, he proceeded slowly between two long parallel lines of distinguished prisoners and paid his respects to each of them.[27]

A legend created much later by writers in Spain claimed the victory as Spanish. It was very far from being that.[28] The battle was not fought in the name of Spain, which was not at war with France; rather it was fought in the name of the ruler of the Netherlands. Control of the campaign was not in the hands of Spain and its Council of War, but in the hands of the Council of the Netherlands, which (as the documents show) made the decisions. The king consulted officials in Brussels and followed their advice. Above all, the finances of the campaign were controlled by Brussels rather than by Spain. The Spaniards of course played an important role, both in terms of manpower and finance, because they were part of the same war effort. Of Philip's total army of some 48,000 – not all of whom took part in the battle – only 12 per cent were Spaniards; 53 per cent were Germans, 23 per cent Netherlanders and 12 per cent English. Moreover, all the chief commanders were non-Spaniards: they included Savoy, Egmont, duke Eric of Brunswick and baron von Münchhausen. The victory certainly belonged to the king in whose name it had been won, but that was because he was ruler of the Netherlands. When Cabrera de Córdoba, writing in Spain half a century later, gave his account of the battle he classified all the personnel of Philip's army as Spaniards ('los de España'), a fiction that has endured in all Spanish textbooks. When later that year Anton van den Wijngaerde produced a masterly engraving of the battle, with convincing detail of its three principal stages, he did so at the direct behest of King Philip, but his talent was expended not on behalf of Spain but of that of his native country, the Netherlands.

One week later, Ruy Gómez, freshly returned from Spain, remarked that the victory had evidently been of God, since it had been won 'without experience, without troops, and without money'.[29] The comment reflected a real problem about what could practicably be done next. Philip, advised by his close friend the governor of Milan, Ferrante Gonzaga,[30] favoured an immediate exploitation of the victory by an advance on Paris, a plan to which all the other members of the Netherlands Council of State were opposed. (The Venetian ambassador Suriano, in Brussels at the time, confirmed the virtual unanimity of their views.)[31] There was no money to pay for a further campaign, the Netherlanders were reluctant to go on the offensive, and France had more forces in reserve. Philip was assured that there was nothing more honourable than retreat when victorious. The arguments seemed irrefutable. He duly accepted the advice, returning to Brussels 'sound, cheerful and full of glory, and to universal satisfaction'.[32] When, some weeks later, the council there told him that nothing more could be done, Philip replied angrily: 'Yes, at present nothing else can be done, but at the time much might have been achieved'.[33]

Historians in the nineteenth century, inspired perhaps by the American historian Prescott, continued to repeat, without any documentary support, an account according to which the king was too cowardly to exploit his success, being afraid to make a further military advance. There was, however, no cowardice on Philip's part, nor any anger on the part of Charles V when he received the news of the action.[34] Philip's own letter to his father, quoted above, demonstrates irrefutably that he wished to press on into France and lacked only the money to do so. He commented glumly to Savoy in October that it was inevitable that 'the army be disbanded at the end of the month because the money has been calculated to last till then. Expenses have increased and mounted more than we expected. I can see no way of finding more money.'[35]

Far from being a coward, the king just over two weeks after the field victory personally led an assault on St Quentin, which was defended by a very small force under Admiral Coligny. This was in effect the second battle of St Quentin, a town of 8,000 inhabitants that had been under siege since 3 August, when Coligny had entered it with a small number of troops and set up defences. The unequal balance of forces left no doubt about the outcome. 'I arrived at my camp on the morning of the 13th,' Philip wrote to his uncle the archduke Ferdinand, 'and thanks to the preparations made since then it was possible on the 27th to enter by force and capture the town, in such a manner that it can be seen clearly as the work of Our Lord.' In a detailed account that he dictated to his secretary, he described the action in the third person: 'In the afternoon of the twenty-seventh, at just before 2 p.m. His Majesty ordered the attack to begin, and our men made such efforts that in little less than an hour we penetrated from every side, killing all the people caught up in the force of the initial assault.'[36] It was his first direct experience of the brutal carnage of war. 'His Majesty at once gave the necessary orders to ensure the welfare and protection of the churches, monasteries, women and children.' Despite the king's efforts to reduce casualties, the town was sacked by the German mercenaries who, reported the earl of Bedford, accompanying the victors, 'showed such cruelty as the like hath not been seen. The town was by them set afire and a great piece of it burnt; women and children gave such pitiful cries that it would grieve any Christian heart.'[37] Admiral Coligny was taken prisoner.

The historian Cabrera de Córdoba, who felt a very personal link with the event since his father and grandfather both died in the first assault on the town, had (as we have noted) no hesitation in attributing the victory exclusively to 'Spaniards'. In his account, there were no troops from other nations.[38] As it happened, few Spaniards identified with the famous victory, and no Spanish artist seems to have had any interest in painting a canvas on the theme. Not until thirty years later did the imagination of an Italian painter, Luca Cambiaso, create a delightful representation of the royal camp in a series painted for the decoration of the king's gallery in the Escorial (see Chapter 7).

With both the Constable and Admiral, France's two most prominent nobles, in his power, Philip had a strong negotiating hand. He had also – as he informed the regent of Spain, his sister Juana – won his spurs. 'Our Lord in his goodness has desired to grant me these victories within a few days of the beginning of my reign, with all the honour and *reputación* that follow from them.'[39] For the king it was a profound experience of personal triumph. Our most direct evidence of his pride in the victory is the magnificent portrait of him painted almost immediately that year in the Netherlands by Antonis Mor. Dressed in a magnificent cuirass adorned by the Golden Fleece, carrying the baton of command in his right hand, with his left hand resting on his sword and wearing a solemn expression as befitted a general who had just accomplished a notable achievement, Philip looked every inch a leader. A text under the portrait, presumably by the artist, states: 'The dress he wore in the St Quentin campaign'. The king's pride in the painting is demonstrated by the fact that he arranged for it to be delivered in 1575 to the Escorial, where it remains. A copy was executed by the artist Alonso Sánchez Coello nine years later.[40]

In October the English troops went home and the king prepared to wind down the campaign. The costs of war, not only in the Netherlands but also in Italy, were already insupportable. Fortunately, the campaign was going favourably in Italy. Alba forced the papacy into a peace settlement in September in an accord that, for the rest of the century, bound the papacy closely to Spain.[41] But it was too early to prepare for peace. In France the duke of Guise, who had just returned from his unsuccessful campaign in Italy, recruited a new army and took the field. He appeared before Calais on New Year's Day 1558. The town, England's last possession on mainland Europe, fell that same week. Its loss infuriated the English, and grieved their queen mortally.

Philip was forced to review his strategy. Writing to the duke of Savoy in January, in despatches that show his perfect familiarity with the geography of the Netherlands and northern France,[42] the king attempted to take control of the situation. French forces continued to make attacks across the border. Then, in mid-July 1558, they suffered a further crushing defeat at Gravelines at the hands of an army commanded by the earl of Egmont. Peace talks became inevitable.

ST QUENTIN, TITIAN AND THE HOLY SHROUD OF TURIN

Thanks to the victories at St Quentin and Gravelines, French power in western Europe suffered a decisive check. In October 1558 the plenipotentiaries of the two kings met near Cambrai. Philip's side was represented by the prince of Orange, Alba, the bishop of Arras, Ruy Gómez and Viglius, president of the Council of State in Brussels; Henry II was represented by the Constable, Saint-André and three others. The final peace between the Habsburgs and France was signed on 3 April 1559, in the little border village of Cateau-Cambrésis. It was one of the decisive treaties of western history. It satisfied France, which despite the military reverses kept Calais and three key fortresses in the Rhineland; it gave – at least for the moment – security to the Netherlands, always fearful of invasions from France; and it immeasurably strengthened Spain, which was confirmed in its domination of Italy. The duke of Savoy was restored to his duchy, and received the hand in marriage of the king of France's sister, Marguerite. Peace returned to Europe. The dynastic enmity between the Valois of France and the Habsburgs was laid to rest. Friendship between France and Spain was sealed when Philip consented to wed Elizabeth Valois, eldest daughter of Henry II and Catherine de' Medici, to which end his ambassadors to the peace, Alba, Orange and Egmont, arrived in Paris on 15 June 1559, bearing a jewel as gift to formalise the marriage proposal. Precisely seven days later a lavish proxy wedding was celebrated in Notre Dame cathedral, with Alba standing in for the king.

The pomp and celebrations[43] had little impact on Spain, where a victory in a faraway country, in a war that seemed not directly to involve Spanish interests and in any case absorbed few

Castilian soldiers, evoked little reaction. By contrast, artists in the Netherlands, like Van den Wijngaerde, were well aware of how far the victory had determined their destiny. The only international artist to produce a picture in response to the battle was Titian, who as one of Philip's official court painters was called upon to commemorate the occasion. In 1559, at the request of the king, he produced a stylised portrait of Saint Lawrence, which was eventually allotted a prominent place beside the altar of the basilica of the Escorial.

Titian retained a version of the same painting in Italy. The work, tentatively dated 1557–9 and which today hangs in the church of the Jesuits in Venice, is in all essentials a copy of the basic theme of the martyrdom of St Lawrence. In both canvases, the death is depicted according to the account given in the old legend of a saint who was roasted alive on a grill (later assumed, without proof, to be the inspiration for the ground plan of the Escorial) and who defied his torturers with the words: 'Turn me over, I'm not yet done on the other side'.

Though the name of St Lawrence probably featured in the early masses celebrated at the building site, the first formal high mass for the saint was not sung until 1571, at the dedication of the new church in the monastery. Thereafter the king attempted to be present each year at the masses for the saint's feast. With the completion of the basilica and the dedication of its high altar, the theme of St Lawrence came to occupy a central place in court ceremonial and imagery. The Italian artist Pellegrino Tibaldi, who had already undertaken a large proportion of the decoration of the church, devoted a central section of the altarpiece on the high altar in the basilica to the saint. Tibaldi died four years later, shortly after returning home to Milan. His stylised Mannerist painting was evidently much to the taste of the king.

The close attention paid by Italians to the barbecued saint demonstrates that in the Catholic world religious themes could never be of merely regional interest. In the same way, the battle at St Quentin was not, as we have already seen, a uniquely Spanish victory. Many other nations had an equally valid reason for commemorating it – a fact too often forgotten. We have noted that it determined events in both the Netherlands and France; for Italy too it had far-reaching consequences.

The earliest reaction to the battle on the parts both of Philip and the duke of Savoy was the recognition that it had been a mercy conceded by God. Neither of them delayed in expressing their gratitude. Shortly afterwards the king founded his monastery in honour of the saint on whose day the battle was won. Duke Emanuele Filiberto soon returned (in 1563) to the territory that was once again his home thanks to the terms of the treaty of Cateau-Cambrésis. To give thanks for the victory, he decided to restore and dedicate to St Lawrence the old ducal chapel in Turin of Santa Maria del Presepe, also known as the Madonna della Neve. In the same years, he transferred his capital from the French-speaking town of Chambéry to the Italian city of Turin. It was a highly significant move, accompanied for the first time by the decision to make Italian, rather than French, the official language of the restored duchy.

At the same time, the duke took active steps to cultivate links with the aristocracy of peninsular Italy, some of whom he invited to become members of Savoy's order of chivalry, the Ordine dell'Annunziata. Finally, in 1578 Emanuele Filiberto transferred the most precious sacred relic in his duchy, the Holy Shroud of Christ, from its previous site at Chambéry (where it had been located on and off since 1502) to the church of San Lorenzo. Magnificent ceremonies in October that year, presided over by the duke and by the archbishop of Milan, Carlo Borromeo, gave the shroud its definitive resting place. Milan was, as we have seen, a ducal possession of Philip II, so the proceedings cemented the friendship between the two dukes.

In the years to come, Savoy and Spain (and, of course, the Netherlands) would continue to be wary of France, their principal enemy. The common ties between the two victorious princes became even closer when, in 1585, they sealed a blood alliance with the marriage of the duke's son to Philip's younger daughter, the Infanta Catalina. It may have been during the visit made by the duke to Spain for the wedding ceremony, which took place in Saragossa, that a small painted copy of the Shroud was presented to

Philip II, who apparently kept it thereafter in his bedroom at the Escorial.[44] Turin, which thanks to the battle of St Quentin became home to the Holy Shroud, confirmed its claims to the spiritual leadership of Italians, and to the political sponsorship of what even then was not too extravagant a dream, the realisation of a new and united Italy. The Escorial became a small, but by no means insignificant, link in the chain of politics binding together the Catholic states of the Mediterranean.

CHAPTER 3

FOUNDATION

Motives of foundation: the battle; Choosing a site for the monastery; The king as builder of palaces; Motives of foundation: filial piety and the supposed pantheon; The basic context: the king as gardener; The king, his architects and his ideas for the Escorial; The Escorial as a repository of art

MOTIVES OF FOUNDATION: THE BATTLE

The king's intention to build the Escorial may have taken shape at any time after the mid-sixteenth century, when he completed his travels through the continent. He would later attach specific importance to the circumstances of the victory at St Quentin, as we shall see below, but the battle was not necessarily a reason for his decision to build, merely a trigger. There were many other events and inspirations (the fruits of his stay in the Netherlands and northern Europe) that also shaped the way in which his idea of the foundation developed. Every influence drawn from Europe was closely related to a context that had its roots in Spain, so that we need to bring together the European and Spanish experiences in order to understand what the building represented. Every aspect of his great project, whether European or Spanish in origin, was of course rooted in the mind of the king, who alone made the major decisions affecting planning. It is sensible, then, to take the words of the king as our point of departure. It is quite possible that he did not explain himself with sufficient clarity to satisfy our inquisitive minds, but his words are there and we are obliged to respect what he himself stated to be his purpose.

In a letter of intent that the king sent to the general of the Jeronimite order in 1561, he stated: 'In recognition of the victory that Our Lord was pleased to give me on the day of St Lawrence of the year 1557, I have decided to build and endow a monastery'.[1] The first powerful motive, then, was St Quentin. Every account of the Escorial written in the past three centuries has pinpointed the fact that the king intended to celebrate the victory over the French at St Quentin, won on the feast-day of St Lawrence, the 10 August. On 22 April 1567, some ten years after the main decisions had been taken and four years after the foundation stone had been laid, Philip issued a formal Letter of Foundation. It is of crucial importance because in it he explains his motives, albeit with a slight difference of emphasis. He begins by reaffirming that the church will be dedicated to St Lawrence because of his own 'special devotion' to the saint and 'in commemoration of the mercy and victories that we began to receive on the day of his heavenly birthday. Moreover, the foundation is to be of the Order of St Jerome, because of the special attachment and devotion that we have for this order, as the Emperor and King my lord also had.'[2]

The king refers specifically to 'victories', meaning not simply the field of battle, at which he was not present, but more surely the storming of the town, which occurred some days later (see Chapter 2) and at which he was not only conspicuously present but about which he had sent a detailed report in his own hand to his sister the regent Juana and to his uncle the archduke Ferdinand (soon to be emperor as Ferdinand I). There were, in short, two victories, not one. The interpretation of victory as a 'mercy' is also interesting. Nearly a century later the English head of state, Oliver Cromwell, would also use the word 'mercy' to refer to military victories conceded by God.[3] Philip had particular cause to consider the victory miraculous because, as his friend Ruy Gómez had commented, it was wholly unexpected. His armies that year had been pitted against both France and the pope, and the outcome in both cases had been successful. He was particularly mindful of the failure of the duke of Guise's invasion of southern Italy, where Alba had been commanding Spanish troops. It was the totality of successes achieved during that summer of 1557 that convinced the king. Did he devote his traditional two-day Corpus Christi retreat to prayer, alone with his God, to secure a successful outcome to the military conflicts which threatened him? As he informed his sister the regent Juana, the events of those weeks confirmed that God gave his blessing to his forthcoming tenure of power. 'Our Lord in his goodness has desired to grant me these victories within a few days of the beginning of my reign, with all the honour and *reputación* that follow from them.'[4] The question of the alleged vow to San Lorenzo, which some commentators mentioned later, does not figure in the letter or in any early account of the matter, and is evidently of lesser importance. 'Everyone knows', Théophile Gautier wrote confidently in 1845, 'that the Escorial was built as the result of a vow made by Philip II at the siege of St Quentin, where he was obliged to bombard a church of St Lawrence.'[5] Long before that, however, Fray José de Sigüenza, librarian of the Escorial and the first historian both of the Jeronimite order and of the Escorial itself, had dismissed the story of the vow as a myth.[6]

There is more of a mystery about the king's 'special devotion' to San Lorenzo. Sigüenza claims that the king had always had such an attachment. There is, however, no known reason for him to have had any interest in the obscure saint, whose mythical origins lay in third-century AD Huesca, in Aragon, and with whom the king appears to have had no connection before the famous battle. It seems more logical, therefore, to conclude that the attachment arose exclusively because of the day on which the victory took place. St Lawrence may safely be set aside as a fundamental *motive* for the establishment of the monastery, but he undoubtedly played a role in the commemoration of the victory, as we know from the reactions of both the king of Spain and the duke of Savoy (see Chapter 2). Five years after work began on the monastery, the king arranged for the transport from Huesca to the Escorial of the (supposed) remains of the parents of the saint. In order to avoid the expected uproar in Huesca, he ordered that it be done 'with the least possible fuss'.[7] Fuss, indeed, there was, in the form of local protests, but it was brief.

CHOOSING A SITE FOR THE MONASTERY

The king, as we shall see, had been elaborating a building programme well before his journeys abroad. During his final stay in the Netherlands, he brought these schemes to completion. As early as 1556 he was sending back sketches of gardens and buildings, in his own hand, to the directors of works at Aranjuez and at Aceca.[8] Philip also arranged for the construction of smaller houses which served as stops on the way, or simply as hunting lodges, and included the accommodation at Fuenfría, La Fresneda, Galapagar, El Monesterio and Torrelodones. More substantial houses, veritable palaces in their own right, were built at Vaciamadrid and Aceca. Together, the palaces and lodges formed a collection of royal residences without equal in Europe. The network of residences in the vicinity of the capital were slowly put in order.

In these months another plan, bold and wholly innovative, took shape in the king's mind. Since the victory at St Quentin he had been considering the possibility of founding a religious house in honour of his military successes in 1557. Sending for Juan Bautista from Italy in 1559 was the first step. The architect arrived in Spain early in 1560 (in circumstances that were unbelievably tragic and contributed to his early death),[9] and was given his instructions: to think about the new foundation and to apply himself meanwhile to the works at Aranjuez, Madrid and Aceca. Philip subsequently contacted the Jeronimite order, whose members were to staff the new monastery. The friars had several meetings with the architect and with Philip's secretary for works, Pedro de Hoyo. In January 1561 a rough sketch of the building by Juan Bautista formed the basis for discussion.

As yet no site had been chosen. Philip wished the monastery to be within reach of his other palaces, so that a rough idea of its situation was already in his mind. There were no substantial towns in the region – Toledo at the southern end was probably the largest – so his stipulation of a country setting was easily met. It was much more difficult to arrive at a setting that would match what he had seen years ago in Ettal, where the combination of valley, wood and mountain could be seen at its finest. Philip's evident priority was for a location that would be completely rural. If we wish to understand his preferences it is sufficient to contemplate not merely Ettal as it might have been in that period, but the view (to which we refer again on page 60) drawn by Anton van den Wijngaerde in 1562 of the palace at Valsaín. The Dutch artist's rendering shows a handsome, isolated country mansion surrounded by hills and woods as far as the eye could see,[10] a choice of environment that the king wished to emulate for his monastery.

In looking for a site, he had the help of a 'committee made up of architects, doctors and philosophers',[11] whose first selection was a site near the monastery of Guisando, in the Sierra de Gredos, in the province of Avila. The site would have satisfied the king, because of the rural environment, and was ideal for the monks, whose order resided in the house at Guisando; but Philip judged the distance from his palaces to be too great. After further searches, by the end of 1561 a decision was made in favour of a place in the sierra de Guadarrama, next to the little village of El Escorial. The village was by no means a picture-postcard location, a subsequent monk and librarian of the Escorial commenting rather that it was a miserable hamlet, where the houses 'did not have a single chimney or window',[12] a veritable hole. The population of the village could have been moved, a practice not uncommon at the time among European nobles who wished to appropriate residential areas for other schemes. Instead, the king decided to make use of it as a base from which to work on the monastery, and he even took up temporary lodgings there at a later date. During 1562 the site of the proposed building was cleared. By March 1562 Juan Bautista had his finalised sketches ready. Philip was excited: 'Bring it when you have finished, and all the better if it's tomorrow.'[13] The next stage was the construction of a model, which was completed by December, after several disagreements.

The king's idea at this stage was summarised by the future librarian and historian of the Escorial, Fray José de Sigüenza. According to Sigüenza, Philip planned a monastery for about fifty friars, adjoining a residence for himself, the royal family and part of the court. Set between the two residences would be a church. Very soon the idea changed and plans were modified, though as yet there was no inkling of the later schemes for a library and a college. But work commenced. On 23 April 1563 the first stone was laid of the building dedicated to San Lorenzo (St Lawrence).

Many modern visitors appear to entertain the idea that what distinguishes the Escorial is the unique combination of monastery and royal palace. In contrast to Philip's other residences, it was the only building in which the two roles, of palace and monastery, functioned side by side. The king, it would seem, wished to be both a ruler and a monk. However, there was nothing novel about this combination. All over medieval Europe, from Russia to the British Isles, rulers tended to be itinerant and visited their territories when the need arose. They had no fixed base, nor did they have the money to settle down and build palaces. For extended stays during their visits, they chose monastic foundations. In early medieval Germany, for example, kings fixed their residences in selected monasteries of the area that they were visiting.[14] The same thing happened in medieval Catalonia, where the austere and majestic monastery of Poblet had a fortified royal residence and, moreover, contained the pantheon of the kings of Catalonia and Aragon. 'A distinctive feature of Iberian monasticism', it has been pointed out, 'was the conjunction of the monastery and the royal palace.'[15] 'In Iberia the princes built and endowed abbeys as spiritual supports for their power, resided in them, and were buried in tombs attached to them.' A Spanish scholar has made a careful study of the way in which medieval rulers, among them Ferdinand and Isabella, chose religious houses as their residences.[16] Even in Philip's own experience, his father – who, as we shall see, had little interest in a fixed abode – chose to spend his last days in a little palace, at Yuste in Extremadura, that was integrated with the adjacent monastery. The king's plan for a building that combined both royal residence and religious house was clearly not exceptional, and accorded with long-standing European practice.

The progress and planning of the structure have been minutely described in many books, most notably in an outstanding volume by the American scholar George Kubler, and will not be touched on here. The work of construction gave rise long ago – it is uncertain precisely when – to the story that the king used to go up into the hills from time to time in order to gain a perspective on the progress below. He chose to sit, or so it is alleged, on a hillside bluff that is today marked out for tourists as 'the Seat of Philip II'. A current tourist guide informs us that 'the Seat of Philip II is a mile and a half to the south of the Escorial and is an excellent lookout, from which the monarch liked to gaze on the view and, down below him, at the progress of the building work. The place is a granite crag overlooking the wood of La Herrería.' There is, however, no written record to confirm that the king ever went up to that spot. More recently, a Madrid university professor, Dr Alicia Canto, has done the best sort of practical research by visiting the hillside site herself; she states simply that the king could not have seen the Escorial from that location.

THE KING AS BUILDER OF PALACES

Philip had sufficient leisure to develop what came to be one of his great hobbies, an interest in building. For some years Charles V had been planning to restore and rebuild parts of the half-neglected royal palaces, notably the Alcázars (medieval fortresses) in Madrid and Toledo. In Toledo the task of remodelling the Alcázar was entrusted in 1537 to Alonso de Covarrubias, and while the work was in progress the emperor and his wife lived in the palace of Fuensalida near San Juan de los Reyes, where the empress died in 1539. In 1543 Charles charged his architect Luis de Vega with the construction of a palace on the site of the hunting lodge at El Pardo. His absences shifted the work on to Philip's shoulders. In May 1545 the prince set up a special department, the Committee for Works (*Junta de Obras y Bosques*), to oversee the royal residences and administer justice on the royal estates, and over time this developed into a major government body. In August 1548 Philip commissioned a report on the Alcázar in Madrid and the house at El Pardo. 'Look into this and remind me about it', runs one of his marginal comments that year on papers related to the palaces.[17] El Pardo was the first building to bear the stamp of his own evident interest in design and architecture. His commitment to its refurbishment dated from the occasion when he and his father had to spend an uncomfortable night in the cramped space available there. When he complained to Charles, the latter replied: 'kings do not need to have residences'.[18] This phrase, memorable and significant as it may appear to us today, did not satisfy Philip. A few days later he set about making his own arrangements for the building. Almost immediately afterwards, as we have seen, he was making preparations to leave the country for his historic visit to Italy, Germany and the Netherlands.

On his return from Germany in 1551 Philip dedicated himself with even greater enthusiasm to his architectural schemes. We can be sure that his head was bursting with ideas he had culled from his extensive experience of the finest palaces of continental Europe. When in 1552 a treatise by the Italian architect Serlio was published in Toledo, the translator (Francisco de Villalpando, who was also an architect) recognised that the prince had 'a taste for architecture'.[19] Sebastiano Serlio (1475–1554) was a leading Italian commentator on the subject. The first published volume of his four-volume *On Architecture* came out in Venice in 1537, and the last volumes were printed in Paris in 1545. The greatest appeal of his work lay in the use of elaborate diagrams and illustrations that made it easier to understand his site descriptions without having to visit the actual places. Philip may have been particularly impressed by Book Three of the work, dedicated to the ancient buildings of Rome and Italy, in which the entire first section was devoted to domes and in particular to the Pantheon, an ancient structure whose distinctive dome became the inspiration of many architects of the Baroque age.[20] Serlio's analysis of the Pantheon would certainly have been in the minds of the architects who at that moment were designing the church of St Peter's in Rome and were soon to be discussing with Philip his ideas for the Escorial. Over a century later, one of Spain's great scholars, Juan de Caramuel, felt confident enough about Philip's expertise to mention the king, the Pantheon and the Escorial all in the same breath:

> Philip was an assiduous student of mathematics, and especially of architecture. In order to leave his mark on posterity, he desired that, just as the Pantheon of Rome was the book from which Michelangelo learnt, so in Old Castile the monastery and palace of San Lorenzo, known as the Escorial, would be the book in which his ideas could be consulted and posterity see them put into effect.[21]

The prince was now well positioned to continue his building plans. In 1553 he replaced Covarrubias as master of works with Francisco de Villalpando, and also made plans for Juan Bautista de Toledo to come to Spain in the near future from Naples.[22] The summoning of Juan Bautista suggests that the prince had already reached his decision, probably taken at some time between 1551 and 1553, to build a religious house that would also serve as a resting-place for the members of his family. These were among the last steps taken by him before his unexpected and prolonged five-year absence from Spain after 1554. The sum total of this activity shows that we should be wary of presenting the prince as an uninformed amateur who began to think about building only in 1559, when he finally returned to the peninsula.[23] He was already formulating plans for a possible structure several years before the foundation stone was laid. For Philip, as has been aptly summarised, 'the building of his palaces was not simply a mental recreation but a serious aspect of government'.[24]

Charles' statement about not needing residences may appear strange in view of the time and money he spent building the new royal palace in Granada. This was begun in 1527, immediately after Charles' honeymoon in the city with Isabel, and formed part of the reforms initiated in the formerly Muslim city (the new cathedral was begun in 1528). Ironically, however, Charles never came to reside in the new palace, which – thanks to the emperor's commitments in northern Europe – was fated to be abandoned almost as soon as it was constructed. As we have noted, this removed the kingdom of Granada, with its notable Islamic heritage, from centrestage and gave a quite different complexion to the building programme soon to be undertaken by the Habsburgs. The situation for royal architecture changed radically when Philip came to the throne, for the new king took building seriously and did not waste money on frivolous residences which he never expected to occupy.

Philip's permanence in the peninsula after 1559 changed the scene decisively. He brought back with him a wealth of new ideas and schemes. As sovereign of the Netherlands and much of Italy he had access to the talents of the principal humanists and artists of his day. As king of England, he had lived in the best that early Tudor architecture had to offer, and knew that Spain's monarchy lacked the dignity of adequate palaces. Despite his state debts, he set aside sums for his cultural plans. In the 1560s he put together a painstaking and impressive programme. Having seen the great palaces and gardens of Italy, southern Germany, England and the Netherlands, he knew that Spain must compete. A new court must be created. It must be dignified as a royal residence, with a fitting environment of art and music. More than this, the monarchy should be seen as the active promoter of science and learning. He chose humanists as tutors for his son. His chief secretary, Gonzalo Pérez, was a renowned humanist. The gains of humanism should be extended by reforming the curriculum in the universities, and by launching a new multilingual version of the Bible. Surveys should be made of all that was known of the world, which was particularly important in respect of the Indies. Official historians and official chroniclers were appointed.

Of all European states, Spain was in a unique position to launch such a programme. In addition to contacts with Italy and the Netherlands, the peninsula could draw on its own internal experience of the cultures of Jews and Arabs. Philip's commitment to Catholic orthodoxy was not in question, but beyond that he kept his pulse on all branches of enquiry, including both the exotic and the informal. While he never wrote down an outline of what he might do, at some time or other in the 1560s, however, he made decisions intended to set all the above into motion. Looking at the enormous range of matters involved, one cannot fail to admire his energy and purpose. At the same time, there were serious obstacles of which he was perfectly aware. Though there were prominent exceptions, as a class the Spanish elite, both nobility and clergy, had little cultural sophistication.[25] An imperial ambassador to Madrid in the 1570s commented that when the nobles spoke of certain subjects they did so in the way that a blind man speaks of colours. They travelled out of Spain very seldom, he said, and so lacked the perspective from which to make judgements.[26] As such, they were unlikely to contribute much to creating a new courtly culture. Moreover, the printing industry in the peninsula was primitive[27] and largely in the hands of foreigners. Good books would have to be introduced from abroad. Indeed, the problem was that nearly everything would have to be imported if any progress were to be made in Spain. The king even insisted on importing his own writing paper,[28] since he found Castilian paper too coarse.

The Spanish monarchy, it must be recognised, arrived late into the company of other princely courts. In the fifteenth century the European Renaissance transformed Italy into the principal magnet for scholars, writers and artists, who took the new ideas back to their noble and princely courts in France, Germany, Burgundy and England. A circle of cultural interchange was created, but Spain lay on its fringes. In the reign of Ferdinand and Isabella, a few scholars had brought from Italy ideas which took some root in the small noble courts and in the court of Isabella. At the same time, close links with the Netherlands confirmed the influence of Flemish art and, later, of the ideas of Erasmus. But the lack of political union among the regions, the non-existence of a fixed royal court and the frequent absences of the emperor made it impossible for these influences to flourish.

Shortly after his return from the Netherlands in 1559, the king was faced with the problem of accommodating his new court, made up not only of Spaniards but of Netherlanders who had come back with him. Previous rulers of Spain, including his father, had had no central capital; they moved around, taking their officials with them. Valladolid was the effective centre of government, but Philip looked around for other options. In 1559 he moved his work place to the more central location of the old capital of Castile, Toledo, but after only a year there he realised that the city was quite unsuitable. It was out of the question to go back to Valladolid, which in 1561 suffered a serious fire that destroyed a good part of the city. Philip was forced to elaborate a completely new scheme for an administrative centre. Nor was his choice of Madrid necessarily determined by its central location in the peninsula; more important was its position relative to the royal residences, which would allow him to commute without difficulty to his hunting resorts.[29] This enabled him to plan for the growth of Madrid and also to develop the royal palaces within a short radius of the town.

In Madrid he renewed his attention to improving the Alcázar. A small palace of Mudéjar style, and occasionally used in the Middle Ages by Castilian rulers, it was enlarged from 1536 onwards by Charles V. From the 1540s Prince Philip took an interest in the works and in improving the surrounding streets.[30] When the decision to move to Madrid became definite, the building programme speeded up. His head full of the splendours of Netherlands architecture and art, he gave instructions to his builders to adapt structures, roofs and gardens to the style he had seen in the north. A report was solicited from the architect Gaspar de Vega, who had been with Philip in the Netherlands and England and had made a special visit to the French palaces in the area of Paris. Flemish experts and artisans were contracted to come to Spain. The extensive reforms carried out by Philip in the Alcázar transformed it into his principal palace, the only one large enough to act also as the seat of government, where administrative councils met and where ambassadors were normally received.[31]

The Alcázar had been, and continued to be, the royal residence in Madrid. Juan Bautista, aided by a number of Italian artisans, contributed. In the refurbished and enlarged building the king chose as his apartments those on the west, overlooking the River Manzanares and the small Casa de Campo. As with all his architects, he was meticulous and demanding over details. His sketches and notes to Juan Bautista were remorseless: 'This has to be the entrance door . . .', 'the horses have to be able to stay under this doorway when it rains. . . .'[32] He got the changes he wanted. By the late 1560s, long before San Lorenzo had taken shape, the Alcázar had been transformed into the crown's biggest and most imposing residence. The point should be emphasised, in order to rid us of the notion that Philip felt any need to build a palace at San Lorenzo, which was always envisaged primarily as a monastery. The Alcázar was the most visible symbol of the adoption of Italianate style and of the abandonment of traditional Spanish architecture. The nineteenth-century art historian Carl Justi[33] informs us that the Alcázar had on the ground floor a large room for Philip's building plans, where the king discussed ideas with his architects; the next floor housed the library, with books on a wide range of subjects; and the top floor boasted a room whose walls were completely given over to the display of Titian's paintings and representations of the *Metamorphoses* of Ovid.

Philip's lifelong dedication to building had two inseparable components. In the first place, he was fascinated by the aesthetic and technical aspects of palace construction. He knew from direct experience that Spain had nothing to compete with the architecture of Italy or the Netherlands. As a result, he was determined to recreate in Castile, as symbols of his power, residences which would be the equal of anything anywhere else. The rebuilt Alcázars of Madrid and Toledo were the end products, within an urban context, of this desire. In the second place, his palace programme was sketched out in its entirety by 1567. No further projects were added to it. The impact of his new ideas could be seen in the palace of El Pardo, which he himself had done much to rebuild in the previous decade. Now, in 1559, he ordered his architect to remove the entire roofing and have it covered in the Flemish style. For technical reasons nothing could be done until 1562, when the king repeated his decision to re-roof it 'in the style of Flanders'.[34] Experts

('Flemish carpenters') were brought in from the Netherlands for the task. The rooms of the palace had recently been decorated in traditional Castilian style. Philip now ordered the entire interior to be redecorated in the Italian manner. Finally, the extensive woods and gardens were put under the direction of a Fleming ('el holandés', the Dutchman). The evocative drawing that Jean Lhermite made of El Pardo at the end of Philip's reign shows off to perfection the balance between countryside and palace which the king desired, the splendid building presenting a typical example of the marriage between Castilian architecture, Flemish influence and Italian art.

Philip's personal pressure on his officials is illustrated by his correspondence with the secretary of works at El Pardo, Pedro de Hoyo. Philip followed every detail with loving care. In one of his reports in May 1562 Hoyo listed prices: 'I did not think it was so much', Philip scribbled in the margin. Hoyo: 'They tell me the orange trees in the Pardo are in splendid condition.' Philip: 'I am glad to hear it.' Hoyo: 'And that the flowers that are sown in double rows have begun to come out.' Philip: 'Tell them to take care when watering.' Hoyo: 'Men need to be hired to weed the slopes.' Philip: 'That seems fine. But they need to be trustworthy men who will not steal the birdsnests or the eggs.' Shortly afterwards – this in Madrid – Philip sent Hoyo a note: 'Send me by dinner tonight the lists of plants so I can check them against what has come from Flanders.'[35]

After El Pardo, the building to which Philip dedicated most enthusiasm on his return from Flanders was Valsaín, frequently referred to simply as 'el Bosque' ('the Woods'), in the woods near Segovia. Originally a fifteenth-century residence, it was modified on the prince's orders in the late 1540s. In the 1550s further works were undertaken to turn it into a small palace. After his return from the north, Philip paid special attention to the gardens and fountains.[36] He drew his own sketches, with comments. 'The paths have to be broad like those you see here . . . and the path in the middle has to be as wide as shown here', he ordered in 1562.[37] When the French ambassador Saint-Sulpice presented his credentials to Philip that year, the king chose Valsaín for the audience. He quickly got the formalities out of the way, choosing instead to regale Saint-Sulpice with the pleasures of the site. The Flemish engineer Jacques Holbecq was in charge of the water and fountains. The gardener was commissioned to import plants and seeds from Italy and Flanders. In May, excited by the glorious display of colour of the flowers in bloom, he wrote to Philip that 'they have never looked so beautiful as now, Your Majesty must come at once to dinner here'.[38] The final touches were put to the interior of the palace in the 1570s. A historian who looks for an insight into the king's character need look no further than the revealing drawing of Valsaín made by Van den Wijngaerde in 1562,[39] in which the beautiful country house nestles into a background of boundless woods and hills, affording the king the happiness he always found in nature and the peace he desired in order to work but also to spend time with his family.

This short discussion of Philip's attention to his palaces serves as a reminder that the Escorial was never his sole obsession. It was not planned simply as a palace, for he already had many. Moreover, it played no effective part in his living arrangements until over a decade after the beginning of his reign, and in no way monopolised his ongoing involvement in building and decoration. His other residences, notably Valsaín and Aranjuez, were equally and profoundly dear to him, and he spent as much time in them as he did in the Escorial. In some measure, each of his palaces reflected different facets of his dreams and lifestyle. However, the Escorial had a unique place in the building programme. Its monumental dimensions and striking architecture reveal that it was intended to be very much more than a palace. The king appears to have wished to express, through one single extraordinary structure, his obligations to his family and his creator, and his cultural aspirations for the monarchy that was now the most extensive in the western world.

MOTIVES OF FOUNDATION: FILIAL PIETY AND THE SUPPOSED PANTHEON

The 1567 Letter of Foundation, when read carefully, helps to clarify our understanding of Philip's motives. If we read it on the assumption that the king, who was always very ordered in his thoughts, put first things first, it becomes clear that the military successes occupy for him a secondary place. The primary motive, to which the king gave due prominence, was the need to assure his father a worthy tomb. This was the purpose of the monastery. The role of the friars was to offer up perpetual prayer for the repose of the soul of the emperor and, with him, of those of the other members of the royal family. The combination of monastery and tomb was, in some measure, an imitation of the emperor's resting-place in Yuste.[40] The prime motive was, therefore, the expression of filial piety, and the desire for a family mausoleum, an extension (as suggested below) of the concept of a pantheon. Everything else was secondary. If we can discern one overarching and profound emotion in the soul of Philip II, it is his devotion to the memory of his mother and his father.

Historians have usually ignored Philip's relationship with his mother, and at times have misrepresented his relationship with his father. Let us begin briefly with his father. His veneration for Charles V shines through in nearly all he did, but detailed attention to it here would plunge us into a theme that covers several decades and a wide range of issues. Philip, it should be noted, probably never felt the emotion of filial love. The courtesies and protocol of that age, comparable in some respects with the type of distant formality between parents and children to be found in the British ruling classes during the age of empire, set a clear barrier between father and son. Their physical separations were also interminable. When Philip arrived in Brussels in 1549 he embraced a father whom he had not seen in six years. During that period the prince had corresponded regularly with the emperor, but very little of the correspondence was private and what may have been private has not survived. During the entire thirty years that the two shared an existence on earth, Philip probably spent less than nine years – mostly during infancy – in the company of his father. Charles was an absent figure who certainly did not have occasion to dominate or over-shadow his son, so that the image offered by the writer Gregorio Marañón,[41] of a timid and browbeaten Philip, fails to convince because it has no evidence to support it. Marañón was unaware that Charles almost never saw his son, making any sort of domination wholly unlikely.

At the opposite pole to the idea of a dominated son is the equally undocumented idea of profound filial piety. The respect felt by Philip for his father was miles away from the 'love and fervent veneration' that some writers have claimed to see.[42] We know from their correspondence that Philip stood up to his father on many crucial matters of policy, so that the picture of a compliant son is amply contradicted by the documents. On many key issues, such as finance, colonial policy, religious toleration and administrative control, there were significant and profound differences of approach.[43] Available correspondence leaves no room for doubt. Very often, Philip's point of view happened to coincide with that of advisers in the peninsula who disagreed with the emperor, so that differences of opinion were not based on personality but on well-founded policy alternatives. There was, one should stress, no antagonism between Philip and Charles. The image of a son who was personally hostile to his father and could not wait to take over the reins of power is wholly misconceived. Though an attempt has been made to present such a picture of Philip,[44] it receives no support whatever from the documents available in the archives at Simancas. The existence or lack of filial piety does not, however, affect the idea of an intended monument to Charles V. There is every likelihood that from the moment his father died, in 1558, Philip decided to resolve the question of where the emperor's final resting-place would be.

The king's devotion to his mother, who was continually by his side in the twelve years of his life until her death in 1539, is undeniable. The empress Isabel, subject of a handsome portrait by Titian, is one of the great neglected figures of Spain's history. The companion of Philip throughout his early life, her influence on him is beyond doubt. Although the prince's education was in the hands of tutors, her personal attention to him was evident, as witness the fragments of her private correspondence that have survived. 'The prince my son is ill with fever,' she wrote to a friend in mid-June

1532, 'and though the illness is not dangerous it has me very worried and anxious.' Three weeks later Philip was ill again: 'I'm very anxious,' she wrote.[45] When Philip's personal papers are further researched, we shall probably learn more of the ties that bound them together.

An example of the available evidence comes from the private papers of the marquis of Ladrada, who was appointed chamberlain to Philip's last wife Queen Anna when she arrived from Germany in 1570. The king had to consider whether any changes were necessary in the style of household that his late queen, Elizabeth of Valois, had maintained until her untimely death in 1568 in a riding accident. Elizabeth had introduced many French customs and had also been a spendthrift. Philip was in no doubt that a complete makeover was necessary. The household, he decided, must revert to the practice of the time of his mother, the empress Isabel. It is one of the moments that his correspondence lets us glimpse his veneration for her: 'It is not acceptable,' he told Ladrada, 'to continue the household practice of the late queen; everything must be done as it was in the time of my mother.' That was over thirty years ago, but 'I believe that the duke of Alba and Ruy Gómez will be able to inform you about it; what used to be done then must be done now'. During the months following his marriage to Anna, he continued to sweep away the customs and changes brought in by Elizabeth. The standard now was to be the peninsular usage of his mother. Asked whether Queen Anna should observe the practice of making an offering in church, he replied: 'I cannot recall ever seeing my mother making the offering. I wouldn't do it.' And on a point of household procedure, he noted: 'It's what I remember being done in the time of my mother.' On the matter of whether the queen should distribute gifts to all her household at Christmas, he ruled that 'in my mother's time gifts were given, but only to chaplains and cantors; giving more in this past period was, I think, an irregularity, like many other matters'. The last phrase was a dig at the late queen's way of doing things. What remained firm in his mind was the need to run the royal household in the way that his mother had done. The drawback was that he now had only a hazy recall: 'I cannot remember what used to be done in the time of my mother'.[46]

Both his father and mother were at the heart of Philip's plans for the Escorial. In addition to filial piety, Philip had a deep-seated consciousness – as all the European Habsburgs seem to have had – of dynastic loyalty and the interests of family. His tutor's reports on his movements in the spring of 1543, when he was sixteen years old, illustrate his attention to family: 'His Highness arrived here this afternoon in good health, he came from Tordesillas which he visited yesterday, and where his grandmother [Juana the Mad] was most happy to see him. He had also spent a happy week in Alcalá with his sisters.'[47] While the visits to his grandmother always formed an integral part of his routine, those to his sisters were, as we shall see, an essential expression of brotherly love. As an extension to family loyalty he had in mind a broader concern, to achieve somehow the peaceful repose in the same place of the kings and queens of Spain who were of his direct lineage. It was the motive, many years later in 1572, for his instructions to Ambrosio de Morales to find out whether there were any medieval royal persons buried in the old churches of Galicia. However, he did not pursue the aim systematically, and in any case he had enough work attending to the fate of immediate members of his family. The dynastic principle excluded, we should remember, any notion of changing the resting-place of Ferdinand and Isabella, who were not Habsburgs and who already had their recognised tomb in the royal palace that Charles V had been building in Granada.

The concerns for family and dynasty were present at every stage of the construction of the Escorial, but it is almost certainly a mistake to assume that Philip's plans included the construction of a Pantheon for the mortal remains of Spain's royal family. Nowhere did he speak of a Pantheon, a word that was well known to him from his studies of architecture. The king's documents and statements show that there were two main aspects to the concern for his family: that the bodies of the members of the dynasty should be brought from elsewhere in Spain in order to be re-interred, and that a community of monks should be created in order to ensure a constant stream of prayer for the departed would be directed to heaven.[48] Both religion and dynasty therefore converged. The enigma in this scheme, however, lies in the question of the alleged eventual mausoleum for the Habsburgs, which Philip never got around to constructing. If, as many think, the building was meant to be a Pantheon, two fundamental questions arise. Why was the resting-place of the royal dead not given priority in the building plans? And why did the king do nothing in over forty years to construct the crypt that now houses the royal remains?

The collection of royal bodies in the church was the first significant act by Philip on moving into the Escorial. The priority assigned to this is irrefutable proof of what the foundation represented for him. Nothing else was remotely comparable in importance. The first move was taken as the result of an event that, curiously, goes unmentioned in most accounts: the death of his younger sister Juana. Philip was profoundly attached to his two sisters. He was extremely close to his elder sister María, who was married in Madrid in September 1548 to the Archduke Maximilian and went to Germany to be his wife and empress. After Maximilian's death, María returned to Spain in 1581, set up her residence in the convent of the Descalzas in Madrid and became an important component of the political life of the capital.[49] She outlived her brother.

Philip's relationship with Juana was exceptionally close, as we have already had occasion to see (Chapter 1). In 1552 Juana was married to the prince of Portugal, and became mother of the ill-fated king Sebastian. She later acted as regent of Spain, at the age of only twenty, when Philip went to England to marry Mary Tudor. In subsequent years, she withdrew from politics in order to devote herself to religion and founded the convent of the Descalzas in Madrid.[50] She was particularly close to Queen Anna. Later she developed an illness, which in 1572 showed signs of being terminal. During a stay at San Lorenzo with the court she was taken very ill and died a week later, on 8 September 1573, with her brother at her bedside.[51] 'The king', Cabrera de Córdoba commented later, 'loved her deeply.'[52] Juana was buried in the Descalzas, but her demise was indubitably the spur to Philip's decision to bring his lost relatives together in the Escorial. That year the reburial of the royal bodies began in earnest.

The bodies of dead royalty were brought in and lodged temporarily in 1573 in the monastic church, until the main church was completed. The first arrivals were Elizabeth Valois and Don Carlos, who had died in the same year, 1568. Then in 1574 it was the turn of the previous generation, brought in from Granada, Valladolid and Yuste. The most illustrious corpse to arrive was that of the emperor, who during his lifetime had entertained various ideas about where his remains should rest. It is possible that he would have liked to return to his beloved Burgundy, but later on he thought of being buried in Germany. His last testament, drawn up in Brussels in June 1554, stipulated the cathedral of Granada; but eventually by a codicil made at Yuste in September 1558 he decided to leave the decision to his son, asking only that he be buried beside his wife Isabel. The other family members who came in 1574 were Juana the Mad (from Tordesillas, though her body was in fact sent on to Granada, to lie beside her husband Philip the Fair), Philip's mother the empress Isabel, Philip's first wife Maria of Portugal, Charles V's sisters the queens Leonor of France and Mary of Hungary,[53] and recently deceased royal children. Mary of Hungary had been buried in the church of San Benito in Valladolid (we know this from the report by the king's chaplain Ambrosio de Morales when he made a visit to the north of Castile in 1572);[54] the king arranged for her remains to be transferred to the Escorial in February 1574.

The building of the great church – the basilica – of San Lorenzo did not begin until 1575, and there appears to be no documentation about a tomb plan for the royal bodies until 1579. Events may have been precipitated in that year by the death of the king's half-brother Don Juan. Aged only thirty-two when he died in office as commander in the Netherlands, on 1 October 1578,[55] Don Juan was buried at Namur, then in the spring of 1579 disinterred and his body brought back secretly to Spain. Nothing shows more clearly the king's insistence on giving his family a suitable resting-place. The event elicited from Sigüenza an unequivocal assertion: 'the principal purpose of this building is to be one sole mausoleum for so many and such illustrious royal persons'.[56] Don Juan's body was cut up in the Netherlands at the joints, packed suitably into leather bags, then accompanied overland to Spain by an escort of eighty. (The arduous journey was deemed preferable to the risk of loss if the body were shipped by sea.) The body was taken to the monastery at Parraces, where it was put together and deposited in a coffin, which was then transported to the Escorial and buried with honours on 24 May 1579. Don Juan was followed there by Queen Anna, who died of the epidemic in Extremadura and whose body was received in the monastery by Cardinal Quiroga of Toledo on 11 November 1580. Because of his absence at the battle front in Portugal, Philip could not attend the ceremonies for Anna.

The royal burials in the Escorial were meant to be temporary, since the final resting-place could not be decided until the basilica was completed and definitive tombs allotted. The construction was not completed until 1584, and only then did the king feel free to decide. After the basilica had been blessed in 1586, he was faced with a crucial decision. One writer suggests that the Escorial 'was raised and endowed with the purpose of building a large royal sepulchre, the Pantheon, in which would be laid to rest the remains' of the family of Philip II.[57] The truth is that the king never stated the intention nor in thirty years took any steps towards putting it into effect. Despite this, it is often believed that he harboured the intention of transforming an unused chapel below the sanctuary into a final burial place for all the royal figures. There are solid grounds for dissenting from this opinion. If the king planned a Pantheon, the big question is why he delayed so long in constructing something that has been presented as a key reason for the existence of the Escorial.

Like other students of Renaissance architecture, Philip was perfectly aware of the fundamental importance allotted to the Pantheon of Rome in Serlio's classic treatise (see page 53). In the Third Book of his treatise, Serlio placed great stress on the theme: 'Of all the ancient buildings that can be seen in Rome, in my estimation the Pantheon is actually the most beautiful, most complete and best conceived.'[58] A visitor to Rome today would have little reason to disagree with this verdict on one of the most striking monuments in the city. Despite this text, Philip did not integrate the idea into his plans. Burying the royal family and dynasty in a monastery was an idea with which he had long been familiar, since he had personally seen it done in the royal monastery at Poblet in Catalonia, where the kings and queens of the Crown of Aragon were buried. Philip had been at Poblet more than once, yet he never got around to imitating the impressive and sacred disposition of royal tombs in the area of the altar there. Philip had also been in Westminster Abbey, where he had seen and admired the tomb of Henry VII and his wife – described by a recent scholar as 'the most triumphant collaboration of the visual arts in the entire English Renaissance'[59] – yet he never took any steps to emulate what he had seen in London. What is certain is that the king had direct personal knowledge of many models that might have served him, had he intended to create a Pantheon. However, he used none of them.

There were two distinct stages in the plans he adopted for the burials. The first stage, completed by about 1580, involved the bringing together of the royal bodies. Time and money were spent on laying them to rest, but still the king revealed no plans for any 'large royal sepulchre'. Only in 1586, two years after the formal completion of the whole edifice and nearly a quarter of a century after the commencement of works, did Philip articulate a plan to re-inter the royal bodies.[60] The basilica had now been blessed, and was a fitting place for a garden of remembrance. We must remember that it was a long-standing practice in every part of the Christian world for the great ones of Church and state to be laid to rest in their family churches, sometimes under the flagstones, sometimes in sarcophagi, sometimes in sculpted tombs. The Escorial was now the family church of the Habsburgs. But what location could serve for the tombs? At first the king had certainly considered moving all the bodies to the underground chapel beneath the high altar (the present location of the Pantheon). His bad health, however, led him to change his mind. At the end of May 1586 he suffered an acute attack of gout, which lasted for over two months and made it impossible for him to conduct business normally. Late in June he was confined to bed for a while and periodically bled.[61] 'Now I can walk around,' he reported in July, 'although a bit lame and still with a stick. I had a bad attack in my hand and have not been able to write.'[62]

The change of plan was explained by Sigüenza as follows: 'he felt that this place [the underground chapel] was a long way away, gloomy, and difficult to enter or leave'.[63] Even today a visitor to the basement chapel has to descend the staircase with care. Had Philip pursued the idea, it would have been almost impossible for him to go downstairs and visit the tombs. His poor health ruled out any possibility of an underground mausoleum. His final decision – made almost immediately after the blessing of the basilica in August – appears in the order he issued from the Pardo palace on 18 October 1586,[64] which directs that the royal bodies

> be moved and transferred from where they now are to the vault under the high altar of the main church, which is the place that I now direct to be fixed for the burials.

The move, stated the king, was final: 'with the said move my wishes will have been observed'. Philip's phrase pre-empts any need for speculation about a hypothetical intention to move the bodies yet again to the underground crypt. The definitive reburials in November 1586 were carried out with care and ceremony.[65] It was a solemn occasion, but too emotionally painful for Philip,[66] who made it plain that he did not wish to be present.[67] Modern visitors to the Escorial are, to my knowledge, never informed that the king's intention was quite the opposite of what the subsequent Pantheon accomplished. Philip wished to place all the members of his family together, which is what he achieved with the 1586 burials. That was an act of loyalty and piety. There was never any intention of separating the kings and queens from the others, leaving the latter to a different place of rest, namely the so-called pantheon of the Infantes which is located in the basement.

When, in 1599 and a year after the king's death, the Jesuit Juan de Mariana wrote a brief survey of the Escorial he made no mention of a possible Pantheon, and limited his discussion of the burials to a description of the steps leading up to the high altar, 'made of green stone inlaid with red, eighteen broad steps, under which lie the tombs of the kings and queens'.[68] It is sometimes claimed that Philip would have constructed the Pantheon had the money not run out. However, the required sum would not have been large and the king always gave priority to the sacred task of caring for his dynasty. His vow in 1563, hidden away in the British Library in a letter that has never been published, is definitive: 'I shall always make an effort to find money for that building [the Escorial]'.[69] He kept to his word: the building was finished as planned, all bills were met, and no contractor or architect ever complained that they had not been paid. The evidence obliges us to conclude that the Pantheon, commenced in fact by Philip III and completed by Philip IV, never entered into the king's plans for the church. When the friar Francisco de los Santos proclaimed in 1650 that 'the glory of the Escorial is the Pantheon', his aim was to heap praise on Philip III while at the same time crediting Philip II for an idea described as the latter's 'royal intention'. In reality, there was no intention nor proof of any, and Santos was unable to document it. Such royal intention as there was remained exclusively that of Philip III, who also chose the architect. A scholar concludes, logically enough, that 'the Royal Pantheon was a work promoted by Philip III and carried out by Juan Gómez de Mora' as architect.[70] When interpreting Philip II's ideas and plans, it is clearly safer to leave out of the reckoning the semi-Baroque garishness of the underground Pantheon.

THE BASIC CONTEXT: THE KING AS GARDENER

A modern-day visitor to the Escorial is confronted by an enormous structure of stone walls and terrace, an immensely sombre perspective. This was not the king's intention. Philip II was the first king to be a lover of gardens in Spain's history, but the fact has tended to be neglected. Students of the Escorial have too frequently ignored the geographical setting envisaged by Philip II, and gone straight to what appears to be the centre of attention, the monastery-palace. It is consequently important to point out that not for nothing did the king spend many months searching for a suitable site. His first concern was less for the building than for the setting in which it would shine. All his life he was a lover of nature.[71] His monastery must have a wholly rural setting, with woods, water and wildlife. These were not irrelevant requirements: the woods were for supplies of timber, the water was for human survival, the wildlife for background effect as well as for hunting. Throughout his life Philip had a great attachment to nature. In the cold midwinter of the Netherlands in February 1559, he wrote to his friend Ruy Gomez that he was going to take a break from work and go hunting in Binche, 'excellent country for it, and for the benefit to my health from the exercise and the open air'.[72] In the 1580s he was repeating to his daughters the advice that nothing was better than fresh air. He never cared for the city as an environment – his first love was always for the open air, for fields and forests, riding and hunting. He regularly insisted to his children as well as to his ministers that they should take fresh air more often, and his workplace had to be within reach of healthy leisure pursuits. If we look carefully at the completely wooded setting of Binche, its environs covered by a dense carpet of trees, or at the wild surroundings of Ettal, cradled in a fold of the Bavarian Alps and woods, we can begin to imagine the hope that Philip nurtured, of finding his desired haven in the forests of Castile.

The visual austerity presented by the vast stone pavement leading up to huge stone walls was certainly not what Philip had in mind when he created the palace. The carefully contoured hedges that run along the south wall today, supplying an elegant setting to soften the mass of granite, are a pale shadow of the gardens that the young king intended to plant on the mountain slopes. Philip was the first king of Spain to have the culture, enthusiasm, time and money to undertake a gardening programme. Generations of writers have been indifferent to this passion, leaving us with few adequate studies of the king as a lover of flowers, plants, grass, countryside and nature in general.[73] There is little information about the king's interest in these matters, even in massive volumes purporting to be dedicated to the theme.[74] A specialist essay on the gardens of the Escorial limits itself to saying that there were no gardens in Spain, except for those that owed their origin to the Arabs, or had been recently cultivated by Italian architects.[75] It is hardly surprising that we should be left with an image of a royal prisoner immured within stone walls if few historians have little more than mentioned the extensive gardens to which Philip devoted hour upon hour of his precious time. The king who constructed the wonder of Aranjuez, conceived as a poem of joy to the world of nature and viewed by a Flemish courtier as a terrestrial paradise,[76] was also the king who planned the gardens of the Escorial.

The love of nature had been with Philip all his life, but he first began to learn about garden design when he undertook his travels in northern Europe. He learnt directly from the gardens of the Italian princes during his stay in northern Italy in 1548. However, one should not exaggerate the quality of what was available to learn. The late Renaissance garden was as yet in its infancy: the famous gardens of the Villa d'Este were begun only after 1560, those of Tivoli only after 1570, and those of the Villa Medici at the same date. Likewise in England, though Hampton Court had gardens in the early century, the principal gardens of stately homes took shape only in the 1570s.[77] The Dutch, who became perhaps the most outstanding gardeners of Europe, did not make their horticultural mark until they had won their liberty from Spain, decades later.

However, enough on the subject existed for Philip to have a clear idea of the enormous difference between Europe and Spain. During the five years he spent in the north for his wedding and his father's abdication, he was already committed to the gardening programme, and must have learnt much from the report he received from his agent Gaspar de Vega in May 1556, on the state of the French palaces at the Louvre, St Germain sur Laye and Fontainebleau.[78] It was in the Netherlands that he first discovered the delights of endless landscapes, and the possibility of combining countryside with palaces. Full of enthusiasm, he brought the idea of the garden back with him in 1559. Philip received further advice from those who had direct knowledge of the estates of Italian princes. He has been described, in one of the few adequate essays on the subject, as 'the introducer into Spain of the new concept of [the] garden that emerged in the Italian Renaissance, to which he added the floral richness typical of the Flemish, German and English world'.[79]

As each garden developed, Philip would pass scribbled lists of plants and ideas to the designers. He sent experts abroad to gain experience firsthand. When one of his designers died he asked for his notebooks to be sent to him; and in particular one 'which says it is of gardens in Italy though I think it refers to France or England, which he did when I sent him to see the gardens there'.[80] In his instructions one phrase recurs: the plants must be like those 'in Flanders'.[81] Under the care of the Dutch and Italian specialists whom he attracted to Spain, and notably under the expert guidance of Juan Bautista, Philip's palace gardens became a superb example of Italian Mannerism.[82] Readily accessible from the capital, they offered a haven of peace to which he could escape from his bureaucratic duties. More broadly, his love of nature also evoked concerns for the environment. A constant traveller through the countryside of central Castile, he was disturbed by the condition of the forests, increasingly consumed as these were by tillage or by the search for firewood. 'One thing I would like to see done', he stated to a government minister in 1582, 'is about the conservation of the forests. . . . I fear that those who come after us will have much to complain of if we leave them depleted, and please God we do not see it in our time.'[83] Above all, the country represented for him the pleasures of hunting, his principal and lifelong relaxation. All his residences, including the Escorial, were developed with hunting in mind.

Following the style Philip had seen in northern Europe, gardens had to be constructed outside the walls of the palace, as a retreat for leisure and walks. Twelve thousand pine trees were purchased from the city of Cuenca and transported to the monastery by river and road.[84] Comparable efforts were made to bring plants from Holland. Fish were sought to stock the ponds. In the spring of 1566 the king thanked his gardener in Segovia for cultivating flowers, and added: 'I sent some on Thursday or Friday to the Escorial, have them put in water, and not too open because they will open soon enough'.[85] The gardens to the south of the monastery emerge clearly in paintings of the time, and even today an enterprising photographer may capture some of the view available to the king.

Filled today only with blossomless shrubs, the gardens in the king's time were a blaze of colour. According to Sigüenza, the Escorial plots were planted in the Arab manner, by scattering the seeds of a variety of flowers. The king was a great lover of flowers, which obviously constituted a vital part of his plan for the Escorial, so much so that he took his work there in order to tend to the plants in his leisure time. Sigüenza observes that during 1576 'the king visited even more often, because the plants needed to be watered more frequently'.[86] The king's grand design has long since vanished under the weight of the indifference of subsequent generations, and visitors are left with views of a landscape in which flowering plants have been almost expunged from the original conception of the creator of the Escorial.

The only garden inside the monastery was in the courtyard of the Evangelists. A modern expert sees the courtyard as 'the only monastic feature of the Escorial to be architecturally distinguished, since the conventual buildings are utilitarian'.[87] It was created by Fray Marcos de Cardona, who had designed a similar one for Charles V in the small palace at Yuste, and its layout was possibly an imitation of one in the monastery of Guadalupe, which was also a Jeronimite house and from which some of the Escorial's friars came.[88] The courtyard was planned to be accessible also to the king. Philip's private chambers overlooked the space with its plants and fountains and afforded him his only contact with nature within the confines of the monastic building. When he wanted to go outside for a while and think, it was the courtyard into which he went. Sigüenza comments that the patio was

> for everybody the most cheerful space in this building, because the monks and members of the royal family go down to it, walk there, pick flowers in summer and enjoy the sun in winter. It is a great solace for the soul.

From the other side of his apartments, the king also had the benefit of more greenery, the whole perspective of the south side, from which he could look out with an unimpeded view onto the gardens, trees and landscape before him. Among the few foreign visitors to have appreciated this view was an American, William Dean Howells, who commented in his *Familiar Spanish Travels*: 'I did think the convent gardens as I saw them from the chapter-house window were beautiful, and the hills around majestic and serious'.[89]

It is not out of place to recall at this point that the creator of the Escorial also created Aranjuez, which we have mentioned earlier. Unaccountably, many have chosen to identify the personality of the king with the gaunt stone of the Escorial rather than with the buildings which were equally his home, Valsaín (noted on pages 59–60) and Aranjuez. After the Escorial, Aranjuez was the site which most benefited from the services of Juan Bautista. With Philip's encouragement, the architect and the master of works Juan de Castro laid the basis for a splendid residence. One of the king's pet schemes, which he pursued throughout his reign, was to make the River Tajo navigable. To this end, at Aranjuez Juan Bautista undertook a prolonged feat of engineering which succeeded in making part of the river more easily navigable.[90] Water for irrigation and watering was an urgent need on this site. Thanks to Juan Bautista, it became possible to transform the entire area of Aranjuez, with a perimeter of nearly 34 kilometres (25 miles), into a huge garden.

Jean Lhermite's contemporary sketch of the site offers an impressive perspective. Five thousand trees were imported from Flanders. Fruit trees were introduced from France.[91] Exotic plants came from the Indies and from all over the peninsula. Dutch gardeners were put in charge of the landscaping. Philip lovingly planned and modified every detail of the gardens. To a large extent, he was their architect.[92] Covered with woods, parks and gardens, in which an immense variety of trees, plants, fruits and above all flowers flourished, Aranjuez was a source of wonder to visitors and of unremitting pleasure to the monarch. As an alternative to the Escorial, he fled there to escape from his papers and to fish in the lakes.

THE KING, HIS ARCHITECTS AND HIS IDEAS FOR
THE ESCORIAL

Although the actual work was in the hands of architects, the Escorial was in great measure Philip's own creation, a projection of his own imagination. In the months of consultation in 1561 between Juan Bautista, Pedro de Hoyo and the Jeronimite friars, the king imposed his wishes at every stage. 'Your Majesty is quite right', Hoyo observed, 'to want to do more for San Lorenzo than any other site. Because apart from the service of God one is also dealing with a question of prestige (*reputación*)'.[93] In his determination to create something durable, in 1562–3 the king rejected key features of Juan Bautista's plan, and accepted instead suggestions by other architects. Construction work began early in 1562 and foundation stones were formally laid on 23 April 1563 for the monastery and on 20 August for the church. Juan Bautista's outline for the building was subjected to the severe (and usually justified) criticisms of the friars, other architects and the king himself. The masterplan underwent major changes, the most important of which was the decision, in 1564, to construct a further storey in order to house more religious. Through his builders and architects, the king managed to give expression to his conception of the Escorial. The building was to be pre-eminently religious, though with provision for a royal residence. It is unlikely that the king had any intention of re-creating the Biblical Temple of Solomon (see the discussion in Chapter 4).[94]

The king's personal interest in his architectural programme was all-encompassing. His role has frequently been reduced to the level of the trivial and the anecdotal, but the reality was different. As we have seen, since the 1540s he had taken a serious and creative interest in restoring all his palaces and his direct experience in northern Europe filled his head with new ideas. His personal contribution to the programme was not simply as paymaster. He sent rough sketches and specific instructions to his architects. Broad schematisation and minute detail were equally interesting to him, for these were *his* palaces and in great measure *his* ideas. In the middle of a busy session with his papers the building programme would break in on his thoughts: 'Although I have a hundred papers in front of me', runs a note, 'I thought I would remind you of the following . . .'.[95]

Attributing the part played by each planner in the evolution of the building over the thirty years it took to complete has given rise to significant differences of scholarly opinion. There is no dispute over the fundamental contribution of Juan Bautista, on whom however the king made incessant demands. His relationship with the architect was close and friendly, but he was careful not to offend his touchy disposition. 'I don't know if I frightened him with what I demanded,' he confessed to Hoyo in 1563, 'I mean in the building.'[96] From our perspective, his demands on the architect do seem inordinate and the work may well have contributed to Juan Bautista's premature death in 1567, though the tragedy of his personal circumstances undoubtedly left their mark. The next major influence on the style of the Escorial was Juan de Herrera, who followed Juan Bautista as principal architect. Though Herrera played an important part in several of the king's projects, his role in the Escorial was certainly smaller than he himself claimed.[97] Our concern here is principally with the king's own role. In the peak building years 1562 and 1563 Philip alternated his political and family duties with visits to all the sites where work was in progress. His works secretary Pedro de Hoyo had to handle memos, notes and letters from the king. 'I shall go tomorrow to sleep in Aranjuez', ran a typical note in May 1562, 'go there and make Juan Bautista go there tomorrow with the sketches of the monastery.' Philip's attention to detail was unrelenting. He was no dilettante, nor did he demand the impossible. He spent long hours discussing plans with his architects, trying to adjust what he wished to what was feasible. There were regular site meetings. 'The weather is so good', he scribbled to Hoyo on a fine summer's day in 1565, 'that we must not waste it, and so I want to go this afternoon to El Pardo and tomorrow to El Escorial . . . and would like you also to arrive there tomorrow.' His instructions were based on informed discussions with his architects.

We have already suggested the possibility that the king's first inspiration for the monastery, as well as his vision of its ideal location, stemmed from his visit to the abbey at Ettal in Bavaria. In the same way it is possible to suggest that some of his early ideas on the structure came out of his direct experience of a building with which both he and Juan Bautista were familiar, the Ospedale Maggiore in Milan. This impressive but unfinished Renaissance structure, planned with interior courtyards and a basilica, had been built around 1460 for the duke of Milan, Francesco Sforza, by the architect Antonio Filarete (see Chapter 4 below). The king, in short, had adequate experience and material of his own to be able to take part in the complex process of agreeing on what could and could not be done in San Lorenzo. By 1567 enough of the building had been completed to allow the monks, the king with some of his court and part of the stables to take up residence. A good part of the king's official correspondence in 1569, for example, was sent from the Escorial. The building now had a small church, with kitchens and other necessary amenities.

The next important stage in construction was the building of the basilica, the central feature of the whole edifice, commenced in 1574. The years spent in erecting the building up to that point were also years in which time and again there were shifts in ideas over what the church should be like.[98] The basilica was to be not merely an imposing church, but the resting-place for bodies of the royal family. Its planning and construction were to be the most problematic aspect of all. Subsequently, other key features of the structure took shape, among them the library, which was completed in 1583. The king's permanent apartments were not ready before 1585; until then, the royal family occupied temporary quarters in the south wing. The apartments, when completed, served not only as a residence but also as a court, with public audience halls. However, this public role never overwhelmed the private character of the palace, a place for retreat and prayer.[99]

The money and effort devoted to the construction programme were impressive. Thousands of workmen were employed for decades. Immense quantities of materials were transported into and across the peninsula. Fleets of carts trundled from the port of Cartagena to the site at Aranjuez with tons of marble imported from Italy; shiploads of nails came from Antwerp.[100] Given the crucial part played in the construction by personnel and material from Italy and the Netherlands, Sigüenza had no hesitation in viewing the result as an all-European product: 'No small part of this building came from all over Spain, Italy and Flanders, and although it was possible to estimate the men who worked on the temple of Solomon it is no easy task to estimate the material for this one, since it came from an infinite number of places'.[101] His description of the men at work is impressive:

> That uproar and noise, that variety of people and different voices, that range of artisans, workers and labourers all absorbed in a single and extraordinary task, caused astonishment and wonder to everyone who saw it for the first time. In the church alone there were twenty cranes, with men shouting to others, those from below shouting to those above, those in the middle yelling at each other, by day and night, morning and afternoon, you heard nothing but pull up, let down, let go, etc, everything seethed and grew at an astonishing rate. The countryside around echoed to blows.[102]

THE ESCORIAL AS A REPOSITORY OF ART

Over and above the overwhelming architecture and its ecclesiastical significance, Philip brought into existence for the Escorial 'one of the finest collections of religious art in Europe'.[103] When more extensive analysis of the collection as it was at the time is eventually undertaken (not an easy task, given the substantial relocation of many of the paintings), we may begin to see that the king made a hugely positive contribution to the visual appreciation of the Christian religion. By the time of his death, it has been calculated, he had donated some 1,150 paintings. The building has continued to function as a sort of art gallery: today it is calculated that it contains 1,600 oils and 540 frescoes by Van der Weyden, Dürer, Bosch, Titian, Tintoretto, Velázquez, Rubens, Veronese, Navarrete, Ribera and later Baroque artists. The emphasis on numbers may, however, mislead us into thinking of the building as a huge art venue. It is certainly more correct and historical to think of it rather as a repository of sacred art that was intended to complement the message of the structure. Art historians have a rich field in which to develop their expertise about the king, his tastes and the cultural environment of the time. The following comments are limited to touching on some aspects that have already been developed magisterially by experts in the field.

Philip II was Europe's leading patron of artists.[104] His tastes, though nurtured against a Castilian background, were shaped and matured by extensive travel. Observers of the time, and readers of his own surviving papers, testify that his interest in art was positive, personal and discriminating. At one time, we are informed by a Venetian ambassador, he himself had taken up painting.[105] Artists were not, for him, mere artisans: he had a profound but critical respect for them. He wrote to them directly, argued with them personally, and bullied them mercilessly. He cast his eye all over Europe in search of the best. The Escorial, logically, was a repository for religious rather than profane art, and does not by itself offer a guide to the whole range of the king's preferences. The crucial contribution of the monastery was, moreover, in *imported* art and artists. The collection was not predominantly Spanish and did not therefore constitute a Spanish input to the Renaissance. During his years travelling on the continent and in England, Philip never ceased to make notes on the pictures he wished to buy and the painters he wished to employ. When he returned to the peninsula in 1559 his ships were loaded down with foreign works of art, and unkind fate decreed that many of them should perish in the storm that hit the fleet just after landfall.

The king's most enduring enthusiasm was for the work of Titian. In Italy, in Augsburg and from Brussels, he commissioned several paintings. Some of the most famous portraits of Charles V and Philip were executed at this time. The most significant canvases of the early period were the series known as 'Poésies', based on themes from classical mythology. The sensuality of Titian's figures, the emphasis on the female nude, the preference for mythological themes, all appealed to a king who at this stage was captivated by the world of humanism and chivalry.[106] A taste for sensuality was not exclusive to Philip; it was shared by other European courts as well. While Titian continued painting for the king well after this, from about 1560, however, there was a change of mood. All further commissions were for exclusively religious subjects. Since we know that the king had not altered in outlook or character, the reason must be sought in the buildings for which the new paintings were intended. The earlier works were intended for the private pleasure of the king, in his country houses at El Pardo and Valsaín. Many of the later works were by contrast public pieces. Titian's *Last Supper* (1564), for instance, was meant for the Escorial. The building of the new monastery, from the 1560s, undoubtedly had a crucial impact on changing the type of paintings that the king commissioned. Meanwhile, Philip had immeasurably enriched his collection of Titians with the paintings he inherited from his father and from Mary of Hungary. The Italian master always remained Philip's favourite artist.

Flemish art was his first love, as we can see from the works he began collecting during his first visit to the Netherlands. His collection of paintings by Bosch is one example of his preferences. He owned at least one work by Bosch in 1564, adding more in subsequent years (the *Garden of Earthly Delights* came very late to the monastery, part of a gift of five Bosch works donated by a noble in 1593). Philip ended up with at least twenty-six paintings by Bosch; most of them were hung in the Escorial, though several were to be found in the Pardo, alongside works by Mor and Titian.[107] The Flemish artist's primitive style, and his obvious moralising, seem to have been the aspects which appealed to the king. José de Sigüenza firmly defended the king's taste for Bosch: the artist, he said, presented 'a satire in paint on the sins of men'.[108] Nor was Philip wholly alone in his admiration for Bosch enjoyed a certain popularity in Spain and his works were often copied by Spaniards.[109]

Among the accomplished northern painters who attracted the king's favour was Antonis Mor, the Brussels-based artist who had painted a portrait of the prince in 1549. When he returned to the Netherlands six years later Philip adopted him as court painter and invited him to Spain. Mor made three visits to the peninsula. No fewer than fifteen of his works came to hang in El Pardo, and the artist ranked as high as Titian in the king's favour.[110] In some matters the king had a decided preference for things Flemish, but in other areas, such as frescos, he was more inclined to use Italians.[111] In the same decade he also invited to his court the Italian sculptor Pompeo Leoni and his son Leone. The latter's son Pompeo became in the 1580s the king's official court sculptor. The priority given to Flemish and Italian art in Philip's court is attested by the roll-call of artists who visited Spain, including Gianbattista Bergamasco, Anton van den Wijngaerde, Luca Cambiaso and Federigo Zuccaro. All the Italian artists were brought in to decorate the Escorial. Among the last of them was Pellegrino Tibaldi, who laboured at the Escorial between 1588 and 1593.

Peninsular artists were not absent from this gallery. From the 1550s the Valencian painter Alonso Sánchez Coello, who had studied with Mor in Brussels, began to produce portraits of members of the royal family.[112] Philip set aside special apartments for him and his family in the Alcázar, and loved to slip in unannounced to watch the painter at work. Alonso produced a large number of accomplished canvases, and found the spare time to father eleven children. Royal favour was also extended to Coello's pupil Juan Pantoja de la Cruz. A particular favourite of Philip's among the Spanish painters was Juan Fernández de Navarrete, 'el Mudo' ('the Dumb'). An obvious absentee from the list of artists whom the king patronised was El Greco. Shortly after his return from Portugal in 1583 Philip had to decide on the future of a large canvas which El Greco delivered to the Escorial in November 1582, *The Martyrdom of St Maurice*. According to a friar who was present, the king rejected the painting (on which the artist had been working for two years) because of its exaggerated emphasis on the figures in the foreground.[113] The rejection excluded El Greco thereafter from the ambit of royal patronage.

Philip's close collaboration with Juan de Herrera is perhaps the clearest illustration of the contact between patron and artist. In the 1560s Herrera was doing minor work for the crown. From 1572 he was put in charge of the development of the Escorial, and assigned tasks on other sites. Seven years later, the king appointed him his royal architect. For over thirty years he worked closely as Philip's servant, obediently carrying out instructions but also imposing, in the process, his stamp on the architecture of Spain. He died in 1597, a few months before his king. Under Philip's direction, Herrera gave a unique character to the royal building programme.[114] In the Alcázar of Toledo, which he modified, he offered a structure of simplicity but also of authority and power. When the king was in Lisbon, he planned and constructed the new royal palace, the Paço da Ribeira, overlooking the harbour. Herrera extended his style to non-royal buildings, such as the merchants' exchange, the Lonja, in Seville, but it was the Escorial which most typified his style and his relationship with Philip. Thanks to their partnership, architecture in Spain seemed to become an integral aspect of royal policy. Philip was no theorist, and nursed no dreams of grandeur. Simplicity and frugality were among his most basic principles, and neither excess nor superfluity can be found in his palaces.[115] But he also wished to give Spain the aesthetic riches that other monarchies already possessed.

By the sheer volume of their output, the artists contributed enormously to the grandeur and standing of the king. Philip established a completely new norm for collectors thanks to the resources at his disposal and the variety of realms over which he reigned. A natural consequence of the ideas and preferences that the king developed during his long years abroad, and of the contacts and influences that were now maturing, the Escorial – it might seem surprising to emphasise, given the standard belief that it is somehow very 'Spanish' – became an expression of universal culture of a type hitherto unknown in the peninsula. Because of this, it never ceased both to surprise and to shock. After his travels through Europe, Philip opted very decidedly for Germanic and Italian culture, since there was no specifically Spanish culture on which he could draw for his purposes. Nor is the word 'Germanic' a misnomer, even though it is habitual to refer only to so-called 'Flemish' influences. In terms of princely and monastic architecture and gardens, with which he was intimately familiar from his travels in Austria, Bavaria and the Rhineland, he probably picked up a great deal from Germany, as he certainly did in matters of books, armour and religious relics. In general, it was not a question of choosing between influences,[116] for he frankly chose all influences. There was, however, always a marked preference for things northern. Despite the extensive use of Italian painters, it is likely that the fundamental artistic influence at work in the monastery was Flemish. The pioneering Danish scholar Carl Justi, who produced the first modern analysis of Philip II's tastes, relates an incident to this effect.[117] Apparently the king paid a visit to the Carthusian monastery in Miraflores (Burgos) and when he saw the richness of the Flemish artwork there, produced at the instigation of Isabella the Catholic, he exclaimed, 'What we have done in the Escorial is nothing!'

However, San Lorenzo was always the apple of Philip's eye. We can see his delight in the project through the receptions he laid on for visitors. If foreign diplomats chanced on him in Madrid rather than in San Lorenzo, he packed them off there immediately so they would not fail to see his creation. As a particular example of how he loved to impress others with the building, we may choose the notable visit by Japanese nobles in 1584.[118] The visit was perhaps the Escorial's first real contact with the world outside Europe, and so fully merits mention here. Christian converts were at the time a growing community in Japan, and their mentors the Jesuits encouraged them to send a small group to visit the seat of Christianity in Rome.[119] The hope was that the trip would encourage more support from the pope for the mission. Four young Japanese nobles and their Portuguese Jesuit guide left Nagasaki in February 1582 and arrived in Portugal towards the end of 1584. In Madrid in November they were encouraged by the king (recently returned from Lisbon) to visit his Escorial. Philip escorted them in person. The visitors were impressed and expressed their admiration for 'so magnificent a thing, whose like we have never seen nor expected to see'. The youths then went on to Italy, from which they eventually took ship on a long voyage that – taking into account delays waiting in port for ships – lasted four years. Their whole visit took an astonishing seven years, and proved eventually to be fruitless, since neither Spain nor the papacy extended any help to the beleaguered Japanese Christians as a result.[120] The fame of the Escorial, however, had for the first time penetrated to the farthest ends of the globe.

CHAPTER 4

THE MAGIC TEMPLE
OF WISDOM

The fabled Temple of Solomon; The Temple of Wisdom; Science and the Escorial

From the moment of its construction, the wholly unexpected vision of a massive and isolated monastery cradled in the hills of northern Castile never ceased to generate wonder on the part of beholders. Since visitors had seldom seen similar edifices – the monastery of Guadalupe in Extremadura was probably the only comparable one in the peninsula – they were liable to conclude that the building was unique, if not a product of fantasy. Commentators were unconvinced by the humdrum idea that it could be related to its immediate environment in Spain, or born out of a normal process of decision-making, and had no difficulty in looking for more exotic explanations. With the passage of time extravagant interpretations multiplied.[1] Among scholarly fantasies, perhaps the most popular was the idea, broached by a handful of researchers in the twentieth century, that the Escorial had in some way been inspired by Philip's wish to copy the fabled Temple of Solomon in Jerusalem. Without any visible evidence, the idea of the Escorial as a mystical reproduction of the Temple has been reiterated by imaginative scholars,[2] which has reinforced the vision of the building as a mystery or enigma.

One should emphasise that in the mid-sixteenth century, when Philip II planned and constructed San Lorenzo, not a single spoken or textual reference was made, either in Spain or in the rest of Europe, to a possible connection between the Jewish Temple once located in historic Jerusalem and the monastery taking shape in the hills outside Madrid. *After* the monastery had been completed, of course, the monks themselves and an occasional writer from outside were proud enough of the building to make comparisons with the biblical Temple. Some observers may even have ventured to claim that the Bible had inspired Philip II's architectural plans. These basic facts have been summarised in the following way by a recent historian: 'The idea of reproducing the Temple of Solomon may not have existed before the building of the Escorial, but it is certain that its final form sought to reflect its image'.[3] Even this 'certainty' is, one may add, open to question.

The absence of any evidence for an architectural connection between San Lorenzo and the Bible has not deterred a handful of writers searching for an exotic origin. Two principal approaches have occupied these commentators in recent decades. First, in 1967 an American scholar, René Taylor, published an intriguing essay (commented on below) in which he argued that ideas related to magic had inspired some of the artists and architects working on the Escorial.[4] This is a perfectly plausible hypothesis. Many creative spirits of that age, including Philip II, took an interest in magic. However, no other art critic has supported or added substance to the hypothesis. Subsequently, in 1979 a German researcher, Cornelia von der Osten Sacken,[5] further developed one aspect of Taylor's argument, on how the planning of the Escorial was influenced by the notion of Solomon as a source of magical ideas. This created a second, if rather less systematic approach, in which researchers began looking for any reference that might conceivably link Philip II to King Solomon. The accumulation of references to the word 'Solomon' was intended to demonstrate that Philip saw himself (even though he never said so) as a new Solomon building the Temple. Was the Escorial, we may ask, an attempt to reproduce the biblical temple?

THE FABLED TEMPLE OF SOLOMON

Since the Middle Ages, the name of Solomon had been associated with wisdom, magic and sorcery.[6] 'God gave Solomon wisdom and understanding exceeding much' (1 Kings 4), and supervised the temple that he built in Jerusalem. To avoid confusion, we need to recall that there were in fact four biblical temples: the one built by Solomon (and destroyed by the Babylonians), the second one built after the return from captivity in Babylon, and the third one built by Herod and destroyed by the Romans. The fourth existed only in a vision: its form was dictated by God to the prophet Ezekiel during the captivity. In practice, sixteenth-century commentators tended to limit their attention to the temple of Solomon, which connected with related themes of wisdom and magic. Moreover, it was the only one explicitly claimed to have been designed and constructed by God.

When the age of printing dawned, publications such as the *Book of Solomon*,[7] an occult handbook, achieved wide circulation and also gained the disapproval of the Church because they were deemed to encourage superstition. The image of Solomon, however, was not limited to identification with magic but also had political relevance. Rulers of state who prided themselves on their intelligence were keen to identify themselves with the wise King Solomon of the Bible. Various kings, from a fourteenth-century ruler of Naples[8] to a seventeenth-century ruler of Great Britain,[9] gloried in being identified with Solomon. Henry VIII liked to be represented as the biblical king, a role that underscored the correctness of his policies.[10] Holbein produced a watercolour miniature of Henry as Solomon receiving the Queen of Sheba, a theme which other artists repeated for other monarchs. The library of the Escorial, for example, has a fresco of about 1586 by the Italian artist Pellegrino Tibaldi representing Solomon and the Queen of Sheba. The fresco seems to have formed part of the scheme of decoration elaborated by the then administrator of the library, the humanist Benito Arias Montano.[11]

In Tibaldi's painting the king, the traditional archetype of wisdom, is evidently explaining something of importance to the visiting queen. Earlier in the sixteenth century the French humanist Guillaume Budé, in dedicating the manuscript of his *Institution du prince* to King Francis I, presented Solomon as the model of wisdom that a just ruler of France should imitate.[12] In England, Francis Bacon dedicated his *Novum Organum* to James I as 'Solomon the Wise', and Rubens depicted the same king as Solomon on the ceiling of the Banqueting House in Whitehall. In the 1550s in Russia, the tsars employed the theme of Solomon not only to enhance their own status, but also to promote the official religion by elevating Solomon to the level of a Christian saint. 'The analogy with Solomon symbolized both divinely inspired kingship and the all-important dynastic theme.'[13] It was, clearly, a commonplace for Christian kings in the age of Philip II to be compared to the wisest king of the Bible.

The reputation for being a 'wise ruler' served, it was hoped, to give confidence to one's subjects, but this was only one dimension of the Solomonic image. The other dimension was substantially more ambitious. Solomon had built the Temple of the Lord in Jerusalem. It was the supreme religious building of the Jewish faith, and Christians inherited the same veneration for it. The task facing kings in their government was by association represented as a building (or re-building) of the Temple. It was in this sense that several commentators of the sixteenth century referred to the tasks facing the emperor Charles V. When Cardinal Pole of England, in a speech before Parliament in 1554, greeted the presence of Prince Philip of Spain and compared his work to that of Solomon, he was following a time-honoured tradition.[14] Pole's message was that Philip might possibly achieve the peace between warring Christians that his father the emperor had failed to achieve. Just as Solomon completed the temple that his father David had begun but been unable to finish, so Philip could be seen as the completer of his father's work. The two notions of wisdom and of construction went together. The Temple of Solomon as a concept, then, represented both state power and religious belief, the two supreme peaks of moral authority. Political leaders who were conscious of the dual significance of the Temple did not fail to exploit the idea. In Russia the sixteenth-century tsar Boris Godunov, a contemporary of Philip II, planned to build a church in the Moscow Kremlin modelled on the presumed layout of the Temple of Solomon in Jerusalem.[15] The plan was not carried out in full, but Russia's leaders did not forget the idea. In the seventeenth century the patriarch Nikon did not go so far as to create a new Temple of Solomon, but he did recreate an exact copy of Jerusalem's Church of the Holy Sepulchre at his monastery of New Jerusalem.

Literary culture drew heavily on what people knew about the Bible, and Renaissance commentators began to adopt biblical references to Solomon when they spoke about the good qualities of their rulers. What did a king need to be if not good, wise and just? The prototype of such a ruler happened to be Solomon, and references to him came up when writers wished to defend the record of their kings. In Spain, however, the notion of Philip II as a Solomon seems to have been completely unknown, and Spaniards (as we shall see) had little concern for the subject before the end of the sixteenth century. Oddly enough, there was no lack of reference to Philip as a Solomon in the events and literature of countries outside Spain. But in what context were those references made?

The earliest identifications of Solomon with Philip II appeared in the mid-sixteenth century, when the likely succession of the prince to his father's titles invited obvious comparisons with the David and Solomon of the Bible. David was the great emperor (identified therefore with Charles V), and his son and successor was Solomon (identified by extension with Prince Philip). Humanist writers, who obviously knew their Bible, drew on the David/Solomon image frequently during Philip's 1548 Fortunate Journey to northern Europe, when the theme of the succession was to the fore. During the prince's tour of the Netherlands, the cities vied with each other to proclaim Philip the destined heir of his father, but the context was always that of the succession, not of any specific virtues of the son. A triumphal arch erected in the city of Ypres bore the motto: 'David senex et plenus dierum regem constituit Salomonem filium suum',[16] and in Haarlem an arch bore the motto in Spanish: 'Solomon is anointed as king, in the lifetime of his father'.[17] The same theme was repeated in city after city – in Ghent, Bruges, Lille, Tournai, the Hague, Leiden – because the purpose of the prince's journey was to be sworn in as heir in each independent province. Haarlem developed the quite original theme of itself as the Queen of Sheba seeking the wisdom offered by Solomon, that is, the prince. Calvete de Estrella commented that the statues on several arches 'represented how Solomon was crowned as King of Israel with the consent of King David his father'.[18]

The references made by Netherlanders to the David/Solomon theme have encouraged some commentators in recent years to argue that the prince felt himself to be Solomon. A recent Spanish university thesis states: 'The relation of the Escorial with Solomon's Temple encouraged the sovereign to present himself as a second Solomon'.[19] In fact, the king never presented himself as a Solomon, and two solid objections may be made to the Philip/Solomon argument. First, during his visit to northern Europe the prince was likened not only to Solomon but also to a wide range of other classical and biblical figures. He was repeatedly compared to the Virgilian figure of Aeneas, bearing his father on his back out of the ruins of Troy.[20] Virgil's lines 'imperium sine fine dedi'[21] were applied to him. Philip was also compared to Alexander the Great and to Julius Caesar, even though he had absolutely no military glories to his credit.[22] Always with a reference to the father/son theme, he was also compared to the biblical son-figures of Isaac, Joseph and Tobias. A further and constantly repeated theme was that of the Pillars of Hercules, the twin columns that were one of his father's emblems, together with the motto 'Plus Ultra', meaning unlimited power.[23] There is no evidence that the prince identified himself with any of these emblems, mottoes and personages, and it is misleading to single out the Solomon theme.

Second, the references to Solomon were without exception limited to the Netherlands, and were made principally within the context of the succession to power in those provinces. They were nearly all made, moreover, several years before Charles V eventually abdicated power to his son, and so had no relevance to events or circumstances in Spain, where not a single writer thought of describing the prince as the biblical king. When the Spaniard Felipe de la Torre published in 1556 at Antwerp a work which he dedicated to the new king of Spain,[24] he compared Philip to Solomon exclusively in the context of being heir to the emperor's task of bringing peace among Christians. The mention of peace among Christians was an echo not only of what Cardinal Pole had said two years previously, in the English Parliament, but also in general of a concern shared by European humanists. What neither De la Torre nor Pole knew was that Philip, drawing in part on his direct experience of the situation in Germany, was a very decided opponent of religious compromise. In May 1557, only a few months after becoming king of Spain, he wrote from London to his uncle the emperor Ferdinand, warning him against accepting any policy of negotiation with religious opponents.[25]

On the eve of his departure from the Netherlands for Spain in 1559, Philip II held a ceremony – as it happened, the last such ever to be held in that country – of the chapter of the order of the Golden Fleece. The sessions lasted from 29 July into the opening days of August. On 7 August Philip opened the session of the States General of the Netherlands in Ghent, and explained to delegates the reasons for his departure. In preparation for these events, the Netherlands Council of State commissioned a young artist, Lucas de Heere, to paint for the cathedral in Ghent a canvas depicting the visit of the Queen of Sheba to King Solomon.

The artist managed to produce his painting in time (it is dated 1559), and took care (obviously, following orders) to give King Solomon the features of the new king of the provinces, Philip II.[26] On the frame of the painting, the Spanish king is described in Latin as *alter Salomon*, another Solomon. These references to Solomon, as we see, were made far away from Spain and in contexts that had nothing to do with the peninsula. The Philip who features in them is the ruler of the Netherlands, not of Spain. By contrast, when Spaniards did take up the theme of Philip II and Solomon, it was not until nearly thirty years later.

The references in Spain to Philip as Solomon can be found only a generation after the Escorial came into existence, and their purpose was clearly to make a pious comparison rather than to insinuate that the king really wished to create an up-to-date Temple of Solomon. In his history of the monastery, Sigüenza, who wrote after the year 1600, made reference to 'the Temple in Jerusalem', but the parallel he drew was explicitly with the Council of Trent, not with the Escorial.[27] Subsequently, when speaking of Herrera's plan for the basilica in the 1570s, he stated that the architect 'greatly imitated the ideas of Solomon himself',[28] which suggests that some idea of the biblical Temple was in circulation. A depiction of the Temple of Solomon in Jerusalem appeared, for example, in the Royal Bible which Arias Montano oversaw and helped to publish in Antwerp in 1572 (see below, and Chapter 8). Indeed, Montano, whose profound interest in biblical texts stemmed from a singular fascination with the figure of King David, logically extended his interest to David's son Solomon. His six years' residence in the Netherlands brought him into contact with ideas and influences that left their stamp on the Escorial, and particularly on the library.[29] The reference made by Montano in the 1572 Bible is illustrated by a sketch of the Temple of Solomon depicting a building with multiple courtyards and, in the innermost courtyard, a Holy of Holies.

Despite Montano's close links with the king, nobody has dared to suggest that his concept of the Temple (which was probably not his alone but based on ideas also shared by others) had an influence on the groundplan of the Escorial. The fact is that the notion of the Temple and the biblical figure of Solomon could be found in several contexts that obviously had nothing to do with the king, and even less with the planning of the Escorial. In 1567 the Spanish explorer Alvaro de Mendaña with two ships set sail from Peru and chanced upon some Pacific islands to which he gave the name Solomon Islands,[30] but it would be hazardous to suggest that this name had a mystical significance connected with the Escorial. Other contemporary instances in which Solomon figures could no doubt be found. There was, for example, a painting of the Judgment of Solomon by the Italian artist Francesco da Urbino, dated 1581, in the cell of the prior of the monastery of the Escorial.

The very fact of a large building with a divine purpose made it inevitable that in later years people would draw a parallel between the Escorial and the biblical Temple. In 1640, for instance, Baltasar Gracián in his *Criticon* described the monastery as 'that great temple of the Catholic Solomon'.[31] The description, made nearly a century after the monastery was constructed, clearly lends no support to the theory that the king meant to reproduce the Temple of Jerusalem in the interior of his lands in Castile. One thing is incontrovertible: not a single statement or document exists to demonstrate that the king modelled his building on Solomon's Temple. He may have been familiar with writings (some in his own library) which touched on the subject, but they appear not to have intruded into his actual plans or those of his architects.

Once the Escorial had been built, nevertheless, its very existence stimulated the proliferation of speculation and theories. The idea of a Christian king building anew the Jewish Temple, and therefore completing the entire message of the Judeo-Christian tradition, goes back well beyond the Middle Ages. Already in the eighth century in England the Venerable Bede had been fascinated by the idea of the Solomonic temple. In the early ninth century when the emperor Charlemagne built the cathedral at Aachen, one of his advisers, the Englishman Alcuin of York, claimed that it was 'completely built according to the principles applied by the very wise Solomon at the construction of his Temple'. Alcuin also compared Charlemagne with King Solomon as well as with his father King David. The association of royal church builders with King Solomon and his Temple is to be found in many medieval churches throughout Europe.

In the case of the Escorial, the notion of Solomon as an inspiration is based in part on the presence, on the façade of the basilica, of six biblical kings, among them David and Solomon. The reason for the appearance of the statues, it has been pointed out, is very simple and has nothing to do with occult influences.[32] When, in 1577, Juan de Herrera drew his masterly sketches of the Escorial, he depicted no statues, proof enough that they formed no part of the original design. The answer to how and when they got there is given by the chronicler of the monastery. Sigüenza explains: 'the idea was that of the most learned Arias Montano, whose advice led to erecting the statues of these six kings'.[33] Montano's interest in biblical figures led him to propose the statues, which were commissioned during the king's absence as king of Portugal and erected just after Philip's return.

The notion that Philip II had wished to imitate Solomon's Temple began to circulate only after his death, when commentators felt they could create their own fanciful vision of the Escorial. The source of the suggestion was a Jesuit, Juan Bautista Villalpando (1552–1608), who was born in Córdoba, entered the Jesuit order in 1574, and spent at least the last twenty years of his life in Italy. Around 1583 the Jesuits in Spain assigned Villalpando to collaborate with a fellow Jesuit, Jerónimo Prado, on a textual study of the Book of Ezekiel. From at least 1592 the two men were working together in Rome. Villalpando was instructed to concentrate on the description of the proposed Temple of Solomon in chapters 40 to 42 of the Book of Ezekiel. When Prado died in 1595, Villalpando took over the work and in 1596 published the first volume of *In Ezechielen explanationes et apparatus urbis ac templi Hierosolymitani*. This first volume was largely Prado's work, but the two further volumes that appeared finally in 1604 were written by Villalpando. Virtually nothing is known of his life and career, and what he says about himself in the book seems unreliable and is probably in part untrue. Possibly in an attempt to boost his own qualifications, he claims in the study that he was a pupil of Juan de Herrera, though there is no evidence for this. He also claims that in 1580 he showed Philip II a sketch of the biblical Temple of Solomon, from which the conclusion we are meant to draw (or which enthusiasts of the occult have drawn) is that the king modelled the Escorial on the sketch. Since the groundplan of the Escorial was obviously completed long before 1580, we may reject the idea of any link between the alleged sketch and the evolution of Philip II's ideas.

Villalpando's work earned him lasting fame. It was the first analysis of the biblical Temple to have been done by a scholar of undeniable erudition (in the languages and text of the Bible) and solid expertise (in mathematics and architecture). Everything in it – the description of the Temple, the map of the old city of Jerusalem – was pure speculation, but it was speculation based on the information supplied by Holy Scripture in the form of the prophet Ezekiel's visions. In the seventeenth century, scholars such as the French scientist Mersenne and the English architect Inigo Jones confessed that they had borrowed from his ideas. Indeed, Inigo Jones' patron King Charles I had read Villalpando's work during his enforced confinement in Carisbrooke Castle in 1648,[34] and, as we have seen, Rubens subsequently arranged for Solomon to feature in the ceiling that he created in Jones' Banqueting Hall in Whitehall Palace. The idea of resuscitating (an imagined version of) Solomon's Temple excited those who saw such a construct as an image of magical, celestial harmony and also as a fulfilment of biblical prophecy.[35] Shortly after the study by Villalpando was published in Italy, a Lutheran theologian, Matthias Hafenreffer, brought out in 1613 a similar book, but without the broader architectural implications. It was the beginning of an obsession that inspired many writers throughout Europe.[36] Already in 1593, in his *Antiquitatum Iudaicarum libri IX* which he published at Leiden in 1593, Benito Arias Montano had made reference to the historical temple of Jerusalem. Perhaps the most insistent on the theme was the Dutch rabbi of Hispanic origin, Jacob Judah Leon, who published in 1665 in Holland his *De templo Hierosolymitano . . . libri IV.*

Central to all these studies was an attempt to offer a reconstruction of the biblical temple. Many, like Montano, discounted Villalpando's theories as unhistorical because they were based not on the real and historical Temple of Solomon but rather on the one which the prophet Ezekiel had seen in a vision. Montano's comments are valuable because they remind us of the necessary distinction between the real Temple of Jerusalem – destroyed both by the Babylonians and by the Romans – and the imagined temple which the prophet Ezekiel saw only in a vision. With good reason the greatest architect of that time, Christopher Wren, dismissed Villalpando's scheme as a 'fable'. In his book Villalpando produced sketches of a huge Renaissance-type palace, which he claimed was the likely appearance of Solomon's temple as seen by Ezekiel. If this was the sketch which he showed to Philip II in 1580, there can be no doubt whatever of the complete irrelevance of his ideas to the building that the king had built. The structure of the temple in the Book of Ezekiel, Villalpando argued, was not simply that of a human building. Its conception and lines reflected a God-given plan that also reflected the harmony of the created universe. It was thus also a divine creation, similar to the divine creation produced by Philip II in the Escorial. The Escorial, according to this view, could be interpreted as a version of the Temple of Solomon.

If Philip ever showed any interest – and there is no evidence that he did – in the drawings presented to him by Villalpando, it would simply have been because he already had direct knowledge of a similar structure. The design of Villalpando's temple shows a striking resemblance to a building with which Philip was certainly familiar from his two visits to Milan, the city that he ruled as duke. The great Ospedale Maggiore (now the state university) built around 1460 for the then duke of Milan, Francesco Sforza, by the architect Antonio Filarete, was uncannily similar in aspect to Villalpando's imagined building. It also had several characteristics that may well have influenced the groundplan of the Escorial. As we can see from the sketch produced by the architect at the time,[37] the exterior aspect of the Ospedale featured several towers that exist in Villalpando's scheme but were discarded in the final plans for the Escorial. More important, however, is the scheme for a number of interior rectangular courtyards, with the main basilica located in the very centre of the whole structure and in the middle of its own courtyard.

When we consider this scheme for the Ospedale, it is clear that the eventual plan carried out for the Escorial was by no means novel; it was drawing on a tradition to which Juan Bautista de Toledo was heir and with which the king was directly familiar.[38] If, as seems more than likely, Juan Bautista specifically drew on personal knowledge of the Ospedale, and if Philip gave his assent on the basis of his own acquaintance with it, the outline of the

Escorial groundplan can be seen to derive in part from an emblematic Renaissance building in Italy.

However, this somewhat down-to-earth account of the origins of the groundplan rules out any exotic origin and deprives us of the excitement of some other mysterious explanation. Subsequent writers in the generation after Philip II, more preoccupied with the search for out-of-this-world aspects than with the mundane realities of bricks and mortar, continued to exercise their considerable intellectual talents searching for deeper meanings. Perhaps the most ingenious parallel between the Escorial and the Temple was made by a Spanish theologian of Czech origin, Juan de Caramuel y Lobkowitz (1606–82), polyglot and polymath, author of an estimated 262 works who published in Spanish (in Italy) at the end of the seventeenth century his *Architectura civil, recta y obliqua: Considerada y dibuxada en el Templo de Ierusalen . . . promovida a suma perfeccion en el templo y palacio de S. Lorenço cerca del Escurial*, in three volumes (Vigevano 1678). Caramuel, a genius who spent his entire professional life as priest, scholar and diplomat outside Spain, shared with other Europeans a taste for the occult. Like those writers who brought the Escorial and Solomon's Temple into their scheme of things, Caramuel was primarily concerned not with the buildings but with what lurked behind them, specific spiritual concepts about the nature of the universe and man's place in it. These ideas, clearly, have little to do with the real history of the Escorial, and even less with Philip II.

It is difficult, all the same, to shake off the interest in exotic origins. In the seventeenth century, the major European philosophers and scientists were schooled in mathematics, which they believed offered a way of measuring dimension, time and all aspects of reality. Like Descartes, they felt that God was the supreme mathematician. Art and architecture were quite obviously part of this mathematical configuration. Some decades ago, the art scholar René Taylor suggested that aspects of the design of the Escorial did indeed point to the influence of occult mathematical ideas linked to non-Christian Renaissance philosophy.[39] He noted that a fresco by Luca Cambiaso on the ceiling over the upper choir in the basilica of the Escorial prominently displayed a cube. The image of a cube, he said, can be found in the works of the medieval Catalan philosopher Ramon Llull and also in a sixteenth-century treatise written by either Juan de Herrera or Juan Bautista. This signified that either of the architects had placed the cube in the fresco for a purpose. The use of the cube as a preferred dimension was to be found in some architects, for simple reasons of construction.[40] Taylor, however, preferred to look for an exotic explanation. Herrera was also known to be interested in the occult, and especially in the works of the mythical pre-Christian sage Hermes Trismegistus (whose ideas are referred to by scholars as Hermetism).[41] Taylor concluded: 'Herrera's manifest interest in the occult prompts the reflection that the Escorial itself may possibly be a Hermetic building'.[42] This 'reflection' about a vague possibility was quickly converted by Taylor into a certainty. Herrera was not alone, Taylor emphasised. He worked closely with the king, who also had a deep interest in the occult and in magic (for which, see below), to the extent that Herrera may have been, according to Taylor, not only the king's architect but also his personal magician.[43]

Villalpando may have been a pupil of Herrera, a tenuous link but sufficient for Taylor to suggest that the Escorial, Herrera's creation (in his view, but not in that of several other scholars), was built specifically as a replica of the Temple of Jerusalem. To soften the force of this startling claim, Taylor adds: 'In considering the Escorial as a copy of the Temple, it must be borne in mind that it was never meant to be a *vera imago*'.[44] In other words, it was a copy and it wasn't a copy, because there was no real physical resemblance. To establish the connection, however, Taylor goes on to point to a number of symbols and diagrams in various parts of the Escorial that presumably have magical significance. In particular, he claims, the fact that the groundplan of the building can be enclosed within a geometric circle confirms that the Escorial is based on an occult design. These fragments of evidence are evidently intended to serve as proof that the monastery came into being in a context deeply influenced by magic.

At every point, one may object, this argument is founded on supposition and conjecture. The famous 'cube' in the Cambiaso fresco, for example, can be found in the biblical text of the Book of Ezekiel (Chapter 41), where 'the most holy place' in the visionary Temple is a perfect cube. Cambiaso could have taken his reference from the Bible without the need to consult Ramon Llull. Taylor's thesis flies so high above the available evidence that it is impossible to disprove, because even demolition of basic premises – for example, his central assumption that Herrera was the author of the groundplan – cannot serve to demolish belief in the aura of speculation that continues to hover elegantly above the Escorial. Architects and artists often play imaginative games with their creations, and those who collaborated in building the Escorial may well also have done so. It is not unreasonable to think that occult symbols lurk in the ceilings and crannies of this vast edifice, but at no point did the fabled Temple of Solomon have any overt or deliberate part to play in the planning or ideas of Philip II's palace-monastery. Taylor cites in support of his thesis the comment by Sigüenza that the Escorial was 'another Temple of Solomon',[45] but omits to explain that the monk-chronicler explicitly rejected any physical parallel between the biblical temple and that of Philip II. Over several pages in which he attempted to refute precisely the idea that Taylor has attempted to propose, Sigüenza argued firmly that there were at least two hundred differences between the two buildings, and that in any case Philip's 'temple' was bigger than that of the historical Solomon.[46]

A recent Spanish commentator, encouraged by Dr Taylor's conclusions, states: 'everything suggests that Philip II opted for the most ambitious of models: nothing less than Solomon's Temple, the most perfect building in the Judaeo-Christian tradition'.[47] It would be more correct to substitute 'nothing' for 'everything' in the quotation. In an exposition that is backed by several erudite references but on close analysis turns out to be based entirely on doubtful premises and pure speculation,[48] this author insists that the king was a convinced devotee of something (never defined, but seemingly a sort of cult) called 'Solomonism'. The conclusion he arrives at is novel, precisely because no reliable evidence is cited in its support: 'on 29 December 1558, at his father's funeral, Philip hit upon the idea that he needed, and that had perhaps been crystallising in his mind. He would model his father's tomb on the foremost example of religious architecture: Solomon's Temple.'[49] The ceremonies in Brussels on 29–30 December[50] were not a funeral but a massive series of obsequies performed in the streets,[51] there is no document to suggest that Philip hit upon any idea at that moment;[52] and the Temple was never a 'foremost example' of religious architecture in Europe, simply because nobody had any idea of what it looked like. Random association and vague allusion continue to be the methods applied by writers who wish to demonstrate that the Escorial was consciously built as part of a vast mystical scheme that embraced continents.[53] The considerable bibliography on this theme is overwhelmingly Spanish in origin and based wholly on imaginative speculation.[54]

THE TEMPLE OF WISDOM

Even while rejecting the link with Solomon's temple, we may reasonably concur that Philip wished to create in his palace a centre of wisdom. The prince had been brought up with care by his father. In July 1534 Charles V appointed a tutor for Philip, ostensibly 'to teach him to read and write', but we may presume that a higher level of training was also included in the programme. Booklets on reading and grammar were specially written for Philip's instruction by a humanist member of the royal household, who also translated Erasmus's *Institution of a Christian Prince* into Spanish for the same purpose. His tutor reported to Charles in November 1535 that 'he shows promise of learning a lot in a short time'.[55] By March 1540, 'he has improved a lot in speaking Latin, and speaks no other language during classes. . . . He has started to write in Latin.' In 1541 Cristóbal Calvete de Estrella was appointed to teach Philip Latin and Greek, Honorat Juan to teach mathematics and architecture, and Juan Ginés de Sepúlveda geography and history. These illustrious humanists and scholars were unable to bring the prince to the level of excellence desired by his father: Philip's command of Latin was better than average, his literary style had no pretensions to sophistication but it was always exact and lucid, and his handwriting though often ill-formed could in moments of relaxation become almost a pleasure to read.[56] Educated as a humanist, he never became one; he had, nevertheless, exceptionally high cultural qualifications for a head of state.

Philip's astonishing capacity for absorbing necessary information showed through in his attention to his duties. Latin, his father had warned him, was essential to his work, so the prince dutifully came to terms with it. In a country where the elite was notable for its ignorance of Latin,[57] this was quite an achievement. During his reign the humanist Juan Huarte de San Juan published a book in which he observed: 'Why is it that the Latin language is so repugnant to the mind of Spaniards and so acceptable to the French, Italians, Germans, English and others? When we look at what they write, good Latin identifies its author as a foreigner, whereas crude and bad Latin points to its author as Spanish.'[58] Philip was an exception in his own country. He was able to compose official letters in Latin and could also converse in it when necessary (with foreign princes, and above all during his visits to England and Germany). It gave him some confidence when undertaking the task of collecting books in Latin. He also understood Portuguese (thanks to the Portuguese circle at his mother's court), and had a working knowledge of French. He read Italian without difficulty, as we can see from the large quantity of state correspondence in Italian that carries his detailed annotations in the margin. By contrast, his Greek, a subject in his childhood curriculum, was non-existent (as it was among virtually all of Spain's elite), so he had to rely on his librarians to assess works in that or other alien tongues. When, in 1547, his secretary Gonzalo Pérez dedicated to him a Castilian translation of the *Iliad*, he hoped that Philip might 'see in his own tongue what many famous princes have read in Greek'.[59]

His refusal to become a scholar did not mean that he did not appreciate the value of scholarship. His tutors, notably Calvete de Estrella, were given funds to build up a library for the prince so Philip grew up surrounded by books written by the flower of western civilisation. Among volumes acquired for him by Calvete in 1545, bought in Salamanca and Medina del Campo but for the most part printed abroad, were works by Sophocles, Virgil, Aquinas, Luis Vives, Bede, Boccaccio, Savonarola, Petrarch, Dionysius the Areopagite, Vitruvio, Copernicus (*De Revolutionibus*), and the collected works (*Opera omnia*) of Erasmus.[60] His library in 1553 contained 'books in different subjects and languages', including works by Dürer, Dante and Machiavelli.[61] The collection grew over the years, as he continued to purchase items on his special interests: architecture and art, music and warfare, magic and theology. The prince undoubtedly dipped into the volumes, but like other rulers of the day he had little time to devote to erudition. The rich selection served rather to stimulate him to amass more books.

His library was perhaps the most ambitious of his projects, since he planned to collect volumes from all parts of the empire. No other monarch of that time, not even the pope, had so ambitious a plan. The origins of his enterprise probably go back to his experience of the famous Fugger library in Augsburg, which consisted of an excellent collection totalling some 10,000 volumes (see Chapter 1 above). After the Fuggers encountered setbacks in their banking business, their friend Duke Albrecht V of Bavaria purchased (1571) the volumes and bequeathed them to the Bavarian State Library, which he himself had founded in 1558 in Munich. Meanwhile, one of the Fuggers, Ulrich (1526–84) had moved from his native Augsburg to Heidelberg in 1564, taking his extensive library, which upon his death passed to the famous Palatine Library located in Heidelberg. We cannot rule out, either, the possibility of an English origin for Philip's ideas. Since he had conversed with Dr John Dee in London, it is feasible that he picked up some ideas from him, among them the proposal (which Dee put to Queen Mary in 1556, a few weeks after Philip left England) for collecting precious books and manuscripts from around Europe and keeping them in a national library. It was a great age for the founding of libraries, and Philip had many precedents to guide him, as well as the assurance that the market in books and manuscripts was a thriving one.

Putting together a large library was a relative novelty in Spain,[62] and Philip's experience of the Fugger collections may have been of decisive importance. A few years later, during his second visit to the

Netherlands, he was presented in 1556 with a petition from a Spaniard, Juan Páez de Castro. 'When one considers', wrote Páez de Castro, 'the amount of coin taken by those who go outside Spain to study, and what booksellers from France and other countries take for books and paper, one sees the importance of having royal bookstores.'[63] Páez de Castro seems to have been thinking of government support for public bookstores as a means of avoiding the export of specie. His most important proposal was that a 'royal bookstore' be set up in Valladolid so that the city's students and clergy could obtain the books they needed. However, Philip's ideas were far removed from such practical issues. The Fugger collection, with its rich manuscript holdings, pointed him in quite a different direction.

In the same period that Páez de Castro presented his petition, a Spanish humanist resident in the Netherlands drew the king's attention to the importance of reading. Felipe de la Torre, whose *Institution of a Christian King* was published in Antwerp in 1556 with a dedication to Philip, emphasised in his third chapter 'how necessary it is for kings to read books, and for men to advise them of the truth'. Throughout his life, the king did indeed read, though he may not have had much free time to do so. He seems to have paid attention to De la Torre, whose recommendation of his fellow humanist Fox Morcillo[64] bore fruit when Morcillo was appointed tutor to the prince, Don Carlos. Although noted as a collector, the king never forgot that books were meant to be read (as witness the letter to his ambassador Francés de Álava in France, noted below).

From the very earliest stage of the Escorial's construction Philip was actively planning his collection. The search for books was, in a sense, a duplication of the search for relics (Chapter 8), and was often carried out by the same people. Indeed, many of the items that arrived were treated with as much veneration as if they were relics.[65] Thanks to his extensive diplomatic network, the king could reach out to every corner of Europe in his search for rare books. It was, he mentioned to his envoy in France, Francés de Álava, a deeply personal enterprise, and one of the fundamental reasons for the Escorial, 'one of the most important things that I wanted to leave there'.[66] The library was not an afterthought, but an integral part of the original plan. His secretary Zayas followed up the royal letter with a note reminding the ambassador that 'His Majesty wishes to build up a library notable for manuscripts and other rare books, and wishes to spend 50,000 ducats on it and to search for the best that there is in Christendom'.[67] Just before Christmas 1567, the king wrote to Álava:

> The cost of the Greek manuscripts that you have found is quite reasonable, though before you agree on them it would be good if you could send a list of all their titles and also of the authors and subject matter, and whether they are really originals or copies of originals, because that is important and in fact is the core of the matter. And since in that university [Paris] there are learned men who know about the subject, it would be wise to consult with someone who is well informed, not saying that the manuscripts are for me but rather for a friend of yours, so that the price does not get affected.[68]

Expanding on the material already to be found in the palaces, from the 1560s Philip built up collections in every known branch of the arts.[69] He also began to pick out those items that would have to go to the Escorial, where the centrepiece was to be the library, housed in a special wing. Where possible, he personally made lists of deliveries, as in 1567: 'Four chests of books are ready to leave for the Escorial, and I had a little more time when I was in the Pardo to draw up a list of them.'[70] Its nucleus was the king's own donation. He persuaded various prelates and nobles to bequeath their books to the collection: in July 1572 an important section of the books possessed by the powerful Mendoza family was sent to the Escorial. In the same weeks a library 'bought in Flanders'[71] was added to the collection. The addition of personal libraries was marked notably by that of the prelate Antonio Agustín in 1587. Philip's agents scoured western Europe in search of rare editions. His ambassador in France in November 1572 was pressed to find out whether some Greek and Latin manuscripts in the library of the king of France

were available for purchase; besides, added Philip, 'they tell me
there is one in Marseille'.[72] The ambassador in Rome in 1572 was
given the additional duty of searching for books. When a bishop
died in 1573 the king wrote to his executor to ask if he could buy
the prelate's library. At the beginning the volumes must have been
stored pell mell; as the precious volumes piled up, even the secretary in charge, Gracián, had to admit that 'it is worse confusion than
the ancient chaos of Hesiod'.[73] Sigüenza dates as late as 1575 the
first important delivery of books: 'This year was that of the first
delivery of books – four thousand – that His Majesty was collecting
here in order to begin constructing his famous library.'[74] It is
certain, however, that there was a pile of books in the area of the
library long before that date.

Within Spain, the programme of collecting publications included
a plan to save from ruin the rare books of remote country parishes.
We do not know how effectively the programme was carried
out, but the plan entrusted to one of Philip's chaplains, Ambrosio
de Morales, met with some success. Starting in June 1572,
Morales spent eight months touring the churches and libraries
of northwest Spain. He found in general that there were very
few books in that region, with the prominent exception of the
cathedral of Oviedo, where 'there are more medieval books than
in all Leon, Galicia and Asturias'. The books could only be taken
after negotiating with the relevant authorities, but Morales was in
no doubt that all available volumes would certainly perish if they
were not removed and saved.[75] The concern for preserving and
ordering documents and books had, it is relevant to remember, its
administrative dimension: Philip was the creator of the state archive
at Simancas, still the main depository of early Castilian documents.[76]

This concern for books, typical of a bibliophile, led the king to
adopt the curious policy of using available space in the library's
deposits to store books condemned by the Inquisition. Although the
idea of saving condemned books has sometimes been attributed to
the Catalan bishop of Vic, Joan Baptista Cardona, who wrote a tract
about administering libraries (*De Bibliotheca*, 1587), Philip's concern

in this regard was of long standing. In 1568 the king's secretary Zayas reported: 'I received the New Testament in Spanish, and sent it on to the Escorial, but His Majesty sent it back to me without reading a word'.[77] It was the first edition of the New Testament that Spanish exiles had just published in France, and the king did not want to fall into the sin of reading a heretical version of the Bible. It was a decade when all western states, including England and France, were actively engaged in censorship, and Philip tried to tread carefully (in Spain the government, rather than the Inquisition, was in control of licences to publish). When, in 1567, the leading French humanist François Baudouin asked permission to dedicate a book to him,[78] Philip looked at the work and commented: 'Its subject matter is very delicate and important, and in these times rather risky, since it is devoted wholly to affairs of state and government'.[79] He ordered that a decision about its quality be made by experts.

Even if a book were prohibited, it did not mean it had to be destroyed. Philip was specially delighted that another of his advisers in the Netherlands (and future librarian of the Escorial), Benito Arias Montano, was able in 1570 to devise a system of censorship by which suspect books could have their offending passages expurgated, thereby allowing the book to circulate without the need to condemn it in its entirety. So pleased was the king with this expedient that he recommended its adoption to the Spanish Inquisition. The condemned books in the Escorial were under certain circumstances available for consultation. In 1577, for example, Inquisitor General Quiroga advised the king that 'the Spanish Bible for the library of San Lorenzo el Real can be kept in a chest since it is a prohibited book, but if someone wants to consult it the librarian may show it to him at his discretion'.[80] In 1585 the prior reported that the library possessed 'many prohibited books sent at different times by His Majesty, and kept there by licence from Don Gaspar de Quiroga'. The custom, pioneered by the Escorial, of having a secret deposit of forbidden books, was later practised by most European libraries including the British Museum.[81] Half a century later the practice must still have been current, for in 1639 the Escorial possessed a total of 932 prohibited works.[82]

Philip's pride in the library was unmistakable. When Queen Anna and the royal princes visited the Escorial in 1575,[83] they took part in celebrations for the king's birthday on 21 May. The day after his birthday, the king and the young archdukes[84] participated in a mounted procession through the cloister. The following evening, 23 May, Philip acted as guide to his wife the queen, his daughters, the archdukes and a large court following. He took them proudly through what was going to be his future library: 'he went along chatting [a monk who was present observed] about all the things in the library, showing and explaining them to queen Anna, so that she saw everything fully and at leisure'.[85]

Philip entrusted Arias Montano with, among other things, the collection of Arabic books – the Escorial ended up with one of the finest collections in the West of works in Arabic, a language that was dying out in Spain. Among a section of the Moriscos it was largely a spoken rather than written tongue; among the Christians, 'even scholarly persons neither understand nor speak it', according to Montano.[86] For the king as collector, Arab books continued to be highly prized. In 1573 he summoned the Morisco scholar and physician Alonso del Castillo to help catalogue the Escorial collection, and let him develop medicines based on the Arab sources.[87] In the subsequent generation, unfortunately, the social position of Moriscos in Castile worsened, and Morisco medicine fell into disrepute. Eventually (from 1609 onwards) the greater part of the Muslim population of Spain was expelled. It is to the credit of the king that, forty years before that event and long before any notion of expulsion was being considered, he fully appreciated the cultural contribution of Hispanic Muslims and converted the Escorial into western Europe's most important repository of Islamic manuscripts.

The library, as conceived by the king, was meant to have readers; it was not meant to be a mere repository. The range of works it housed was intended to be universal. Arias Montano left his stamp of universal learning on the growing collection.

Philip wrote from the Escorial in 1567 to Francés de Álava in France:

> On the matter of books, I have given orders for a sizeable quantity of them to be collected here, though I would still be glad if you could purchase the rarest and most attractive that you can find in Paris, because I am fully in agreement with you, that this is one of the principal memorials that can be bequeathed here, both for the monks as well as for the public benefit of all men of letters who may wish to come and read them.[88]

The phrase 'come and read' merits attention. Credit should be given to Philip for entertaining the theory that a library was for readers. At that period, it seems to have been more normal for book-collecting to be an exercise in cultural status rather than one to serve the public. A scholar has observed that the famous late sixteenth-century library of the count of Gondomar 'was conceived as a kind of museum, whose purpose lay in the skilful conservation, ordering and display of the contents, not in their use'.[89] It was meant to be a display of the power over knowledge that befitted a Renaissance noble. The library of Gondomar (which by the time of his death amounted to around seven thousand volumes) was not meant to be of any practical use. The king, on the other hand, had a somewhat different idea and wished his books to be consulted. In the end, this seems not to have occurred, and there is no record of readers going to the Escorial. Indeed, critics at the time applauded the idea of a library at the monastery but thought it was too far from anywhere, and therefore impossible to consult. The Jesuit Juan de Mariana was certainly referring to the library of the Escorial when he commented, in a work published just after the king's death, that 'it would be good for rulers to pay more attention to learned men. What is the use of books that are, so to speak, captive and prisoner?'[90] The volumes, Mariana felt, were inaccessible and therefore of little service to knowledge. Clergy with their own reasons for hostility to the Jeronimite order also joined in the chorus of criticism, some even questioning the intellectual capacity of the monks entrusted to oversee the books.

For his own private use in his suite at the Escorial Philip II had a more modest collection, totalling around forty items, some of them in manuscript.[91] Half the books were printed abroad, mainly in Antwerp and Paris (the king never – despite an impression to the contrary – restricted the importation of foreign books). The private collection included some missals, the complete works of his chaplain Luis de Granada, the works of St Teresa of Avila, an item on the Virgin of Guadalupe and one on the Virgin of Montserrat. Evidently, they were intended exclusively for pious late-night reading. His own personal and cosmopolitan preferences are perhaps reflected more accurately in the books which he bequeathed in his last testament. They include Boethius's *Consolation of Philosophy* (in French), Froissart's *Chronicles* (in French), books on warfare and on hunting (one in French), the works of Dante and Petrarch, his secretary Gonzalo Pérez's translation of the *Iliad*, and Calvete de Estrella's volume on his own travels to the Netherlands when he was prince.[92]

Philip's ambition to do great things in the world of books was continually frustrated by the unsophisticated state of both printing and learning in the peninsula. Authors who wished to have their books well printed were as a rule driven to look for publishers abroad.[93] Spain remained very much on the periphery of European book production,[94] and relied heavily for book imports on the other states that made up the empire in Europe. The king himself had to have books printed in Flanders or Italy. The extraordinary contribution he made through his efforts at the Escorial (including, as we shall see in Chapter 8, an attempt to give the monastery a monopoly in book distribution) may be contrasted with the lamentable state of Spain's theoretical storehouses of wisdom, the universities.[95] Bonaventura de Smit, a humanist from Bruges who was in Spain as secretary and librarian to the cardinal archbishop of Burgos at precisely the time when Philip was constructing the Escorial, gives us a sad picture of empty universities, professorial chairs unfit for non-Spaniards, studies suspended for five months in the year, scholarship in medicine and letters moribund; in short, a woeful contrast with Italian and Netherlands colleges.[96]

SCIENCE AND THE ESCORIAL

The king was, like other intelligent persons of his time, both fascinated by and sceptical of the occult.[97] His collection of books on magic was substantial, and over the years he continued to add to it. In common with his contemporaries, he treated the unknown with respect. He made use of several astrological advisers (such as the Neapolitan Gian Battista Gesio); was keen to know what comets, eclipses and other unusual phenomena might signify; and consulted horoscopes. When he was in London he had his horoscope drawn up by John Dee, the well-known English magus. But, unlike some other European monarchs, he never gave active credence to the occult. When informed that the Romans had paid attention to the significance of comets, he retorted that 'the Romans were not Christians'. In 1579 he scolded himself for not ordering the archbishop of Toledo to discipline astrologer-priests. 'I am shocked that they believe in these things, and they certainly do wrong, besides it being a mortal sin.'[98] In matters of magic, as in matters of politics, he collected information without necessarily committing himself. He laid great stress, for example, on searching for the works of the medieval Mallorcan occult philosopher Ramon Llull. Many Spaniards, among them Juan de Herrera, had long shared an admiration for Llull's doctrines and from at least 1577 the king began collecting all Llull's works for his library in the Escorial. Translations of Llull's two principal works were made, 'in accordance with Your Majesty's wish [noted the translator] to facilitate the teaching of all sciences'. Llull, for Philip, was an important example of the informal and exotic aspects of knowledge.

The king adopted the same attitude towards all experimental sciences, and notably alchemy. He kept an open mind about several attempts which were made in the 1570s, with his approval, to try and transmute base metals into gold. 'Although I don't believe in these things,' he commented on one experiment, 'I am not so doubting about this one.'[99] The repeated failure of the experiments strengthened his scepticism. When in 1574 his ambassador in Rome Juan de Zúñiga offered to send him an alchemist, Philip commented that the matter could be 'a hoax like all the other results of this science'.[100] He was, however, more tolerant of other aspects of experimental science, particularly those connected with medicine and his large collection of animal horns, mainly rhinoceros but also including six 'unicorn' horns,[101] may have been connected with their alleged medicinal value. Curiosity about scientific instruments gave rise to the rich collection which he transferred to the library of the Escorial in 1597.

Spain never became noted for its science, but the king had an extraordinary interest in the subject. His fascination for medicine and medicinal plants is well known,[102] and from 1557 he encouraged the importation and cultivation of ginger and other spices of possible medical value. Herbs and spices entered within the bounds of his curiosity, but there were two great obstacles to their diffusion which the king never overcame and that in the long run dictated that Spain be a country without exotic herbs. In the first place, Spain had almost no access to Asian spices, which were largely within the ambit of the Portuguese empire. When he became king of Portugal in 1580 Philip made an attempt to intervene in the spice trade, but there is no record of him achieving any success. The second reason for his failure was the inability of oriental flavours to find favour with the Spanish diet. Even today, most Spaniards avoid Asian spices, and tolerate them only if relatively mild. Some have suggested that spice imports to Spain increased significantly under Philip,[103] but there is no credible evidence for this. In all the information about Spanish eating habits in early modern times, there is no indication that many spices were consumed. Nor is it likely that Seville was a major point of entry to Europe for Asian spices. Even less credible is the suggestion that the importation, and growing of such spices 'highlights [sic] the scientific culture of Spain under Philip II'.[104] Science is normally associated with research, philosophy and experiment, not with cuisine.

The king, certainly, had a deep interest in the exotic. Those who spoke with him were always impressed by his interest in all aspects of art, science and culture. The age in which he lived favoured the spirit of enquiry. Not only in traditional branches of learning but also in the sciences and pseudo-sciences, new frontiers were being explored. Among the king's own generation, the New World had been the greatest stimulus to the imagination. As Spain came into contact with the Americas and with the lands beyond the Mediterranean, the exotic began to form part of everyday reality. From America the bean, the tomato and, later, maize entered the peninsular diet; tobacco took its first, fatal hold.[105] As king of a universal empire, Philip was in a unique position to obtain information and specimens; he became, inevitably, a collector *par excellence*. Royal pharmacies were set up in Madrid and San Lorenzo.

Spanish contacts with the outside world in the early sixteenth century were very slow to make an impact, even on the thinking public, but bit by bit perspectives began to change. Discoveries across the ocean, knowledge of hitherto unknown civilisations, exchange of information among travellers and scholars, all these affected perceptions, enabled people to question what they had always accepted and encouraged them to explore new frontiers. The excitement of that generation is visible in the letters, treatises, books and discourses of those who committed their ideas to paper. It was, for some, the rediscovery of the universe.[106] The achievement, however, must not be exaggerated. In the 1560s Spaniards, like most Europeans, were part of a society with massive illiteracy and immense ignorance of the world outside. It was into this world of sharp contrast between the culture of the few and the ignorance of the many that the Escorial imposed its presence.

Influenced by the conviction that knowledge was the basis of adequate administration, Philip set in motion an unprecedented drive to collect facts and data. Nearly all the results ended up in the Escorial. Shortly after his return in 1559, Philip invited Anton van den Wijngaerde to come to Spain and make a survey of its cities.[107] He launched the triangulation of the Iberian Peninsula by mathematician Diego Esquivel. The survey was never completed, but what was done 'is kept by His Majesty in his study' in the Escorial.[108] It was the most impressive survey of its kind undertaken in any European state of the sixteenth century. In 1575 he sent out questionnaires for the *Geographic and Topographical Survey* of provinces in Castile; a year later he did the same for New Spain. He commissioned various general works, including the so-called Escorial atlas of Spain and Portugal, and the numerous histories of the New World undertaken by various chroniclers. He ordered his territories inventoried and portrayed, their fauna and flora catalogued.

The many faces of the Escorial may be considered through perhaps the most ambitious of all Philip's projects as collector, his commission to Francisco Hernández to go to the New World to seek specimens of plant life. Philip's interest in America was profound. In 1571 he appointed Juan López de Velasco as 'cosmographer-chronicler' of the Indies, to draw up a survey of America and also compose an official history of the conquest. This was the period when other great cultural enterprises, such as the monumental *History of the Things of New Spain* by the Franciscan friar Bernardino de Sahagún received royal backing. At the political level, the king ordered a geographical survey of the colonies to be made. His ambitious plans to suspend all conquest in the New World (1573), and substitute for it a programme of exploration and conversion, extended to the natural sciences, where his chosen agent was Dr Francisco Hernández. Hernández (1515–87) had been since 1567 one of the crown's doctors, and in January 1570 was entrusted with an expedition to America, to which he set sail in September that year in the company of his son. In Mexico he undertook an exhaustive programme of cataloguing plants, laying special emphasis on their medicinal properties.

Hernández's plan of work was identical to that of Sahagún, and like Sahagún he prepared his texts in Latin, 'so that this great gift may be communicated to all nations, because this is the common tongue'.[109] 'New Spain alone will take six years to complete', he reported to the king in 1573, even while affirming his intention to go also to Peru (a possibility he had ruled out by 1575, for health reasons). His entire massive enterprise, of which he was the sole director, was made possible exclusively because of help from Mexican aides, who were the true authors of the work. All the artists, researchers and workers who helped him were Mexicans, and in his correspondence he expressed his special gratitude to 'the Indian doctors of Mexico' and all his other native assistants ('there are so many of them that they cannot all be identified'), for whom he recommended cash payments directly from the royal treasury.[110] Unfortunately, from 1575 onwards he was continually ill, and eventually returned to Spain earlier than expected, in 1577. Prior to this he sent back to the king sixteen folio volumes (six of text and ten of paintings) of his work. He himself on his return brought with him a further twenty-two volumes.

The *Natural History of New Spain*, to give the work the title by which it is best known, was the most extensive survey ever made of the botany of Mexico and has never yet been published in its entirety. It includes a description of over 3,000 plants, 40 quadrupeds, 229 birds, 58 reptiles, 30 insects, 54 aquatic animals and 35 minerals, with an emphasis in the case of the plants on their medicinal applica-tion.[111] The volumes were stored in the library of the Escorial, with scant hopes of seeing the light of day. The king in 1580 appointed a doctor from Naples, Nardo Recchi, to come and prepare for publica-tion a selection from the vast work. Recchi took his copy of the text to Rome, a most fortunate event, for the king's sixteen volumes perished in the fire that devoured part of the Escorial in 1671. The Recchi version did not itself see the light of day until finally published in 1651, under the auspices of the famous Roman literary society, the Lincei. Meanwhile, others had not been remiss in their attention to Hernández's unpublished labours. A version of the Recchi text turned up in Mexico and was published there in 1615, while various Spanish and Dutch scholars also managed to look at the surviving originals (protected by the Jesuits in Madrid) and published extracts from it.[112]

As an active scientific enterprise, the labours of Hernández may rightly be seen as the crowning glory of the plan to turn the Escorial into a temple of wisdom. Like much of the other pioneering work of the century – notably the *History* by Sahagún – it had the misfortune to have no adequate production or printing technology to back it up. The crown, which had already invested substantially in another great printing enterprise, the Royal Bible of

Arias Montano (see Chapter 8), did not have the means to sponsor production, nor in fact was there any adequate audience for which such a work could have been destined. Spain lacked the interest, the publishing expertise and the likely readership. The Escorial stood out as a solitary, isolated repository of the wisdom of the universe that a testy but conscientious king had spent years in accumulating and storing.

CHAPTER 5

THE PRISONER OF THE ESCORIAL

A king who knew only Spain?; 'A gloomy king, born to be an inquisitor';
The prisoner of the Escorial; Symbol of Spain's isolation from the outside
world

From the exterior the gigantic granite mass, its three storeys of
seemingly endless windows stretching almost to the horizon, may
convey to some visitors the grim aura of a prison into which entry
seems prohibited and from which escape is surely impossible. The
guides habitually recite the sum total of what the building possesses.
The walls stretch 675 feet by 530 feet: they contain 4,000 rooms,
2,673 windows, 1,250 doors, 16 courtyards, 88 fountains, 45,000
printed books, 5,000 manuscripts, 1,600 paintings, 540 frescos.
They might be talking of Alcatraz (as it used to be) in San Francisco,
or the Lubyanka in Moscow. In the 100 miles of corridor, one may
easily lose one's way. There is no satisfactory explanation of why
the king built on so large a scale, but it is easy to understand the
impression of a stronghold in which the residents must have been
virtual prisoners, and none more so than the king himself. Those
who have written about Philip are in little doubt about the picture.
The dark, grey mass is a reflection of solemnity, austerity and
withdrawal. One modern writer refers to 'the sterility of the regime,
whose perfect monument is the Escorial.'[1] A webpage is of the
opinion that 'the giant, gloomy building made of gray-black
stone looks more like a prison than a palace'. At the heart of

this ominous structure there is, of course, the royal occupant. The nineteenth-century traveller Richard Ford commented that Philip II died in 1598, 'having lived in his vast convent fourteen years, half-king, half-monk, and boasting that from the foot of a mountain he governed half the world'.[2] The king never made the boast, and never lived shut up for fourteen years. Ford's two simple fictions illustrate precisely how opinions on the Escorial have been recklessly formed.

Distinguished scholars have done as much as anyone to perpetuate the legend of Philip II as the prisoner of the Escorial. An English study offers the following portrait:

> Philip II must be the prototype of all monarchs who have tried to rule without rising from their desks. Austere, penitential, tireless, ensconced in a solitary study in the gloomy Escorial on the barren plateau outside Madrid, he strove to enforce a spiritual and administrative uniformity which the variety of his vast dominions would never permit. The dream of 'one monarch, one empire, one sword' was relentlessly pursued. . . . But God, like Philip II, did not smile on Spain.[3]

The building has been presented as an enormous fortress, not only physically but also symbolically. The king is supposed to have enclosed himself in the same way that he enclosed his realms and cut them off from contact with the world. A scholar of great merit lets slip the claim that 'the Renaissance prince was interred in that foundation'[4] of the Escorial. Like Moscow's Kremlin, which was built in the same period and which also – apart from its primary purpose of defence – included the functions of monastery and palace, its high walls shutting off from the outsider any view of what lurked within, the Escorial was an ideological symbol and Philip became its incarnation.

Yet only a portion of the great building was reserved for the king. A fundamental perception, too often forgotten by later commentators, was that of space. The structure (let us remember) was intended to be primarily a monastery and a basilica, rather than a royal palace. The king therefore reserved little space for himself in it, nor did he decorate the royal residences in the way that the palaces in central Castile were embellished. In an overview of the building published in 1599, Juan de Mariana calculated that the monastery occupied half the space, the boys' seminary a quarter and the royal palace a quarter.[5] The 'royal' space was in practice even less than this quarter. If we exclude the public chambers of the crown, possibly less than 10 per cent of the constructed space of the Escorial were allotted to the royal apartments, rooms where the royal family would be lodged. Within that area, the king occupied a tiny section, consisting principally of his antechamber and his bedroom in the wing reserved for the monastery.

The area reserved for the king was termed from the beginning 'private apartments of His Majesty', located in the extreme southern end of the building, beyond the basilica. It was small, and its function was minimal. Was he shutting himself off? Did he hate the world outside? In practical terms, his effective public space was of course very much larger than his royal suite, and included the audience chamber, corridors, chapels and the entire basilica, not to mention the special sections such as the library, and all the patios and gardens. In terms of available space, therefore, his residence was small but his life was by no means monastic or deprived. At no time would he have had the sensation of being enclosed. He was constantly on the move, as he had been throughout his life, so that the idea of his immobility is an illusion created by commentators rather than a reflection of reality. There was ample space at his command. In any of his non-monastic palaces, whether in the Alcázar of Madrid or in Aranjuez, palaces where he spent as much time as he did in San Lorenzo, he had more living space than possibly any other European monarch of his day.

The consideration of space makes it essential to realise also that the Escorial had crucial functions of both work and leisure. If we contemplate what the building represented for the king, in terms of how he spent his time there, it is possible to draw up the following list. First of all, the building (above all, the monastery) was an ongoing work of piety, in which the principal objective was to pay homage to his mother, father and family. Philip therefore spent an enormous amount of time attending to tasks of construction, decoration and prayer that were connected with this homage. Second, the building was not a court, in the sense that Madrid later came to be and as it was actually described (*el corte*). Rather, it merely served as a temporary location for 'the court', understood in the traditional sense of the ruler accompanied by his advisers and retinue. The Escorial and its environs never became a social centre for aristocratic society (a reason, as we shall see in Chapter 9, for hostility to it); it was therefore not a place for receptions but rather an administrative office, to which the king took his papers and to which his ministers and ambassadors sometimes came for instructions. Third, the country setting made the exterior of the building an active centre of recreation, in which he expected the entire local community – monks included – to participate. On all three counts, Philip was not only fully occupied but also constantly on the move. The notion of sedentariness is out of place in this scenario.

A KING WHO KNEW ONLY SPAIN?

Despite all the received opinions to the contrary and subsequent exaggerations, the astonishing fact is that Philip II was – after his father the emperor – the most travelled monarch in Spain's history. Ferdinand and Isabella knew the Spanish realms better and had journeyed extensively through them.[6] Ferdinand also knew the Mediterranean and Italy. But Philip outdid them both in the sum total of his travels throughout the entire peninsula and western Europe.

In comparison, prominent monarchs of the time such as Elizabeth I of England and Henry IV of France seem positively sedentary. No Spanish ruler of early modern times (the emperor Charles V excepted) had a better direct knowledge of the geography, topography, climate, culture and human environment of northern Italy, central Europe, the Rhineland, the Netherlands and England, all of them key territories of the European political landscape. When he asked artists such as Wijngaerde to draw up cityscapes for him, they happened often to be cities with which he was personally acquainted and had visited more than once. Which other European ruler could, like him, give an informed judgement on vistas of London or Amsterdam or Milan? Of the great nations, he failed to visit only France, though he had made brief visits to France's Mediterranean coast. He had conversed face to face, and in their own countries and their own environment, with the Protestant princes who backed the German Reformation, with the leaders of the Netherlands nobility (among them William of Orange), and with Princess Elizabeth of England. Few European heads of state are privileged to have a close, even intimate, knowledge of those who will eventually become their greatest enemies. Philip knew them all. He had consulted in person with Elizabeth, dined, hunted and jousted with Orange. He knew most of the popes of his day personally and was the only European ruler of his time to assist first-hand at a general council of the Catholic Church. It is easy to summarise his early travels: in the period that he governed Spain, before his accession to the throne, he spent fourteen months in England, a year and three months in Germany, and five years in the Netherlands. They were momentous years, and he grew in stature and in experience with them.

According to some foreign diplomats, Philip returned to the peninsula in 1559 because he yearned for Spain. As we have seen, of the sixteen years since 1543 that he had been in control of Spanish affairs, he had spent eight out of the country. 'So as', the English envoy in Brussels reported, 'it is said that upon his getting into Spain he mindeth not to return unto these parts.'[7] But the return home in 1559 was a severe disappointment. In comparison with the sophistication of the Netherlands, Spain seemed a backwater. The king, his courtiers claimed, would love to go back. 'We greatly miss Flanders, and though His Majesty pretends otherwise I suspect he feels the way all of us do', a noble wrote to Granvelle. An intimate of the king, the count (later duke) of Feria, had the same impression: 'I swear to you that His Majesty wishes so much to return that I would not believe it if I did not see it'.[8] Feria had an English wife, which influenced his own preferences. 'Spain is the most backward province on the face of the earth, and devil take me if I do not round up half of all I have and return to Flanders. Besides which, my wife pleads with me every day to go back and has not had a day's good health since she came.'

The notion of a king who yearned only to shut himself up in Spain is pure legend. The testimony of his own courtiers about his wish to return to Flanders is confirmed by his own words. Hidden away in one of his letters to Cardinal Granvelle written a few weeks after his return is a phrase that reveals his yearning to go back: 'I have a deep affection for these states and love them dearly, and more now than ever.'[9] Once back in Spain he became more and more tied down to the routine of government, but he did not cease to travel. His lengthy and onerous journeys through the peninsula had not even begun. Multiple images of the ubiquitous king at hunts in the Black Forest or in the woods of Bavaria, at balls in Binche and Milan and Barcelona, jousting in the great court before the Palace of Westminster or in the grounds of the castle of Mariemont, sailing down the river Rhine and the Danube, or at picnics in Hampton Court or on the lakes in Valencia, accord ill with the still too widely accepted picture of a ruler who wished to flee from the world, bury himself in the Escorial, immerse himself only in his work and deny himself any worldly pleasures. The notion of a gloomy and melancholic king is so openly contradicted by the documents that one may well be wary of writers who not only avoid quoting the documents but make claims for which there is no visible support. A prominent art historian asserts that 'the idea of withdrawal and remoteness was obsessively present' in Philip's palaces, and that 'the idea of the Hidden King reached its peak in the reign of Philip II'.[10] As it happens, this ingenious concept has no basis in fact whatsoever.

'A GLOOMY KING, BORN TO BE AN INQUISITOR'

All these details, readily accessible not only in archival documents but in printed accounts by contemporaries such as Calvete de Estrella, were glossed over by the king's critics when they came to write about him after his death. In part, the blame lay with those who failed to look at the simple mathematics of Philip's travels. Some years ago I asked a well-established Spanish historian, a specialist on the sixteenth century, if he knew that Philip II had spent more time during his reign in the crown of Aragon than in Portugal, where everyone knows he was absent for over two years. He refused to believe that this could have been possible. When I further asked whether he was aware that Philip had lived for over a year in Germany, he confessed that he had no idea of Philip having been there. If the experts were disinclined to ferret out the truth, despite their knowledge of the documentary sources, it is no surprise that long-standing misconceptions about the king should continue to prevail in the pages of popular works.

The image of a caged and hidden king was invented in the nineteenth century by a handful of Spanish and European writers who felt they were justified in creating the likeness of a fanatical monk-like figure shut up in his cell, oblivious to the freedom and progress available in the world outside. There were, of course, contemporary descriptions to help give credence to the idea. The Venetian ambassador said in 1584 that Philip's character made him 'love retreats and solitude, and flee from nearly every kind of pleasure'.[11] Another Venetian ambassador, Contarini, reported in 1593 that the king was 'a lover of solitude, he favours deserted places', and that 'he delights in San Lorenzo of the Escorial, where he retires molto tiempo'.[12] Other Italian diplomats, little inclined to favour the cause of Spain, disseminated similar versions throughout the reign. It remains, as we shall see, a question of what 'molto tiempo' actually means. By identifying the caged king with superstition, writers managed also to create an image of the building as a fortress of darkness.

The favourite adjective for the king and/or his monastery became 'gloomy', used incessantly in texts and even today in Spain by the official web page of the Escorial, which refers to the building as 'bleak and gloomy, like Philip II's character'. Philip remains, as *Time* magazine continued (in 2007) to characterise him, 'a gloomy king'. The biographical entry in the old *Encyclopaedia Britannica* claims that the building 'embodied the gloomy and ascetic spirit of the king and also blended with the stark and forbidding landscape of the Guadarrama mountain range'. Verdi, the composer of *Don Carlo*, the famous opera that immortalised the likeness of a fiendish

Philip II, is said to have declared on seeing the Escorial that 'it is severe and terrible like the savage monarch who built it'. Travelling through Spain in 1840, Théophile Gautier summed up the stock image when he referred in an essay on the Escorial to 'the gloomy Philip II, a king born to be a grand inquisitor'.[13] A modern Spanish historian, heir to the image constantly projected by others over the preceding century, summarised the king's character as 'lugubrious, sombre, fanatical, despotic and cruel'.[14]

Legends about Philip's melancholy disposition extend to his manner of dress.[15] The image of gloom has been driven home incessantly by claims that his state of mind made him prefer to dress always in black. He can be seen in black in the splendid portrait (*c.*1575), now in the Prado, by Sofonisba Anguisciola;[16] and several other paintings show him in various stages of black. Throughout his life the colour was used for two comprehensible purposes, for solemn occasions and for mourning. On the Fortunate Journey in 1548, when barely in his twenties, he frequently dressed in a combination of black and gold. Black helped to set off the Fleece round his neck and the colours of other ornaments on his person. When he received the Venetian ambassadors in an audience in Madrid in 1571 he was dressed partly in silver, with a black silk doublet to set off the gold of the Golden Fleece round his neck.[17] But, as numerous portraits painted throughout his life show, he frequently wore other colours. For purposes of mourning, black had a special significance in Spain. It had to be worn for at least a year, whenever there was a death in the family.[18] Philip had more than his fair share of bereavements. When the rest of Seville was celebrating his visit in 1570, he was still dressed in black for his son and his wife, who had died two years before.[19] But his smile, observers in the city noted, could not have been happier. Above all, after the death of his beloved queen Anna in 1580 he seldom emerged from his condition of mourning, and black became his habitual colour after that date. The truth is that it was difficult for artists to catch the king at a moment when he was not in mourning.

We can pick out at random two or three happy moments in his life when black had no part to play. At his wedding to Mary Tudor in

Winchester Cathedral in 1554, the king stood at the high altar 'dressed in hose and doublet of white leather bordered with silver adornments, and a French cloak gifted by the queen, richly worked in gold and covered with many precious stones and pearls, wearing an exquisite golden sword, and on his head a black velvet cap decorated with white feathers'.[20] His next marriage, to Elizabeth Valois, was formalised on the morning of 31 January 1560 in the palace of the dukes of Infantado in Segovia. The bride was almost fourteen years old, with a dark Italian complexion, bright eyes and long flowing black hair. For the wedding, she wore a silver dress bordered with pearls and precious stones, and a magnificent diamond necklace. Philip was nearly twenty years older and twice a widower. He presented himself in a white doublet and a crimson cloak. An observer noted, 'the pair were most happy to be together'.[21] A banquet and a ball followed the ceremony.

Did Philip, the so-called 'hidden' king, really hide himself from the people? By way of answer, one has only to pick out, at random, moments from Philip's leisure hours. In 1564 he made an official visit to Barcelona and was met at Molins de Rei on 6 February by the city authorities. 'He came on horseback, dressed in a velvet doublet, cloth cloak and hat of black taffeta with a white feather.' He made a formal entry into a city bedecked with Renaissance arches and flowers. An ambassador commented that Philip wanted to 'recover from the boredom of having been four and a half months in Monzón' (where he had been obliged to take part in the lengthy meeting of the Cortes of Aragon). 'There are frequent masked entertainments, when he goes mingling with everybody.'[22] The visit coincided with Carnival, one of the king's favourite entertainments, and there were 'dance, sounds, masks and costumes as never seen before'. The count of Aitona put on a great two-day feast in his house, 'and the king went one day masked to visit the celebration and the ladies'. This – it may be objected – was the young carefree Philip, not the sourpuss that he turned out to be. However, this was no young Philip, but an adult of thirty-seven years who had been ruling the country for eighteen years and had been king for eight of them.

For further evidence, we may pick out the king as he was twenty years later, no 'youngster' now but a mature, aging man. The occasion was Philip's state visit to the city of Valencia in 1586. The party entered Valencia city on 19 January, to a multitudinous welcome. 'The windows everywhere were full of beautiful girls, whom His Majesty greeted courteously.'[23] For the first few weeks of his stay he deliberately abstained from work, and alternated leisure with participation in the festivities (which Philip thought were 'very fine') put on for the royal party.[24] On 4 February, a Tuesday, he went to visit the port of Valencia, the Grao, and inspected the sea-wall. He delighted in the views of the fields and countryside. On Thursday, the entire royal party went for a picnic beside the lake of La Albufera. The ladies ventured out in boats and were rowed by local fishermen.[25] On Saturday, a bull-run was held; the king watched from a palace window.

The French ambassador reported in those weeks that Philip had never looked better or more relaxed in ten years:

> Since he came to Valencia the king has attended very little to business, not because of any indisposition but because it seems he wants to come and rest for a month in a place of leisure, where every day the joy in this kingdom becomes more evident and many festivities are prepared for him. His Majesty has not looked so well in over ten years.[26]

Philip did not shun company and his pleasures were everyday ones – the point must be made because of the vast quantity of writing, from his day to ours, that has asserted the contrary.[27] He lacked neither humour nor vivacity. He enjoyed celebrations, feasts, dances and jousts.[28] He delighted in the outdoors, in riding, hunting and walking. During his early years, his fondness for women was obvious (he was faithful to only one of his wives, Anna). The French soldier Brantôme, whose career coincided with Philip's lifetime and who knew him personally, has left us a description of the king that is somewhat different from that given by others. Philip, he says, 'was elegant, handsome and pleasant, fair-haired, and dressed very well, as I myself have seen'.[29] All his pleasures were indulged in discreetly rather than flagrantly. Some observers referred to his reticent nature as 'melancholic', but the king seems never to have suffered serious melancholy or depression. The outstanding exceptions to this are his reactions to the arrest of Don Carlos, and his response to the Armada defeat;[30] both events, for different reasons, left him in a state of profound shock.

Philip has been presented as essentially shy and withdrawn, afraid of stronger personalities,[31] his reticence sometimes being seen as a sign that he suffered from a feeling of inferiority. The interpretation is interesting, but there is no proof for it. All his life he was a man of silences. He spoke little, and when he did he always expressed himself carefully and courteously. It was precisely his silence that unnerved others. In audience with him, they were given the right to speak first, something which immediately made them feel they were under scrutiny. Worse, the king never interrupted, waiting until the end before he responded, no matter how long the speech.[32] 'He listens patiently', a diplomat observed in 1567. 'He is amiable to those who speak to him, and accompanies his replies with a friendly smile.'[33]

THE PRISONER OF THE ESCORIAL

When tourists are taken round the Escorial, they are shown the little room where the king spent the last few weeks of life. That room is the visible basis of a legend. It is tirelessly presented as the place where a solitary and religious king preferred to shut himself off from others and from reality.

In fact, only a small proportion of the king's existence was tied to that room. He occupied it continuously for the last few months of his life, because it gave him a direct view of the altar in the basilica, and because he literally could not move. The myth of the room will continue, regardless of the facts. In practice, the king's apartments at the Escorial did not cut him off from the real world of Spain. The view he enjoyed from them was ample. Philip had direct contact with the mountains, the sky, the gardens and the whole profile of one side of the Escorial, a recent scholar stating that 'from the apartment of Philip II, looking out to the east and south, one enjoys the full view of the whole building as it extends limitlessly, in an infinity of shades and tones, to the very horizon'.[34]

It is possible that the king who had travelled extensively through Europe prior to 1560 may in later life have grown disinclined to travel. Illness and advancing years, quite understandably, had their part to play. 'Wandering about one's kingdoms for pleasure is neither useful nor becoming,' he is reported to have said. 'The prince should have a fixed base.'[35] However, the document from which the quotation is taken dates from after Philip's death, and there is no reason to accept it as authentic. Moreover, the sentiments do not echo those of the king, who did indeed go 'wandering'. He was never stationary. Like his great forebears the Catholic Kings, he was continually on the move, his principal area of peregrination being within the radius marked out by his palaces and Madrid. But he also travelled through much of the peninsula, more than any subsequent member of his dynasty. Quite apart from his extensive travels in the kingdom of Castile (Granada was the only large city he never visited), after he became king Philip spent two years and four months in Portugal (1580–3), and three years altogether in the crown of Aragon.[36] As one might suspect, the travels were always occasioned by obligations of state,[37] but Philip never failed to exploit to the maximum the possibilities of tourism and entertainment. He knew the periphery of the peninsula as well as he knew its core, and had visited all the great ports except Bilbao.

In the last ten years of his life, when illness kept him bedridden for long periods, he evidently moved less. In the preceding forty years, by contrast, he never stopped. The image of a cloistered king exists only in legend. Although Madrid was the seat of government from 1561, the king did not tie himself down to living there. The duty of ruling could be carried out wherever the king was. Philip and his immediate household distributed their time between the several residences in the central area of Castile. There were eleven of these, ranging from fortresses (the Alcázars of Toledo and Madrid) to substantial palaces (Aranjuez, El Pardo) and country houses (Aceca,

Valsaín). From the late 1560s the monastery-palace at San Lorenzo joined the other residences in the permanent cycle of movement. The palaces, hunting lodges and cottages owned by the crown supplied a network of residences that allowed the royal family to make regular outings to ease the boredom of staying in one place. In 1564, for example, the king's base was the Alcázar in Madrid, but he made regular two- or three-day excursions to go hunting at the Pardo, visited the Escorial from time to time to see how the building was progressing, and spent entire weeks in Valsaín and Aranjuez.[38] In 1566 he stayed for two weeks in October at El Escorial, probably in a temporary residence in the village, then chose also to spend Christmas that same year in the same location. It is not unlikely that he was already sleeping within San Lorenzo.

The first extended change of routine appears to have occurred in 1567. 'On 17 March the king went to the Pardo', it was reported, 'and from there to the Escorial, where he is spending Holy Week and will still be on Easter Day.'[39] He also spent most of August at San Lorenzo.[40] Moreover, he spent the Christmas season of 1567 in San Lorenzo, which is where – after Don Juan of Austria had ridden from Madrid to inform him of the situation – on Christmas Day he took the momentous decision to arrest Don Carlos.[41] Though other writers suggest a much later date – as much as four years later – we can state categorically that from 1567 the king was already resident in the Escorial.[42] Progress with the building work had made space available for the large number of court officials who had to accompany him.

The entire first half of 1568 was spent in Madrid, where Philip could watch over his imprisoned and mentally disturbed son. Don Carlos' sudden death changed the situation, and in July the king went to the Escorial to escape the crisis, after announcing a year of mourning for the court. From that period the king's sojourns in the Escorial were a normal routine. Naturally, this implied that the government had to be in attendance as well. This was not easy to arrange, since the royal apartments did not cater for the residence of ministers, and there was no room among the monks. So from the 1570s, as the king stayed longer and longer there – not necessarily because he liked it, but rather so that he could oversee the building work – the officials also had to be lodged. I first came across this circumstance in the exchange of letters between the king and his secretary Mateo Vázquez, when during a very cold period the king warned Vázquez to safeguard his health and keep well wrapped up, since it was much colder '*abajo*' ('below') than '*arriba*' ('up here'). At first I thought this must mean that Vázquez was living in the basement of the Escorial, which seemed strange; and in any case why would the king write to someone living in the basement? Then gradually I realised that '*arriba*' meant San Lorenzo and '*abajo*' meant 'the village of El Escorial'. This meant that for long periods the officials were lodged in the king's vicinity, and effectively contributed to the development of the village that today has grown into a flourishing country retreat.

In May 1572 Philip informed the queen's chamberlain that his own departure from the Escorial 'could be on Monday afternoon for El Pardo, spending Tuesday there, returning on Tuesday to Las Rozas, and on Wednesday morning to El Pardo, then from El Pardo to Galapagar, lunching at Torrelodones. On Thursday [the queen and family] can go to mass, then lunch at La Fresneda, where I will lunch with them, leaving the queen's attendants to go straight to El Escorial where they will dine and sleep that night. This I think will be a good arrangement for the outing.'[43] This somewhat giddy pace was quite normal. Because of the distances involved, and also because he was accompanied either by his family or by his papers, the king normally travelled in his carriage. For short distances, he continued to travel on horseback.[44]

Philip seldom stayed in San Lorenzo, or any other palace, for more than a short time. For him the Escorial was the perfect office, a place where he could work peacefully, away from administrators, ministers and petitioners. Fray José de Siguenza testified that 'he completed more business here in one day than in Madrid in four, because of the tranquillity'.[45] The family on these occasions was usually encouraged to stay in some other palace, such as the Alcázar of Madrid. Despite the separations, at no time in the 1570s was business given precedence over family matters. Philip was in constant touch with Queen Anna and the children, writing to her about twice a week during separations, and she did the same. When their letters crossed, 'it was not necessary to write yesterday [he informed her chamberlain] since I have seen the queen's reply to mine; and you may now hand the queen the present letter'.[46] Over and above their correspondence, the royal couple would make regular outings (*jornadas*) to see each other, and in this way would manage to visit the various palaces in turn.

The king could not afford to stop work completely. When the queen and his family came to see him at San Lorenzo on 22 May 1572, he spent most of his time with them; but in the evening he returned to his papers. It was a particularly splendid spring that year, and the outings continued regularly through May and June. After a few days in San Lorenzo, with or without the queen, the king would dash off somewhere else, accompanied by his papers and secretaries. 'I'm off this afternoon', he wrote from San Lorenzo in mid-June that year, 'because I have things to do in Madrid; the queen can leave tomorrow afternoon, but if they are happy here and she wants to stay longer she may, though I think they will want to go tomorrow.'[47] Appointments with her were respected. 'Because I have agreed with the queen to go to the country,' he informed his secretary during a stifling July, 'I shall not call you at the moment.'[48] When there was no help for it, she assisted him with his office work. In one of the most appealing of all vignettes of his role as king, we see Philip in the summer of 1573 at the Escorial, working at his papers in the company of Anna and the two girls. 'He busied himself in dispatching business with the close help of the queen and the princesses, so that he would write and sign, the queen would sprinkle sand on the papers, and the princesses would take them to a table where Sebastián de Santoyo (the king's office assistant) was preparing the packets and bundles to send to the secretaries.'[49]

It is important not to think of the Escorial only as a summer residence, because such a notion ignores entirely the real function of the building. San Lorenzo was primarily a monastery. In consequence, it was chosen as the centre for the king's religious duties, not as a shelter to escape from the heat. Philip would just as frequently spend the hottest months of the year in Madrid, where the month of August for example can be insufferable. We may choose one of many cases. The second half of July 1572 he spent in the heat of Madrid, then in early August he moved to the Pardo and from there to San Lorenzo. But in mid-August he was back again in Madrid. The constant movement continued after September, which he spent in San Lorenzo. On 4 October he went off to Madrid. On the 15th he went to Aranjuez to spend ten days with his family. On the 25th he was in the Pardo. Three days later he was back in San Lorenzo. In normal years this pattern of movement was the king's standard routine. Later in the reign, reasons of health made him avoid passing the summer in Madrid. A memorandum from his ministers in 1591 recognises that the king was at the Escorial that summer 'because of his health, which is the reason why he tends to pass the summers in San Lorenzo'.[50]

Religious priorities, rather than health, were the reason why Philip also chose to spend inclement periods of the year at San Lorenzo. He preferred to spend Christmas, and winter, there even though the cold can be intolerable. In 1572, for example, he arrived at the monastery on 22 December, after leaving the Prado, and spent the whole Christmas season there, leaving on 8 January.[51] He preferred to make his Easter retreat also at San Lorenzo. Thereafter he tried to spend all the great feast days there, alternating his stay with visits to other residences. After All Saints, 1 November, he would set off to spend most of the month in El Pardo. At the end of the month he left for Madrid, in order to arrive there by St Andrew's Day, 30 November, when he would celebrate in the company of his knights the founding of the order of the Golden Fleece. The whole Alcázar was usually illuminated and decorated for the brilliant ceremony.

As he travelled between his duties, he commented ruefully on things he was unable to do. Journeying to Madrid in spring 1572, he could not afford to stop and wander through the countryside. 'I believe that the woods will be beautiful, and regret the many times that I have passed by them without having visited one which they say is particularly attractive. If I ever have the chance I must see it.'[52]

Even when he was tied down in one place, he contrived to go out into the countryside to lunch. After hours and days of paperwork, he yearned to break free, if only for a while, to relax and go into the country with his family. 'When I finish this', he wrote after a trying day in San Lorenzo, 'I shall leave here and go to sleep today at La Fresneda and tomorrow at El Pardo, a roundabout route in order to go through some woods. After that I have to leave San Lorenzo on Friday at two, after lunch.'[53] The Venetian ambassadors in Madrid interpreted his wish to escape as an urge for solitude. In reality he was simply trying to get away from being pestered by them.

The Escorial was the king's own creation, and it is logical that he should have been excited by the idea of staying there. But he had to wait a long time. If we take the year 1567 as the beginning of his substantial residences, we can see that he had to wait roughly six years for the monastery-palace to be finished. His stays in San Lorenzo may be divided into two periods. From 1567 to 1580, he tended to stay only for short periods; these years coincided with his marriage to Anna (in 1570) and were in effect the happiest of his life. The following illustrates his movements in the year 1572: he was in Madrid from January to April, then April to May in the Escorial, then June in Madrid, early July in San Lorenzo, late July in Madrid, early August in El Pardo and the Escorial, late August in Madrid, September in San Lorenzo, October in Madrid, Aranjuez and El Pardo, November and December in Madrid. If we add up the months, he may have spent up to four months that year in the Escorial. But this is not the whole story. Even while he was based in San Lorenzo, he moved around to his other palaces. During these years, we may conclude, he was by no means a prisoner of the Escorial.

In his notes on the visit of Queen Anna to the Escorial in 1576, when she spent the summer weeks up to the end of September with her husband, Sigüenza gives us a description of delights that reveals why the royal family might choose to stay there. The king and queen, he notes, went for outings to the local woods,

> which in summer are extremely beautiful gardens, full of flowers and fruits, good hunting, with a variety of fowl and a rich supply

of fish, so that both inside and outside [San Lorenzo] represented for the royal pair a stay full of pleasure and entertainment. When the sun goes down a soft breeze arises that cools the harsh heat of the day, and the queen and princess and princes used to go out in the gardens that surround the monastery.[54]

In the 1580s, reports Sigüenza, 'in order to advance the building work the king used to come here from Madrid with some frequency.'[55] The autumn of 1583 he exercised his sense of humour on the friars. Among the trophies he had brought from Portugal were an Indian elephant and a rhinoceros. In October he arranged for the elephant, driven by a black boy, to saunter round the cloister, up the steps and into the cells of the astonished Jeronimites. (Elephants were not a total rarity in Spain: King Sebastian of Portugal had sent one to Madrid in 1561 as a present for Don Carlos.[56]) A week later it was the turn of the rhinoceros, which was not quite so cooperative. It grunted bad-humouredly and refused to eat the food it was offered.[57]

San Lorenzo was a convenient base for both business and pleasure. After Anna's death, the king invariably came accompanied by Prince Philip and the princesses, who afforded him company and relaxation. In 1584, once again, he celebrated the great feasts in San Lorenzo. The last week of April and the first of May were spent at Aranjuez: 'on most days they went hunting, the king always taking the princes in his coach, and in the afternoon they went by boat on the river'.[58] On 8 May the royal family took boats upriver to the palace at Aceca, which they reached four days later. The French ambassador reported that it was habitual for the king to spend much of April and May in Aranjuez, 'because of the beauty of the gardens, the pathways and the house'.[59]

A full-scale deer hunt was arranged at Aceca on 12 May. The method of hunting used by the court was one common at that time in Europe. Beaters, blowing horns and aided by dogs, were sent out to enclose an agreed zone. The required animals in that zone were then driven, terrified, into a target area. The king and members of his family would be waiting in the royal carriage, from which they would pick off the animals they chose.[60] On this occasion fifty carriages participated in the hunt, and notched up twelve deer. The royal party then set off for San Lorenzo, which Philip made his base from 17 May to 2 October. He spent the whole week of his birthday confined to bed by gout, but after Corpus Christi he was well enough to get about. Every afternoon in June, he was able to make outings with the children to Fresneda (his preferred site for fishing) and the other residences in the Castilian countryside.[61] Much of October was spent in El Pardo, where on Saturday the 20th a pastoral comedy was staged in the evening in honour of the Infanta Catalina's betrothal to the duke of Savoy. The performance lasted from seven to ten in the evening. 'His Majesty enjoyed it greatly and left well content.'[62]

The Escorial, as we have seen, played a due but by no means dominant part in the movements of the king. There were occasions, certainly, when it was neglected. During his lengthy journey to the crown of Aragon in 1585, when he assisted at his daughter Catalina's marriage in Saragossa and made a grand tour of the three realms of Aragon, Catalonia and Valencia, Philip was effectively out of touch with the last stages of the building work. The king and his numerous escort eventually returned from Valencia in February 1586, making their way back to Castile through the wintry landscape. Philip regretted leaving behind the green of the Mediterranean coast, so green, he wrote, 'that it's unbelievable'. Instead, as they approached Castile they were buffeted, he complained, by 'much cold and a terrible wind always in our faces'. The hills were covered with snow and it was bitterly cold.[63] Philip's first care on his return was to see how, after fourteen months of absence, the building programme in all his palaces – not simply San Lorenzo – had advanced. 'We thought Aranjuez was terrible, at least I did. We were there four days and then came to Madrid, where I found that the building work I had left was in good shape, though not finished as I had wished. I stayed there four more days and came one evening to El Pardo, where much less has been done than I had thought. Then I came here [San Lorenzo] where a great deal has been done.'[64] He arrived in San Lorenzo on 26 March and spent Easter there. In early May he was in Aranjuez, where the French ambassador observed Philip during the fortnight that he was there:

> In the time that the King has been in Aranjuez he has been hunting and enjoying the beauty of this place, its gardens and its walks, surrounded by all the contentment that springtime and a beautiful residence can bring.[65]

At the end of May the king and the court returned to San Lorenzo, to spend the early weeks of the summer of 1586. Again, there was no question of being tied down in the monastery, even though he suffered a serious attack of gout there and had to remain through the month of June. In July he was back in the Alcázar of Madrid, but returned to San Lorenzo during August in order to be able to preside over the final great ceremony that brought the construction work to a close: the blessing of the basilica (see Chapter 8). In October he was off to El Pardo, then returned to the Alcázar in November and December. At the end of the year he came back for a few days to San Lorenzo in order to pass Christmas there, but was back again in the Alcázar, where he spent the next four months until April, immobilised in part by his illness. Philip made an effort not to let poor health interfere with family pleasures. Even in Armada year, 1588, when he was suffering frequent pain, he was mindful of his duties as a father: 'This summer,' noted Sigüenza for that year, 'the king went out with his children to visit the surrounding countryside. He sometimes went to Fresneda and Herrería, they went hunting, and fishing in the lakes.'[66]

After the Armada and in the last ten years of his reign, roughly from 1589 to 1598, Philip was forced by his illness to remain for extended periods in specific residences, and in consequence could not go to others. One result was that his absences from certain palaces – even the Escorial – became longer. In April 1589, for example, he noted: 'I've finally decided to make an outing to Aranjuez, it's nearly two years since I was last there.' From about 1590 he also walked everywhere with a stick. It was impossible for him to move as much as he used to. The years of illness in the 1590s created a quite new pattern of consistent *absences from* the Escorial, which he visited much less frequently. An important casualty was his long-standing practice of spending Holy Week in the monastery-palace. 'The year 1590,' notes Sigüenza, 'His Majesty did not come here for Holy Week, because he was afflicted by the gout.'[67] He arrived there only in the first week of June. At the beginning of 1591, he was seriously ill for the same reason, so spent Holy Week and Easter in the monastery of San Jerónimo in Madrid. When the religious holidays were over, he went out to the country, but this time to Aranjuez.[68] Sigüenza reported that the king also had other commitments that kept him away from San Lorenzo: 'he had the festivities of Corpus [Christi] in Toledo, and had to go to the *auto de fe* celebrated by the Holy Office' in that city on Trinity Sunday. Likewise, in 1592 he did not come for Holy Week 'because the gout detained him', and instead came briefly a month later. However, the king made up for it by spending the summer months there.

An exception seems to have been the year 1593, when the king 'spent the greater part of the summer in the Escorial, for the conclusion of the paintings, shelving and floor of the main library, and the majority of the books were shelved in his presence.'[69] He reverted, however, to absences from the Escorial in the years just before his death. Writers today continue to describe him as confined to the monastery by illness, but precisely because of his illness this did not happen. In the spring of 1595 he was, reported the Venetian ambassadors, confined to his bed in Madrid. From that year, he began to use the famous chair that can still be seen on display in the Escorial. Its inventor, Jehan Lhermite, called it a 'gout chair'.[70] According to him, the king 'stayed in it from the morning when he got up, to the evening when he went to bed'. It had the advantage of being adjustable so that it served both as chair and as litter. Its main use was not, despite what the tourist guides at the Escorial often maintain, to bear the king to the monastery. In practice, Philip used the chair wherever he went, above all in Madrid. His most frequented home was his official residence in the palace of the Alcázar, which is where he spent Holy Week and Easter in 1596, when illness prevented him from travelling. Once again, after the religious feast days, he escaped from Madrid by going to Aranjuez and to Aceca.[71] In Aceca he was again taken unwell, and left after a few weeks only in order to go and convalesce in the Alcázar of Toledo, until the end of August.[72] In 1597, the year before his death, Philip stayed the summer months in the Escorial, but not entirely locked up. Instead, the monks were pleased to see him diverting himself hunting (inevitably, from within his coach).

SYMBOL OF SPAIN'S ISOLATION FROM THE OUTSIDE WORLD

The king accepted that his duties cut him off from many normal pleasures, and from the company of others. But he disliked solitude. He loved to be accompanied by his children, and hated the separations, as his letters to Isabel and Catalina from Lisbon amply demonstrate. Very shortly after his return from Lisbon he was unfortunately separated once again from Catalina, who was (as we have noted) married to the duke of Savoy in Saragossa in 1585. After she sailed for Savoy (fated never again to see her father) the king wrote to her. 'I have been very lonely', he told her, 'which has also brought back the loneliness I feel without you.' The example illustrates a simple case of human solitude, but like all evidence needs to be set in context. The king had to divide his time between various obligations, and some of them – such as his regular religious retreats, or his professional duties – made solitude necessary. Other obligations, such as those of his family, made him flee from solitude and seek pleasure in company. Both these types of obligation had their part in the social life of the Escorial, where Philip combined religious duties, administrative work and family entertainment. It is a mistake to identify the monastery-palace too closely with the idea of isolation.

On the other hand, the very fact of being king imposed a certain remoteness from others. All over Europe the monarchy was beginning to distance itself from its subjects, for two main reasons: cost and security. The phenomenon has been well studied in the case of England, less so for other countries, and not at all in the case of Spain. The rising cost of moving around the kingdom was beginning to separate rulers from their subjects. Royal 'progresses' (ceremonial journeys in which rulers travelled through the country, to affirm their presence and to receive oaths of loyalty) were conducted in England and France till the late sixteenth century, but were becoming less common. By the end of the century, they had almost disappeared. In Spain, Ferdinand and Isabella made interminable progresses, but the practice virtually ceased under Charles V. Philip was, as we have seen, the last Spanish ruler to tour his country extensively: he did so in 1564, 1570 and 1585, on each occasion for several months.

However, although the king may have been concerned for his people, he had little effective contact with them. This was a perfectly normal situation in an age when, throughout Europe, there was no regular means of communication between people. Philip felt that his accessibility to the public on feast days – a practice which he tried to maintain all his life – was adequate. 'As you know,' he pointed out when urged to pay more attention to popular opinion, 'people talk to me on Sundays and give me petitions'.[73] As often as feasible, he had his lunch 'in public', but this involved no more than lunching (alone) in one of the large reception rooms of the Alcázar, where members of the court and public might see him.[74] It was, nevertheless, a practice which he urged his son to follow. He made a rule of being accessible to private petitions while going to or from Sunday mass and deliberately walked slowly so that people would have a chance to catch up with him.[75] 'On all feast days until now', a courtier reported in 1583, 'he has gone out, listening to everybody and accepting their petitions.'[76]

Kings all over Europe were no longer in a position to cultivate a common touch. Their duties inevitably tended to separate them more and more from the public. In any case, personal security had to be assured. Political murder was commonplace in western Europe, and kings were in the direct line of fire. An abortive attempt was made on Philip's life in Lisbon in 1581. Thereafter he used greater caution. In 1583 a Frenchman acting suspiciously was followed by officials,[77] who feared another assassination plot. In practice, the king's distancing from his subjects cannot be blamed specifically on the Escorial. In the mid-1570s, when he had only recently added the monastery to his list of residences, one of his officials, Luis Manrique, suggested that the king 'had deliberately and bit by bit made himself inaccessible and shut himself in a tower without doors and windows'. Dedicated only to his papers, Manrique said, Philip had isolated himself from his subjects. Throughout Spain 'the people are despondent, expecting that everything is going to collapse'.[78] This was written a quarter of a century prior to the king's death and long before the Escorial had begun to play a major role in his movements. Whatever the relevance of Manrique's words, the accusation of being 'shut off' was obviously not valid at that stage. By the end of the reign, nevertheless, there were certainly voices, such as that of the visionary Lucrecia de Leon (see Chapter 9 below), that began to associate the Escorial with isolation.

However, the relative distancing of the monarchy from its subjects in France, Spain and elsewhere, a phenomenon that is easy to identify, is qualitatively distinct from the other image, of an anchorite in the Escorial who cut his country off from contact with civilisation. This image is an ideological fiction, still widely prevalent. The legend of the Escorial as a monastic prison is employed in order to present the picture of a king who was timid and nervous, a physical coward, and verging on insane. The strong walls of the Escorial (it is argued) gave him a protection, a solidity, a reassurance, that his own spineless and craven character yearned for, so he buried himself in it and eventually died there. Meanwhile, he worked to isolate Spain as he had isolated himself. The country, runs the argument, possessed immense economic and cultural potential but thanks to Philip II it remained backward because Spaniards were not allowed contact with foreigners, could not trade with them, could not study abroad, and were forbidden to read foreign books. In the nineteenth century, the historian Modesto Lafuente had occasion to denounce 'the isolation from the intellectual movement in Europe that Spain suffered from the time of Philip II'. This presentation, which I (in common with other students of the period) have had reason to analyse on several occasions,[79] was created a century and a half ago by a group of Spanish Liberal historians, and thanks to subsequent political ideologues has enjoyed a long and unmerited lease of life. In order to rescue the

Escorial from this bizarre fantasy, it is worth repeating what should be obvious to those who know Spain's past. Spaniards, at the centre of an inter-continental empire, were never cut off from the outside world. In an age when Spain was Europe's principal power, thousands of Spaniards, of all ranks and condition, including clergy, nobles, students, soldiers and adventurers, left the peninsula and wandered everywhere in the continent or emigrated to America. In the same way, visitors came to Spain. Some even managed to make their way to the Sierra de Guadarrama, to catch a glimpse of the gleaming citadel that the king had constructed on the forested mountain slopes.

CHAPTER 6

A BRACE OF EAGLES

Images of Power and Monarchy

The Escorial and royal absolutism; The Escorial and the imagery of royal power; Queen Elizabeth and King Philip: a brace of eagles

THE ESCORIAL AND ROYAL ABSOLUTISM

Confronted by the enormous granite structure of the monastery and its unquestioned dominance of the visible landscape, observers had little problem identifying it with the absolute power of the monarch. 'Nothing can give you any idea of the Escorial,' Alexandre Dumas *père* wrote in 1846, 'not Windsor in England, nor Peterhof in Russia, nor Versailles in France. It is like nothing but itself, created by a man who bent his epoch to his will, a reverie fashioned in stone, conceived during the sleepless hours of a king on whose realms the sun never set.'[1] It is easy to understand why the first impression that strikes the viewer is one of might. The extensive area of stone unequivocally communicates solidity and authority. Dumas had no doubts on the matter: 'once in the course of centuries there comes a man, typical of his own times, the mirror of a whole epoch, who leaves behind him a monument to make his spirit known to all future generations'. The immense visual impact, unfortunately, was such as to encourage observers to give free rein to their imaginations, as we know from the wide variety of responses they set down on paper. Historians, artists, novelists, philosophers, all claimed to have obtained a special insight into what the building represented. Above all, they saw it as an obvious expression of absolute power and authoritarian kingship. In what sense were they right?

Half a century after Dumas, another citizen of France, the great historian Ernest Lavisse, saw the building as an expression of the despotism of Philip II and a prefiguring of the authoritarian rule of Philip's direct descendant Louis XIV.[2] The idea of comparing Philip II with Louis XIV was launched in the nineteenth century by French republican intellectuals who viewed Louis as a Spaniard (both his mother and his wife were from Spain's royal family, making him a direct blood relative of Philip II), and considered his absolutism an alien Spanish import. By definition, they felt, something as bad as 'absolutism' could not be wholly French – even though, of course, they admitted that only the French, in the person of Louis XIV, were capable of perfecting it – and must have drawn its origins from outside. Theories about the political significance of the Escorial exist precisely because they are informed intuitions, based on the physical power of the building, that seem to promise some basis in historical reality but in the end fall short on hard evidence. The association of Philip II's monastery with Louis XIV did have some basis, but the idea took concrete shape in the mind of an architect, not a king. One hundred years after the death of Philip II, Louis XIV's minister Louvois chose the architect Libéral Bruant to construct a military hospital on the banks of the Seine. Bruant deliberately modelled his building, which was completed in 1674 after three years' work, on the plan of the Escorial. The impressive church, with its dome that recalls San Lorenzo, was constructed shortly after by the architect Jules Mansart. While the final layout of the imposing Hospital des Invalides that we see today differed in many respects from the original idea, the similarity in 1683 to the groundplan of the Escorial is nevertheless striking.

With time, the Escorial came to mean many different things to many different people. The structure was so vast and complex that it was bound to provoke a variety of interpretations. Most commentators saw no problem in identifying it as a concrete expression of the psychology of its maker and of his will to power. In practice, it was very hard to demonstrate through textual citations that the building represented any expression of Philip's own worldview. Indirect evidence had to be sought, or manufactured.

In his volume on the epoch of Spanish dominance in Europe,[3] the French historian Henri Hauser saw the Escorial as a clear image of the unlimited power of Spain's king. For him, the event that most symbolised the rule of Philip II was the 'macabre' reburial of royal bodies in 1574. Hauser's analysis was evidently an inheritance of the view, found generally among French novelists and dramatists of the previous century, of Philip as a 'king of death'.[4] Even Fernand Braudel, whose general approach was far more measured, felt – in his masterly survey of the epoch of Philip II[5] – that a comparison with France was possible: 'Philippe II à l'Escurial, c'est Louis XIV à Versailles'. Seldom has a single building served so much to influence historical interpretation of a ruler simply because of its daunting immensity. The same fate awaited Philip's contemporary Ivan the Terrible, who came to be interpreted according to the gaunt immensity of the walls of the Kremlin in Moscow. The new Kremlin – reconstructed from the end of the fifteenth century on the basis of plans by Italian architects Fioravanti, Solari and Ruffo – was, however, conceived more as an exercise in self-protection than as an essay in power. Its mammoth walls, built of red brick and eventually exceeding 2 kilometres in length, constituted a veritable fortress. No such purpose of protection lay behind the construction of the walls of Philip's monastery. Was the Escorial nevertheless an image of power? Did the king possess any images of power?

One fact is fundamental: whether inside or outside the Escorial, the king could not have had dreams of power, because the Spanish monarchy did not square with such dreams. The 'monarchy', as contemporaries called it – or 'empire', as some modern usage has it – was an alliance of different territories that were independent from each other, had different styles of government, and shared only a common allegiance to the same ruler. They had come together mainly through marriage alliances and continued to preserve their own laws. It would have been extremely difficult to rule arbitrarily in those states or provinces that did not permit it. The king, consequently, always

1 The abbey of Ettal, Bavaria, founded as a Benedictine monastery in the thirteenth century by Duke Ludwig IV of Bavaria.

2 View of the town of San Quentin, beside the River Somme, engraving from the early seventeenth century.

3 Philip II shortly after the battle of San Quentin, portrait by Antonis Mor. The Escorial.

4 High altar of the basilica. Monastery of San Lorenzo del Escorial.

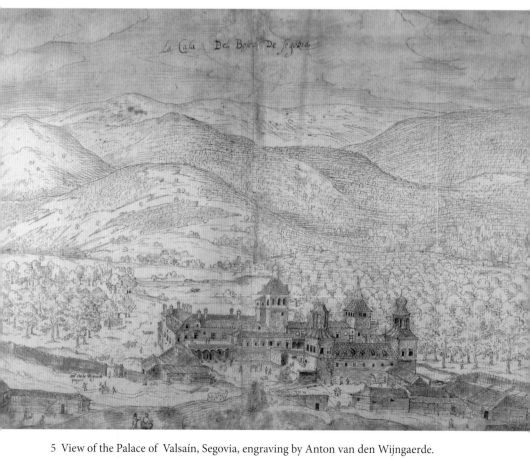

5 View of the Palace of Valsaín, Segovia, engraving by Anton van den Wijngaerde.

6 Pantheon of the Kings, in the Escorial.

7 View of the Escorial.

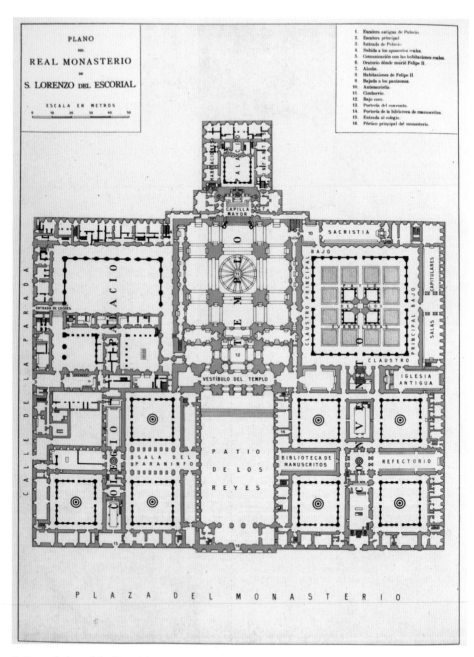

PLANO
DEL
REAL MONASTERIO
DE
S. LORENZO DEL ESCORIAL

ESCALA EN METROS
0   10   20   30   40   50

1. Escalera antigua de Palacio.
2. Escalera principal.
3. Entrada de Palacio.
4. Subida a los aposentos reales.
5. Comunicación con las habitaciones reales.
6. Oratorio dónde murió Felipe II.
7. Alcoba.
8. Habitaciones de Felipe II.
9. Bajada a los panteones.
10. Antesacristía.
11. Cimborrio.
12. Bajo coro.
13. Portería del convento.
14. Portería de la biblioteca de manuscritos.
15. Entrada al colegio.
16. Pórtico principal del monasterio.

8 Ground plan of the Escorial.

9 'Building the Escorial', drawing attributed to Fabrizio Castello and Rodrigo de Holanda. Hatfield House.

10 *Solomon and the Queen of Sheba* by Pellegrino Tibaldi in the library of the Escorial.

11 View of the main façade of the Escorial.

12 The Escorial library.

13 The Escorial, southern façade of the Friars' Garden.

14 Private rooms of Philip II in the Escorial.

15 View from the apartment of Philip II in the Escorial.

16 Hospital of Les Invalides, Paris, in the seventeenth century.

17 Tapestry by Willem de Pannemaker, from the series *The History of Noah*, commissioned by Philip II. Royal Palace, Madrid.

18 *Equestrian Portrait of Philip II* by Rubens. Museo del Prado.

19 Façade in the Courtyard of the Kings, the Escorial, with statues of the kings of Israel.

20 Funerary group of Philip II and his wives, facing the high altar of the basilica, by Pompeo Leoni.

21 The Hall of Battles.

22 One of a series of canvases on *The Battle of Lepanto* by Luca Cambiaso, in the Escorial.

23 *Allegory of the Battle of Lepanto* by Titian. Museo del Prado.

24 Detail from a fresco on the battle of St Quentin, Hall of Battles.

25 *The Dream of Philip II* by El Greco. The Escorial.

26 Title page of The Holy Bible, printed for Philip II by Christophe Plantin in Antwerp.

trod with care. Top-level affairs of war, peace and law and order were seldom in practice his sole preserve. At the beginning of his reign in 1559, he referred everything, down to the smallest detail, to his councils and advisers, and never made decisions based only on his own opinion or preferences.[6] 'Very rarely does he depart from the advice of his ministers', noted the Venetian ambassador Tiepolo. Important decisions always affected many people. The king never acted by himself, and never failed to consult before acting. A generation later, he still proceeded with the same caution. Faced by a grave crisis, he intervened with an army in Aragon in 1591, but only after receiving written opinions from leading officials throughout Spain,[7] and in those months he did not move a finger without first having favourable advice. There could be many stages in the decision-making process where he did not personally prepare the decisions. Quite obviously, specific military decisions, as for example during the wars in the Netherlands, were beyond his control. Many orders, measures and decisions were issued in his name but it would have been impossible to give his direct consent in each case.

The multinational nature of Philip's monarchy encourages some writers to believe that he exercised immense sway, which the king (they argue) continued to emphasise even further through propaganda. Philip, it is felt, cultivated images of his power. A recent historian affirms: 'The presentation of Philip II was done through images of his power, whether through writings or through icons. The production of these images led to a global discourse of the representation or imagery of Philip II, the core of the imagery of empire.'[8] The problem is that Philip appears to have lacked kingly images, and there were (as the present chapter will argue) none in the Escorial. If the monastery was really his most emblematic structure, why did he not use it to proclaim his authority?

We now enter the realm of interpretation, and it is useful to define clearly what we are talking about. Philip II was the most powerful monarch of his day, and the Escorial – massive and uncompromising – was his most memorable creation. Its appearance and dimensions betoken strength; indeed, one cannot deny that the Escorial is a statement of moral power. However, did the king use the building to put forward, through the use of art, imagery and sculpture, assertions of his own monarchical authority? Did he, through the imposing structure of the monastery, try to augment religious authority, or vindicate his own position in Spain as the summit of throne and altar? If the answer to these two questions is 'No', it seems reasonable to conclude that the Escorial looms over us simply because of what it is, and not because it contains some hidden agenda nurtured by the king.

It is a stimulating exercise to claim that Philip II was obsessed by symbolism and imagery, but unless the assertion is documented through texts it cannot be taken seriously. Scholars have often allowed their imagination to run free, and a recent writer has claimed that 'Philip formulated the concept of absolute monarchy', and that he was 'the most significant theocratic ideologist of the modern era'.[9] Such views, for which not the slightest evidence exists, exceed the bounds of fantasy. Other monarchs of that day, above all in France and England where the ruling dynasties were highly fragile and needed to reassure supporters about their hold on power, took great pains to promote their public image. Philip II, the most unassailable and therefore in theory the most powerful ruler of the time, did just the opposite. He downplayed the status of monarchy, and paid little attention to symbolism or images. As emerges clearly from Roy Strong's study of royal Renaissance spectacle, Spain remained on the outer margins of courtly images and splendour.[10] While other monarchs spent time and money on marvellous displays such as the Field of the Cloth of Gold, the only spectacles indulged in by Spanish royalty took place *outside* Spain, in the Netherlands and in France.[11] The emperor managed to mount at least one significant spectacle in Spain, at Barcelona in 1535 just before the Tunis campaign, but it was put on expressly for the stellar concourse of international princes and prelates who had come to the Mediterranean for that campaign. We may gain an idea of how impressive the occasion was through the famous Tunis tapestries (see below, pp. 155–6). Philip II, for his part, spent no time on extravagant spectacles in Spain, and there is no visual record, painting or tapestry, to commemorate any of the modest family celebrations that he did hold from time to time.

In various tracts that were published during the late sixteenth century, some of his courtiers were anxious to create a truly royal, even imperial, persona for him, but they failed spectacularly. Four relevant points may be briefly emphasised.[12] First, not a single significant work favouring absolute kingly power was published in Spain with his approval during his reign. Since other monarchs of that time – notably in France[13] and in England – never hesitated to promote publications that gave support to their pretensions, this is a striking detail. Despite the image of Philip as a despot, sixteenth-century Spain lacked any doctrine of absolute monarchy and even produced the most eloquent anti-absolutist thinkers of the age. All the theorists who were active during Philip's lifetime favoured consultative monarchy, and those who wrote just after his death were even more emphatic that royal authority be strictly limited.[14] The Castilian magistrate Jerónimo de Bobadilla, who published an important treatise touching on royal power just before Philip II's death,[15] pointed out that any attempts that might be made by a Spanish king against individual conscience, or religion, or nature, or provincial laws, were inherently invalid; he also emphasised that the concept of *raison d'état* had no place in Spain.

Second, not a single 'power' portrait of the king was painted by artists in his lifetime, with the unique exception of an imaginative royal portrait done of him as king of Portugal (produced at a time – around 1581 – when he certainly needed propaganda in his support). Third, he never claimed – there is an irrefutable absence of any such claims – special powers as king in the crown of Castile, and never favoured extending the power of Castile over the other realms of the peninsular monarchy. Finally, he had no pretensions to international grandeur, and never attempted to claim the title of emperor or showed interest in the Imperial crown of Germany. Philip's respect for his father's decision on the Imperial crown is unquestionable.[16] Contemporaries who persisted in fostering the image of a king who lusted after kingdoms and titles either did not know Philip or were deliberately distorting the truth. Philip had no interest in ruling over Germany; as early as 1555 he had informed the Spanish ambassador there that he had no intention of claiming the Imperial title.[17] Seven years later, it was the same story: 'As to the succession to the empire,' he reminded his ambassador to Vienna in 1562, 'in the present state of affairs it is not to my interest to claim it, and I wish to help the king [of Bohemia, Maximilian] obtain it.'[18] By contrast, in Italy, where his powers were extremely limited anyway, he insisted on retaining as much authority as possible, in order not to lose what little he had.[19]

THE ESCORIAL AND THE IMAGERY OF ROYAL POWER

The undeniable fact that Philip had no pretensions to monarchical splendour is brushed aside by writers when they come to contemplate the imposing structure of San Lorenzo del Escorial. The monastery, according to one scholar, was a visible affirmation of power, 'a symbol of the triumph of authoritarian kingship over the disruptive forces of anarchy'.[20] Since Philip never saw himself as an authoritarian king, nor faced anarchy in Spain at any time in his life, any 'symbol' lies exclusively in the eye or the imagination of the modern beholder. It has no convincing roots in reality. Those who gaze on the building without taking into account either the context or the evidence are liable to weave somewhat unreal images. It has been claimed that 'Philip II's emblematic image of total order' inspired the building of the Escorial, and that 'the powerful assertion of the architecture was necessary to connect this order with the power required to produce it'.[21] The twice repeated assertion of 'power' serves as emphasis. The same author also considers this and other buildings to be 'architectural equivalents for Philip's chosen style of kingship', and believes 'Philip's authoritarian rule' to be 'fully embodied in the Escorial'.[22] These perceptions of a power-hungry king, as it happens, have no evidence to support them. In reality, almost nothing in the Escorial is a reflection of this presumed image, and the view that 'total order' and 'authoritarian rule' symbolised Philip's approach to art is extremely difficult to substantiate.

Choosing the Escorial as an exclusive image of the mind of Philip II, while omitting his other creations such as Aranjuez or the Alcázar of Madrid or the new palace in Lisbon, the Paço da Ribeira,

all of which might feasibly be described as 'authoritarian', is to
define him arbitrarily in terms of one single construction. The
method is unwise, just as it would be imprudent to define an artist
by one single painting. El Greco cannot be interpreted solely
through his vision of the city of Toledo, and the king's ideas cannot
be viewed only through the prism of one building constructed in
the hills outside Madrid. Let us consider the royal palace which
might be considered, far more than the Escorial, a statement of
power. If there was any one moment when the king seemed to be
on the crest of a wave of triumph, it was after he settled into his new
kingdom of Portugal in 1581. In Lisbon, the existing waterfront
palace of the Paço da Ribera was modified. Its great windows
looked directly out over the ships in the harbour and afforded
a panoramic view of the ocean. A new four-storey domed tower,
the Torreão,[23] was constructed by Juan de Herrera and Filippo
Terzi. It overlooked the harbour, which it dominated like a light-
house,[24] and contained – like the Escorial – a library as well as a
ceremonial throne room and royal lodgings. The Torreão was
lavishly furnished, and visibly represented kingly success. Yet Philip
made no attempt to convert the building into an expression of
imperial triumph.[25]

One may, of course, argue that all the palaces of a king are built
in order to enhance the notion of their power. This is an argument
that is both valid and unquestionably true, since palaces betoken
authority. But affirming power through palaces was never a priority
of Spanish rulers. Ferdinand and Isabella did not have a centralised
monarchy and therefore did not devote time and money to building
palaces. Quite simply, they had none. Charles V had no interest in
building palaces (see Chapter 3 above), and spent most of his reign
outside the peninsula. The only palace he ordered constructed, in
Granada, was one he never managed to occupy. That did not make
him indifferent to the necessary assertion of his power. It was left to
Philip II, however, to become the first Spanish king to carry out a
considered, intelligent and artistically sophisticated programme of
palace-building. Not all his palaces and residences shared the same
purpose, and not all were intended to emphasise the notion of

power. The Alcázar of Madrid, for example, was certainly an exercise in power, not only because of its commanding position on the outskirts of the town, but also because it served as the regular centre of royal administration.[26] The ministers and committees of the government held their meetings in specific rooms of the Alcázar, which was for Spain what Capitol Hill is for the present-day United States. By contrast, the Escorial was primarily not a palace but a monastery; ministers did not hold their meetings there; and the perception of a presence of power there was moral rather than political.

Scholars have attempted to find arguments for Philip as an absolutist by exploring the available imagery of the king, but they have been unable to come up with any convincing results. A leading expert on Philip, Fernando Bouza, concludes that the king's artistic creations (the buildings, as well as the paintings he commissioned) do not lend themselves to an unambiguous political interpretation: 'It is neither possible nor reasonable', he writes, 'to put a political gloss on Philip II's artistic and cultural patronage'.[27] He offers some good examples of image-making, but the Escorial does not figure among them.[28] Bouza also considers the use of propaganda by the king, but it is significant that his evidence comes from the one authentic moment of propaganda in his reign, when Philip was trying to win international support for his dynastic claim to the throne of Portugal,[29] and invited leading European experts to offer their views. The king in that period was attempting to promote dynastic right and save Portugal from falling into the hands of the English or the French. At no time did he use propaganda, either then or later, to enhance the political status or ideological prestige of himself as a ruler.

In brief, Philip expended little energy, inside or outside the Escorial, on trying to construct a royal image. Others constructed it for him if necessary, though it would be difficult to demonstrate that he took part either consciously or actively in the process. All the imagery associated with him up to around 1554 (when he became king of England) was, as we have seen (Chapter 4), related to the imperial power of his father, Charles V. Subsequent imagery, particularly in the Netherlands, was intended to affirm the rights of the king of Spain in those provinces and did not form part of a programme to promote Philip's power within Spain.[30] If the imperial image of Spain was developed by European writers and artists in later decades, it was certainly not because of active encouragement from Philip. For example, a famous illustration of 1581 by the German artist Heinrich Bunting depicts Spain as the imperial head of a body that has its heart in central Europe, more explicitly Bohemia. The intention, as the late lamented and distinguished Czech historian Josef Polišenský once pointed out to me, was quite clearly to promote Bohemia rather than Spain.

Perhaps the principal fallacy in the notion of a Philip II anxious to promote his own image is the idea that kings of Spain were unsure of their position and felt a need to enhance their personal status. We know that the monarchy was uneasy in England and France, mainly for dynastic reasons, but in Spain after the small-scale 1520 rebellion of the Comuneros the government could feel secure. Neither Charles V nor Philip II made any effort to disseminate royal propaganda. A recent essay has suggested that we may think of three principal ways in which the image of the king was promoted in early modern Spain: through the dispersal of portraits, through the building of palaces and through the collection of art.[31] It is doubtful whether the three can be applied with much exactitude to Philip II, since the projection of an image requires a public to receive and be impressed by it, yet neither Philip's portraits nor his collections were available to the people of Spain. We may admire them in hindsight, but they had no impact in their day. The king had a small number of portraits painted, notably by Titian and Sánchez Coello, but they were lodged in private places inaccessible to the public and were never used as state portraits nor seen by any but a small group of political figures. A specialist who has studied the portraits of that time concludes: 'the public, in general, were able to have sight of the images of their kings only in the houses of powerful persons. Portraits for display to the public, set out in public places, do not appear to have existed.'[32]

Normally, the closest that people came to seeing the face of the king was his profile on official coinage, where the motive was not primarily promotion of the king's power. Philip, of course, did not dislike portraits: he liked them greatly but kept them in his study, not in a public hall for everyone to gaze upon. All the surviving portraits of the king are conspicuously lacking in symbols of royal power.[33] Their subject usually restricted himself to simple attire, and to one principal decoration, that of the order of the Golden Fleece.[34] The only truly grand portrait of the king was executed, as we might expect, in relation to Portugal. If it was painted from life, Philip must have posed for it in Lisbon just after 1580. The painting shows him dressed magnificently in cloth-of-gold (a fabric that, according to the Venetian ambassadors, he disliked and always avoided), and carries the wording 'Don Felipe I de Portugal y de Castilla', a description that is technically correct since the political entity 'Spain' did not yet exist and the claim to the throne of Portugal derived from the royal family of Castile. There is no information on how the painting arrived where it now reposes, in the Museo de San Carlos in Mexico.[35]

The king's face appeared in many illustrations and on medals. A survey of some printed books deposited in the National Library in Madrid has yielded up some 139 small black-and-white engravings of Philip, about 100 of them limited to the bust (i.e., head and shoulders) and about 30 showing the full body.[36] The figures are not elevated, when we consider that he governed the country for over half a century, and that thousands of books mentioning him were in circulation. Recent research confirms that there is a surprising lack of images of the king in printed books, and, what is even more surprising, that virtually no Spanish artists and engravers produced published images of the king.[37] His features also appeared, of course, in many books published in Italy and the Netherlands, and the use of image in these contexts was clearly for illustrative as much as propaganda purposes. The king's profile could also be seen on occasional medals. In the belief that all the images associated with the king reflect pretensions to power, scholars have suggested that a small medal created by the Italian designer Iacopo Nizzola da Trezzo in 1555, just after Philip's wedding to Queen Mary of England, was a blatant affirmation of imperialism. The medal bears the emblem of a sun, with the words 'Iam illustrabit omnia' ('it will soon shine everywhere'). One interpretation is that Philip was claiming to be the sun, a new god Apollo or a sort of 'Sun King' before the real Sun King (Louis XIV of France), and that he hoped to have the whole world in his orbit. By extension, the Escorial was a building inspired by the sun, and based on astral premises.[38] This would be a fascinating thesis if any supporting evidence could be found for it. None has.

Within the limits of what we know at present, the medal of 1555 may justly be seen as simply an expression of triumph at the royal wedding of 1555. Philip had just been proclaimed king of Naples and was now marrying the queen of England, thereby extending to the Atlantic the dominion of his father the emperor Charles V in Europe. It was something of which any ruler would be justly proud, but it was clearly an expression of dynastic satisfaction rather than of aggressive imperialism, since Philip at the time was not even king of Spain. The motto 'Iam illustrabit omnia' was in any case not exclusive to Philip II. It can be found subsequently reproduced in publications all over Europe, by authors who wished to earn the approval of Spain.[39] It was reproduced by Girolamo Ruscelli in his *Imprese Illustri* (1566), and then in the *Imprese di diversi Prencipi* of Battista Pittoni (Venice 1568). The motto, always forming part of a beautifully illustrated page in a work, was later used in other publications to apply also to Philip III. Philip II had no monopoly of it.

At different times during his life, Philip opted for different symbols, mottoes and medals. When he was prince and regent of Spain, for example, he adopted a special medal to symbolise his authority. When he made his triumphal entry into the city of Antwerp in 1549, the device he used on public monuments was *Nec spe nec metu* (neither in hope nor in fear).[40] Each royal event elicited its corresponding device, and no single device was a firm or unique reflection of Philip's ideas. Medals were made and distributed to commemorate specific occasions, rather than to promote personal authority. Some medals might take the form of seals for use on official letters (see page 159). The creators of the medals were always Italians,[41] and the medals were not usually part of the Spanish political experience. Every member of Philip's family had medals made, and the king himself collected their medals because they were family mementoes. Each medal, it has been suggested, 'breathed an air of family and home intimacy'.[42]

Though medals might assert authority, it is less convincing to claim that the king was using them to express *ambitions* of power. The motto 'Non suffict orbis' ('the world is not enough', implying – it is suggested – dreams of imperialist expansion) was used on a medal coined in Lisbon after the successful annexation of Portugal, and English sailors came across it in Santo Domingo during a notable raid on the city in 1586. But there is no indication that the device was either inspired by or originated with the king (despite a recent study that suggests it was), and in any case it was never officially sanctioned.[43] The motto had been used years before by a sculptor for Charles V who placed the words on a fountain of the emperor's (never inhabited) Renaissance palace in Granada, to illustrate a carving of the famous conqueror Alexander the Great.[44] It was also used by a king of France, Francis II. The idea that Philip coined a medal to express his dreams of conquest has been entertained by writers who are seemingly attracted by the coincidence of the motto with the title of a James Bond movie. The notion of a macho imperialism backed by Philip II, however, has a basis only – like Bond films – in fantasy. A similar observation may be made about the claim, referred to above, that Philip dreamed of being a Sun King. Popular writers of the twentieth century plucked the idea out of their air, and returned to it persistently.[45] The Escorial has bathed for over four centuries in the sunshine of Castile, but has never, in any statement by the king himself or by his admirers, been directly identified with the sun.

In the same way, Philip's love of armour should not be interpreted as a crude assertion of royal power.[46] Philip's obsession with armour was limited to his years as prince, and ceased completely when he became king, so that it has no connection with his theories of kingship. The wearing of armour by princes and nobility, extremely rare in an age when military armour was rapidly going out of fashion, demonstrated less a will to power than delight in a masculine, exotic hobby. There are striking examples of Philip's armour in the Armoury of the Royal Palace in Madrid, but evidently none in the strictly religious environment of the Escorial. In any case, all examples of Philip's interest in armour date exclusively from his days as a prince, when he had the time and agility to play at chivalry.[47] The striking suits of armour in Madrid were designed for him during his visit to Augsburg in the days of the Fortunate Journey. The ironsmith Desiderius Colman made at least two full suits for him in 1549 and 1550.[48]

Philip insisted on being painted when wearing his precious suits, and the portrait he ordered done immediately after St Quentin shows him off to perfection in the suit that he wore in the victory parade on the battlefield (see Chapter 2). It was in all probability the last time that he donned armour. When he embarked on his career as king, Philip no longer had the opportunity to indulge in his hobby. In 1565 he initiated the building in the Alcázar (now the Royal Palace) of the Armoury that was specifically intended to house not only his own suits but also the priceless collection inherited from his father the emperor. The word 'priceless' is not out of place. Suits of armour were toys, but they were very expensive toys. In 1550 Colman was paid for Philip's suit three times the amount that Titian received for his famous portrait of the emperor (clad, of course, in armour) on horseback.[49]

In the sixteenth century a particularly striking method of displaying political messages were tapestries, which through their size, colour and complexity were able to impact the viewer far more effectively than mere paintings.[50] It was an art form that by the fourteenth century flourished almost exclusively in the Netherlands, a fact that the emperor Charles V exploited to great advantage. He hired the Flemish artists Jan Cornelisz Vermeyen[51] and Pieter Coecke van Aelst to accompany him on an expedition against the Turks, so that they could base their designs for tapestries on direct observation. The result was the magnificent series of twelve tapestries, executed by Willem de Pannemaker, dedicated to the Tunis campaign of 1535, an international enterprise set in motion against the Muslims in North Africa. Woven of Granada silks, French wool and threads of gold and silver, the tapestries were the most expensive that Charles ever commissioned. Completed by 1554, the full series of twelve pieces was sent to England as a wedding gift for Philip and Mary, then brought back to the Netherlands in 1556 to be hung at a session of the knights of the order of the Golden Fleece.

During these years, Philip also proved to be a great patron of tapestries.[52] He began buying them from 1550, at the end of his first visit to the Netherlands.[53] In May 1550 he bought the seven-piece series entitled the *History of Solomon*, which was sent back to Spain. He inherited pieces from his family, notably from his father and his two aunts, Mary and Leonor, but also became a notable collector himself. The collection of tapestries in La Granja de San Ildefonso displays those that the king ordered from Brussels. From 1555, the period of Charles's abdication, Philip made even bigger purchases, notably a series on the *Apocalypse*, part of which was lost in the vessels that capsized when he returned to Spain in 1559. Willem de Pannemaker had a hand in the making of some of that series, which included panels illustrating St Michael and the angels slaying the devil, an expression of the permanent struggle between good and evil.

There was a fundamental difference in theme between the tapestries commissioned by Charles and those by Philip. The emperor, as we see from the *Tunis* series and also from a previous series (completed in 1531) on the imperial victory over France at Pavia, gloried in the magnificence of war. One of the *Tunis* pieces does not shrink from depicting the brutality of the occupation of the small Muslim coastal town. In contrast, all the series commissioned by Philip were of biblical or mythical themes. When he transferred some of his tapestries to the Escorial, the king restricted himself to two pieces each from the sets *Apocalypse* and the *History of Noah*. No pieces from *Tunis* went to the monastery where, as we know (see Chapter 7), war had no place. (Today, the visitor may consult them instead in the Royal Palace in Madrid.) Despite his love of tapestries, the king appears never to have commissioned any with the specific theme of celebrating his own victories; he always accepted his own status and dignity, but saw no need for propaganda about them. His father had ordered that one of the *Tunis* pieces place the boy Philip centre-stage in the pre-embarkation ceremonies in Barcelona in 1535.[54] When the boy grew up, he may have thought that the reference was adequate tribute to his collaboration with his father. He did not find it necessary to place his own face in any of the tapestries that he ordered.

Perhaps the only occasion when the king saw fit to use his tapestry collection was when, for the first and only time during his reign, he entertained a visiting head of state. This happened in 1576, when he had a meeting with his nephew, King Sebastian of Portugal, in the monastery of Guadalupe near the Portuguese border. The two kings arrived at Guadalupe in the third week of December and had their first meeting on the 22nd. The chief advisers of both kings were in attendance. In deference to his guest, Philip ordered Sebastian's rooms to be hung with tapestries from the royal collection. Thirty-three rooms were decorated in this way, with the ten pieces from the *Noah* series in pride of place.[55] In vain did Philip try to reason with his wayward nephew. Sebastian, however, was interested only in concrete offers of help for his plans to invade Africa, a scheme which ended tragically several months later when on 4 August 1578 the army of Portugal, comprising the flower of its nobility with the young 25-year-old king at their head, was wiped out by Berber forces at the battle of Alcázar-el-Kebir.

The use of tapestries at Guadalupe in order to flatter the pride of the king of Portugal, rather than to emphasise his own power, was typical of Philip's behaviour. It is difficult, if not impossible, to find a situation in which he used visual imagery to enhance his own status. When still a prince, he entered his duchy of Milan in a triumphal procession in 1548 and was greeted by street arches that bore the words 'Hispaniarum Rex' at a time when he was certainly not king of Spain.[56] An over-zealous historian might read this as evidence that Philip was plotting to become king, when the truth is that the language of street banners was planned by the city and not by the visiting ruler. In the later years of the emperor, art had begun to be used as a means of reinforcing Charles' image of power. Paintings (such as the formal portraits by Titian), tapestries (notably those of Pannemaker), statues, documents and treatises all helped to build up the notion of imperial authority as expressed in the person of Charles.[57] The duke of Alba, who became Philip's chief military commander, was also a follower of the vogue for tapestries, and always with the intention of glorifying his own military role.[58] The duke's vanity on such matters subsequently clashed with the ideas of the king, who ordered that a self-aggrandising statue erected in Antwerp by the duke be taken down (see page 161).[59]

By contrast, the art chosen to decorate the Escorial had no propaganda purpose. Just as the king excluded entirely the theme of war (see Chapter 7), so he excluded images of power or portraits of himself that might insinuate a desire for power. An inventory made of his tapestry collection at the end of his reign shows that he had 701 complete series, an impressive figure that, curiously, is seldom mentioned by art historians. Of the collection, 40 per cent is devoted to gardens and scenes from nature, 16 per cent to mythology, 14 per cent to allegorical themes, 13 per cent to scenes from ancient history, and 13 per cent to biblical themes. Contemporary history – a category that includes his father's *Tunis* series – represents only 4 per cent.[60] They are figures that confirm the immense wealth of the Habsburg family that amassed the collection, but the themes also confirm the absence of war and power as a priority in the chosen imagery of the king.

A decisive piece of evidence for his reluctance to use artistic images of power is the absence of equestrian portraits of Philip. In royal portraiture of the period, artists placed their subject on horseback when they wished to enhance their dignity and communicate the notion of power. Equestrian portraits of European rulers abound, especially in the Baroque age; but they were also to be seen a century before. In Renaissance Italy, the ruler on a horse was a symbol of power.[61] Francis I of France is shown on horseback in a panel portrait executed by François Clouet in 1548 and now in the Uffizi Gallery, Florence. Perhaps the most famous portrait of Charles V, done by Titian in 1548 and now in the Prado, shows him mounted on a horse before the battle of Mühlberg; his contemporary, Henry II of France, also figures in at least one equestrian portrait.[62] In the same way, in a famous painting Elizabeth I of England is depicted riding a horse as a symbol of her power when she addresses the troops at Tilbury, while the Spanish Armada looms threateningly in the background, unaware of its impending defeat.[63] Half a century later, Van Dyck raised the equestrian portrait to a peak of perfection. By contrast, Philip II did not favour equestrian portraits. There were exceptions. During his visit to the Netherlands in 1549, at least one print of the young prince mounted on horseback was published, but it was issued by his hosts, not by himself.[64]

Seals were another matter. Even before he became king of Spain Philip used a representation of himself on a horse for official seals, as witnessed by a beautiful gold seal preserved in the Vatican archives.[65] When he was ruler of Spain, there was an equestrian image of the king on his royal seal after the 1580s, a clear case of the horse as a (discreet) symbol of power. Drawings of him mounted can be seen occasionally in publications celebrating public occasions,[66] but the king did not allow equestrian paintings and the only known portrait of him on a horse is an imaginative work painted after his death, by Rubens in 1628.

The refusal to accept the horse as a symbol of power in art was of course at odds with Philip's great love of horses, riding and hunting. It has been argued that the much prized Spanish breed of Arab horse was a creation of Philip II, who cultivated the strain in his stables in Córdoba from 1567, shortly after his decision to construct the Escorial. His enthusiasm for the horse was notable, yet no symbolism of the animal in relation to royal power decorates any corner of the Escorial. We cannot doubt that the king was perfectly aware of the role of the horse as an expression of authority, since where possible he habitually made use of it. At Winchester for his wedding to Mary Tudor he arrived in state on horseback: he entered the city at 6 a.m. 'riding on a fair white horse, in a rich coate embroidered with gold, his doublet hosen, and hat suite like, with a white feather in his hat'.[67] When he opened the Cortes held in Córdoba in 1570, he rode through the city on his horse towards the steps of the building where the Cortes were about to be held. When he made his entrance into Seville in those same weeks, he did so mounted on horseback (but dressed in mourning).[68] At every stage of his career, then, he used the horse as a symbol of his dignity.

When he left Madrid for royal progresses he always insisted on riding out of the city on horseback. Once beyond the city confines, he would immediately dismount and continue the journey in his carriage. After his royal visit to the kingdom of Valencia in February 1586, he entered the kingdom of Castile in March 1586, and chose to do so with all formality, as a diplomat of the time observed:

> He entered several towns on the way into Castile, riding a horse, and shortly behind him the prince and the princess in a horse-carriage, all still wearing black in memory of the death of the duchess of Parma.[69]

Towards the end of his life, when despite his illness he had to undertake a long journey to take part in person in the Cortes of Aragon, held after the troubles of the Antonio Pérez affair, he was conveyed for the most part by litter. The king reached Tarazona on the last day of November 1592. Making a special effort, despite his condition, he transferred from his litter and passed into the city riding a pure white horse.[70] 'It caused wonder in all of us', recorded a Flemish courtier who was present.[71] The king, in short, was perfectly aware of the status a horse conferred, and made used of that knowledge whenever necessary. But he did not use the symbolism in the Escorial, or indeed anywhere else in the penin-sula. All the same, it is interesting to note that when he wished to present an image of power to a far-distant oriental potentate, he did so using the image of a horse. In 1580 the artist Sánchez Coello sent the king a bill of account for four large paintings that he had been asked to prepare for export to the emperor of China. One of them was 'a life-sized portrait of Your Majesty on horseback, in armour and with a baton, and another of the prince, also in armour'.[72] One of the four portraits was of the emperor, indubitably a copy which

Sánchez Coello had made from the Titian portrait depicting Charles on horseback at Mühlberg.

The low-key use of imagery, both inside and outside the Escorial, may be underlined by touching, finally, on the role of statuary. Since classical times, political figures had enhanced their status through the erection of public statues. The practice was resurrected in the nineteenth century by, for example, the British, who placed statues of their great men not only in Britain but throughout the British Empire; and also by the French.[73] I still distantly recall, from my childhood in colonial India, the grand marble statues that the great ones of British India erected for themselves in key spots of the parks and thoroughfares, posing always as though they were Roman pro-consuls. The Spanish monarchy, in contrast to the practice of Renaissance Italy, had no interest in public statuary of political leaders. A sixteenth-century writer, Diego de Villalta, observed that though statues were a normal form of displaying power, 'our princes and kings have always avoided and dismissed this type of vanity'.[74] The rejection of public statuary for living personages was a firmly held conviction. As we have noted above, when the duke of Alba had the effrontery to erect a statue to himself in a public square in the Netherlands, the outrage in Spain was so great that the king personally ordered the statue to be demolished. 'People in Spain complained', a historian of the subsequent generation reports, 'of the duke wishing to sing his own praises, and it was the main topic of conversation at the king's court. King Philip was displeased with the statue, and four years later he ordered it demolished in order to avoid offending the Netherlanders.'[75]

Philip II gave statues a limited role in the decoration of his residences. The Escorial, in particular, is notable for the complete absence of statues or busts representing either the king or the royal family. By contrast, in the gardens there were a substantial number of decorative statues on mythological themes, a feature that the king and his architects borrowed from the Renaissance gardens they had seen in Italy.

The only statues to be found in San Lorenzo fall into two distinct categories. First, a number of figures, such as those adorning the entrance to the building, represent biblical kings, in this case the kings of Israel, who stand prominently on guard over the entrance. In the interior Patio of the Kings, the façade of the basilica is also surmounted by statues of six of the kings of Israel.[76] Do those kings simply represent a homage to biblical kings who had served God? Or do they mean, rather, that King Philip II was identifying himself with them? An eminent scholar offers the following conclusion:

> The Escorial epitomized Philip's conception of his dual role as king and priest. At the front of the basilica he placed statues of biblical kings of Israel, descendants of David and ancestors of Christ.[77]

On this view, it seems, the king of Spain saw himself very much in biblical terms. In reality, the evidence suggests that the king never thought of himself as a priest (Chapter 8, below). Nor did he ever present himself specifically as a successor of the kings of the Bible. Since all monarchies of the time tried to base their authority on biblical origins, moreover, the appearance of effigies of kings at the Escorial is quite unexceptional. The origin of the statues in front of the basilica has already been touched upon (Chapter 4, above), and we can be certain that Philip 'placed' no statues there. The person who placed them there, as Sigüenza affirms unequivocally, was Arias Montano, who commissioned the kings during Philip's absence in Lisbon. The king himself had no particular enthusiasm for statues.[78]

Second, the only statues of royal personages inside the building are the funerary groups facing the high altar of the basilica, representing the emperor and Philip with their wives, work contracted to the sculptor and architect Leone Leoni as early as 1548. Memorial statuary was an art form that dated back to the Middle Ages and of which there are many examples in sixteenth-century Spain produced exclusively by Italian masters. Thanks to their work, we have access to the likenesses of important Spanish nobles and prelates. The two royal groups in the Escorial basilica, completed by Leoni's son Pompeo Leoni in the 1590s, were not aimed at emphasising royal eminence to the exclusion of other nobility. On the contrary, both groups expressly face the tabernacle of the high altar, in attitudes of prayer and worship. They are there to praise the power of God, not their own. It is significant that, apart from the memorial groups, the king refused to allow any representation of himself in a posture of public power, just as he rejected portraits on horseback. In the same way, no other distinguished contemporaries in Spain had their statues in public places. A statue of Charles V dating from that time exists, but in Brussels. A public statue of Don Juan of Austria also exists, but in Messina not in Spain.

Within this context, the only significant statue of Philip of Spain, now in the Prado, merits comment. It is a full-sized figure (5 ft 6 in high, 169 cm) made of bronze, showing a proud and handsome young man wearing armour, with a baton of command in his left hand and a sword girded to his right hip. Some scholars have hastened to identify the elegant figure with Philip II's lust for power and a desire to 'shape his monarchy in the mould of the unapproachable god-king'.[79] This might be plausible if the statue had seen the light of day and been positioned in a location where it would attract admiration for the 'god-king', or if it had been commissioned by the person whom it represents, or even if it represented Philip II. But none of these conditions prevailed. The statue does not represent King Philip II of Spain, but rather the young prince Philip as he was in 1551 at the end of his Fortunate Journey, before he even became king of England. The creator of the statue, Pompeo Leoni, saw fit to add the words 'Philip King of England' to the base of the figure, as an afterthought, but the work had been completed a year before Philip arrived in England. The figure was not made for Philip, but for the private collection of his aunt Mary of Hungary. It was finished in Milan in 1553, but for various reasons never reached Mary's residence in Valladolid, and instead remained gathering dust in the studio that Leoni subsequently possessed in Madrid.[80] Only in 1608 was it brought out and moved to the palace of the Alcázar.

The Apollo-like statue of the young prince, neither commissioned nor ever seen by him, clearly cannot be utilised in ingenious theses about Philip's ideas. However, ideologues of a later generation felt quite free to make use of Philip for their own purposes. In 1961 the dictatorship in Spain ordered the casting of a bronze copy, twice life-size, of Leoni's statue in order to celebrate the fourth centenary of Philip's decision to make Madrid the seat of his court. The new statue, commemorating the so-called 'capital status' of Madrid (in fact, Philip never at any point declared Madrid capital of Spain),[81] was set up in front of the new cathedral of the Almudena. The incident underlines the fact that all known statues of the king were ordered by private clients, not by Philip. There are several examples of public statues to the king in Madrid and other Spanish cities, but they all date from two hundred years after his death. The known busts of Philip were also all contracted by others, usually foreigners. The bronze bust in the Prado, attributed to Jacques Jonghelinck, was for example probably commissioned by Cardinal Granvelle. A further salient example is the bust of Philip by Leone Leoni, housed in Windsor Castle, which was commissioned by the duke of Alba in about 1555, just before the prince became king of Spain.

The idea of the Escorial as a monument to royal power is even less convincing when considered in relation to the core of the building, the basilica. The church, it has been suggested, was 'essentially a demonstration of power', and the choir a theatre where Philip acted out the role of a god.[82] A visitor to the basilica can have little doubt as to the spiritual power of the surroundings, but it is less convincing (and of course undocumented) to imagine the king in a divine role. There was but one power in the Escorial, the power of the God to whom Philip prayed every day. The king had no pretentions to any role save that of a humble suppliant, and certainly never attempted to be God. He voiced his humility before God many times, and it would be superfluous to repeat his words here. If there were human actors in the theatre of the basilica, they were exclusively members of the Habsburg dynasty commemorated in the memorials, statues and tombs. And they were commemorated not because of pretensions to power, but because they were now with God, the supreme power of the universe.

The suggestion that the Escorial was a symbol of monarchical pretensions is, one must conclude, difficult to sustain. Had any message of power emanated, directly or indirectly, from the Escorial, it would have collided with the reality – well known to Philip – that half of Spain had deep-rooted regional constitutions which did not tolerate any mystical or symbolic idealisation of the king of Castile. Nor, indeed, did Castilians themselves – the testimony of political theorists such as Castillo de Bobadilla, Juan de Mariana and Francisco Suárez is unequivocal enough – entertain such ideas about their monarchy. An observer today, of course, may read and interpret in different ways the undoubted power of the mammoth building. This type of interpretation is, however, quite different from any attempt to identify San Lorenzo with a programme that Philip never entertained. From the moment when he gazed in wonder and admiration at the lines of the abbey of Ettal in the mountains of Bavaria, the young prince nursed a clear intention to found a monastery that would be testimony to the power of God alone. The power of kings was a much lesser consideration. Nothing in the groundplan of the Escorial was meant to promote royal authority and, without exception, all the imagery was dedicated to glorifying one sole purpose: the eternity of God and the temporality of man. The most astonishing feature of the building is that there are nowhere any inscriptions or statues to indicate who was the begetter of this great work. A valid comment on the matter comes from Jonathan Brown: 'It may be tempting to interpret the stern style of the Escorial as a total metaphor for Philip II and his reign. Any such evaluation would rest on fallacious assumptions derived either from facile psychotherapy or crude historical generalization.'[83]

QUEEN ELIZABETH AND KING PHILIP: A BRACE OF EAGLES

The year 1988, which marked the passage of four centuries since the great Armada was sent against England by Philip II, itself saw the launch of a powerful fleet of scholarly studies dealing with the respective roles of England and Spain, but among English historians there was a curiously stubborn attachment to the old image of a good Queen Bess and a bad King Philip. In England a lengthy tradition dating back to the sixteenth century unfailingly pinned the label of expansionist on Philip, and leading English experts on Spanish history tended to reinforce the same image, which recurred in textbooks as well as in the cinema. Ten years after the Armada tributes, the year 1998 in Spain commemorated the fourth centenary of the death of Philip II, and a prominent English specialist on the king published a study in which the contrast between Elizabeth and Philip was very clearly drawn.[84] Elizabeth does not, it is true, occupy a central role in the book, but she is clearly seen as the intended victim of a king who has undisguised and obsessive ambitions of world supremacy.[85] A decade has passed since then, but no other historical study has emerged to back up the image of an expansionist Spain threatening its valiant victim, England. The following pages attempt to look again at the question, by suggesting briefly that there is little to distinguish the policies and ambitions of King Philip from those of Queen Elizabeth: both monarchs had more in common than we realise. As a Spanish scholar has appositely commented, King Philip was a person 'who can only be compared with Elizabeth of England'.[86]

One of the astonishing consequences of the failure of Spain's monarchy to find a home in the heart of its subjects – a problem that, as we shall see, also played some part in defining attitudes to the Escorial as a building (Chapter 9) – was the way in which some of Spain's political leaders came to admire the ruler of their great enemy, England, more than they admired their own. A precedent for this had already been set in the 1580s, when the impending threat of the Armada focused European attention on the small island kingdom. It was observed by an Italian diplomat that at the Spanish court 'everyone is amazed to see how cleverly that woman manages in everything'. 'The Spanish say that the king thinks and plans while the queen of England acts.'[87] A further sign of this tendency was the comment made by the pope in Armada Year, 1588. His Holiness did not disguise his admiration for Elizabeth. 'She certainly is a great queen,' he said, 'and were she only a Catholic she would be most dear to us. Just look how well she governs. She is only a woman, mistress of half an island, yet she makes herself feared by all.'[88] There were indeed many Spanish admirers of the English queen in the very highest ranks of the administration. The year after the Armada a royal official, Juan de Silva, count of Portalegre, commented to a high-ranking military administrator that 'only England preserves its spirit and increases its reputation. I think that other princes should exchange advisers with the queen, because she alone assaults with impunity the most powerful crowns of the world.'[89] When Philip II died, Silva wrote to the king's chief minister Cristóbal de Moura: 'these last twenty-two years that the queen of England has spent in the service of the world, will be the most outstanding known of in history.'[90] The chief minister wrote back, expressing agreement. From his direct knowledge, Silva cited the case of a man he knew, an Italian military commander from Milan, who was visiting him and on seeing a portrait of Elizabeth in the study began to utter prayers to her.[91] The parallels between Elizabeth and Philip were, indeed, so striking that there would be good reason to present them both as two eagles who, despite profound differences in outlook, faith and ideology, shared a comparable vision that (whether they liked it or not) served to mould their respective empires.

Our point of departure is an essay by British historian David Armitage on 'The Elizabethan Idea of Empire', published in 2004.[92] After pointing out how previous historians had identified the rise of England's claims to imperial destiny with the later Tudors, he stressed that they were mistaken and that 'this idea of empire was exemplary in its errors', because Queen Elizabeth I did not really have any firm view of expansion and did not 'possess any exalted ideas of her own imperial status'. His argument distinguishes between what commentators both at the time and much later contended (down to Frances Yates in her 1975 book, *Astraea: The Imperial Theme*), and what the queen really thought. Commentators, he suggests, have exaggerated, for the queen herself had no such ideas. 'The Elizabethan idea of empire', he states, 'was belated and unelaborated.' In order to stress the undeveloped nature of Elizabethan theory, he chooses to emphasise that 'the contrast with the comprehensive apocalyptic imperial vision of her adversary Philip II of Spain is especially striking'.[93] The two opposing poles of the imperial thesis thus seem to be clearly set out, but the unwary English reader is given no hint that the reference to Philip II's 'comprehensive apocalyptic imperial vision' rests on little tangible evidence and is based on the authority of one sole scholar, whose work on the king has always been invaluable and pioneering but whose thesis in this respect is neither proven nor provable.[94] The reality, as we shall suggest, is that every comment Armitage makes about Elizabeth and her absence of imperial theory can be applied with equal force to Philip of Spain, whose vision – despite Armitage – was very seldom comprehensive, never by any stretch of the imagination apocalyptic and only in the perspective of his enemies imperialist.[95]

A glance at the reality of European politics in their day reveals that in effect there was not much to differentiate the vision of Elizabeth from that of the king of Spain. Did Elizabeth reject ambitious ideas about inheriting the globe? So did Philip. If visions of empire in England 'outran the ambitions of Elizabeth [and] most of her councillors',[96] so too did those in Spain. There were always theorists who put forward claims that flattered the crown and exaggerated its pretensions, but did not necessarily reflect the crown's thinking. This in some measure was what happened to Elizabeth, whose supporters were eager to emphasise her imperial power at a time when she herself took no steps in that direction.[97] Under Charles V some Spanish writers laid claim to 'universality', by which they meant moral rather than imperialist authority.[98] The majority of them, however, particularly in Castile, were hostile to a German-based imperial programme, which they felt would be detrimental to Castilian interests. There was always, therefore, a clear ambivalence about Spanish participation in the imperial programme of Charles V.

When the young Philip of Spain, still only twenty-one years old and not yet confirmed as heir to his father, visited the Council of Trent in 1548, the city of Trent extended across the main street an arch with a quote from Virgil: 'Huic ego nec metas rerum/ nec tempore pono/ imperium sine fine dedi'.[99] It would be unwise to claim that this reflected Philip's imperial ambitions, since the motto was chosen not by the prince but by the city fathers, who were anxious to show that they supported the 'imperium' of Charles V. The arches erected by the cities of the Netherlands during Philip's visit of the provinces were in the same vein.[100] In Brussels, arches bore the motto 'Plus Ultra', and the symbol of the Pillars of Hercules to show that Philip's power was unlimited; the young prince, who had never yet participated in a military campaign, was also compared to Julius Caesar.[101] Neither reference, clearly, proves that the prince, who may not even have seen the words, was an imperialist. In any case, the mottoes, the symbolism and the references to Caesar were all taken directly from the emperor's own fund of images. There were arches, similarly, with the phrases: 'Dedit Abraham cuncta quae possederat Isaac', and 'Haeredem statuam populis te totius orbis', which presumed that Charles wished to pass on the imperial crown to Philip, but the phrases cannot be cited as proof that Philip himself sought imperial or universal dominion.[102] Street banners, then as now, reflected the aspirations of the street; they were not a statement of the political philosophy of the dignitary in whose honour they were displayed. This was as true in the Netherlands as in Spain, where towns rejoiced and celebrated when the king visited, but made no attempt to glorify his status or emphasise his power.[103]

If 'there is no evidence that the queen possessed any exalted idea of her own imperial status',[104] the same may be said of the king. If Elizabeth's ideas were 'unelaborated', so too were those of Philip. Nowhere among Philip's statements is there any unusual emphasis on the rights of kings, or on his personal power. Like most rulers, he was attributed 'absolute' power. The concept of *poderío absoluto* in Spain was late medieval in origin, and implied no more than the independence (or indivisibility)[105] of royal power. It was employed habitually by kings of Castile in the fifteenth century, and appeared several times in the will of Isabella the Catholic.[106] It was also applied to Philip when he resumed the government of Spain on his

return from Flanders in 1551.[107] In his last testament, over a generation later, he referred to 'my absolute power'. But he did not use
the phrase during his reign. Charles V had paid little attention to
the concept, but at the same time encouraged the use of the title
'Majesty', little known in Spain until then.[108] 'Majesty' was also
claimed for Philip in the year that he became king, by a Spanish
humanist writing in the Netherlands.[109] But he had little need for
theory. While university professors in Spain debated political principles, the king avoided any theoretical discussion about his powers,
exercised his authority within traditional limits, and was eventually
(in 1586) even to discourage the title 'Majesty' in favour of the very
much humbler form of address 'Sir'.

If Elizabeth rejected high and mighty titles and courtly flattery
(as Armitage claims), so too did Philip. 'It is one of the significant
peculiarities of Philip's rule', I pointed out some years ago, 'that
flattery was unknown at his court.'[110] If Elizabeth discouraged
expansion and settlement in the New World, so then did Philip,
who in 1573 took the historic step of decreeing that all further military expeditions in America should cease. If the 'Elizabethan idea of
empire [was] belated and unelaborated', so too was Philip's. As
noted below, no coherent Spanish theory of empire ever came into
existence.[111] If Elizabeth's sense of power was 'tinged with the sense
of isolation, backwardness and anxiety', so was Philip's. At every
point, Philip's perception of his role – and his attitude to the part to
be played by the crown in literature, music and art[112] – was similar
to that of the Elizabeth presented by British historians. The parallel
may be pressed yet further. In some aspects, in fact, a comparison of
the two regimes leaves that of Elizabeth in a strikingly unfavourable
position. The Escorial has been used as a symbol of the despotism,
cruelty and oppression of Philip's regime, but the oppression exercised by the regime in England was at many points far worse. When
we consider the mechanics and consequences of English rule in
Scotland, Ireland and the New World, it is difficult to exclude the
use of terms such as 'cruelty' and 'oppression'.

Despite his firmness over royal power, the king did not – because
he could not – become a despot. Previous rulers of Castile and

Spain had consciously rejected many of the symbols of power used by monarchies outside the peninsula.[113] They did not consider their office sacred, did not claim (like the rulers of France and England) any power to heal the sick and enjoyed no special rituals at the time of their birth, coronation[114] or death. The imagery of magical power, common in other monarchies, was notably absent in Spain. Philip followed this tradition perfectly. He encouraged no cult of his person, as Elizabeth of England did in subsequent years[115] and as Louis XIV was to do on a grand scale later. Like his predecessors, he firmly asserted his authority to rule, and the trust he received from God, but he did not inflate these claims into a mystique of royal power. Observers who knew something of Spanish politics were in no doubt, a correspondent writing from Madrid to Prague in 1564 commenting:

> Although it may appear that the king has great armies, great power, great income and revenue, his armies are scattered and thin, everyone is extremely dissatisfied with His Majesty, the treasury is deeply in debt, and outside of Italy he does not have the absolute power and command over his subjects and estates that would enable him to rule at will.[116]

By contrast, the cult of Elizabeth converted her into a virtual goddess: the rule of Elizabeth, it has been pointed out, was 'the most successful Protestant version of a sacred kingship in the English Reformation'.[117] In the literature, she was treated variously as goddess, queen, Venus, mother and even as man. She performed the ritual magic of the medieval kings, touching those sick with scrofula and healing them. She gave wealth to the poor in the form of the Maundy alms (her reign saw a conspicuous growth in poverty among the population). The cult of the queen, heightened by the crisis of national defence in the decades when there was fear of a Spanish invasion, made it easy for Englishmen to pass over without comment the less savoury aspects of the reign.

If the English were 'left without any substantial or distinctive conception of empire for most if not all of the reign',[118] the same – one should emphasise – was true of the Spanish.[119] One of the amazing – and even admirable – aspects of the Spanish imperial system was that its theorists spent most of their time arguing *against* the empire, and in favour of the rights of the peoples who lived in it. In 1539 the Salamanca professor Francisco de Vitoria set out in a lecture the argument that peoples who are conquered (the reference was to America) do not necessarily forfeit their natural rights. His theories were endorsed by other Spanish clergy in the subsequent century, and were even taken up by foreigners. 'There is a strong sense', we are reminded, 'in which the members of the school of Salamanca and their heirs were anti-imperialist.'[120] This tendency to define and limit the authority of Spaniards in other lands was also pursued from a slightly different direction by Bartolomé de las Casas, and effectively impeded the growth of any formal imperial theory. Spaniards – especially the soldiers among them – were proud of the world role they enjoyed, and expressed themselves in an aggressive way, but they seldom used the word empire to refer to the entity they served. Indeed, some spent a great deal of time arguing that the notion of empire was 'a children's story',[121] pure fantasy.

Philip, for example, never aspired to crush the autonomy of the kingdoms in the peninsula. He used an army to maintain his claim to Portugal, but that claim rested primarily on hereditary succession rather than on conquest. One of the things that most irritated the duke of Alba, who led the army that occupied Portugal in 1580, was Philip's refusal to admit in any way that the campaign was one of 'conquest'.[122] Philip, however, had good reasons. How, he argued, could he 'conquer' what was already his, not only by right of succession but also by the express will of the Cortes of Portugal? In the same way, Philip respected fully the constitutional rights of the other kingdoms of the peninsula. The most relevant example is Aragon, which was also invaded by a royal army. That army conquered nothing, occupied nothing, and left the constitution of the realm almost completely untouched. By contrast, Elizabeth's forces in Ireland acted with substantially more rigour.

In practice, of course, there is no sense in downplaying Elizabeth's system and drawing an unfavourable contrast with that of Philip II. Both rulers controlled similar mechanisms of power; both organised sytems of espionage for collecting information in their own defence. Few adequate studies have been done of the king's extensive (and poorly organised) international network of spies, but we know that it existed and that it worked.[123] In the same way, Elizabeth enjoyed the benefits of an intelligence system operated by her chief ministers.[124] Both lacked any imperialist Grand Strategy, but they were not so foolish as to be unaware of the rules of the imperial game. They knew that in order to maintain the advantage they had to resort to any means, both fair and foul, that might be necessary. Here the parallels between Elizabeth and Philip are so close that it is almost impossible to distinguish between their strategies and methods. Philip resorted where necessary – and always, of course, on the advice of his ministers and agents – to blackmail, sabotage, military intervention and assassination. So, too, did Elizabeth.

The similarities and parallels fall down when we consider the projection of images. Philip, as we have observed, had no concern to broadcast his image. He did not retire into the Escorial (see Chapter 5), but neither did he indulge in a flurry of royal progresses through the nation. One key illustration highlights the contrast immediately. In the Wingfield Digby collection at Sherborne Castle there is a painting of Queen Elizabeth in procession, borne high in a litter on the shoulders of her nobles and courtiers. The portrait of Her Royal Majesty carried aloft by her faithful subjects has no parallel in any work of art produced anywhere in Spain during the reign of Philip II. No divine adulation greeted the rulers of Spain on any of their public appearances, and when they dismounted from their ceremonial horses they limited themselves, as Philip did on all the recorded occasions, to walking among the people on terms of equality. Philip did not need, nor did he seek, public magnificences.[125] His throne was secure. By contrast, Elizabeth cooperated fully with her advisers and her subjects in promoting her own image. It was essential to do so in order to protect her dynasty (threatened by alternative pretenders, notably Mary, Queen of Scots) and her succession (threatened by the obvious lack of an heir). From the beginning of the reign, the day of her accession to the throne was always celebrated with popular rejoicing and bell-ringing. In times of crisis, pageants were put on in which she was allotted a central place. From the 1580s, and in particular after Armada year, the portraits of her carried messages of mystery and power. Her reign 'stands as a perfect illustration not simply of the inter-connectedness of art and power, but of the complex exchange between authority and subjects in the production and dissemination of a successful image'.[126]

The Escorial, vaunted by many as the arch-symbol of the king's power, offers us a final commentary on the comparison between the king of Spain and the queen of England. Approximately around Armada year, Juan Pantoja de la Cruz[127] produced an impressive portrait that belies any myth of pretensions to imperial grandeur (see Chapter 9). His painting of an elderly Philip stands prominently to one side of the Escorial library and reflects perfectly the wastage of the years. Philip stands erect, dressed from top to toe in black, with the Fleece as his only ornament. His face is ashen pale, the same colour as his beard and hair. The lips sag. His eyes are old and weary, the lids half-closed. Did the king ever see the portrait? At what moment was it installed in the library? Philip's correspondence demonstrates that he was not afraid of old age or of death, and he had no qualms about displaying the portrait.

The imagery of Elizabeth, by contrast, was entirely different. In her portraits Elizabeth barely ages. She is the permanent, immortal Virgin Queen, a 'timeless icon, never ageing and ever youthful'.[128] As late as 1600, portraits of her – when she was the same age as Philip in the Pantoja painting – present her as a queen of beauty, eternally young.[129] One must concede that artists in England at the time were far more accomplished than those in Spain, and were able to flatter without falling into undue exaggeration. The king of Spain, however, was not one for exaggeration. Conscious of his infirmities, he accepted the reality of age and death. A flattering portrait would have earned his displeasure. Their different approach to portraiture was indisputable evidence of their different approach to power. Elizabeth welcomed the consciousness of contact with her people. Philip in the Escorial, less preoccupied with the people, had his eyes fixed already on God.

CHAPTER 7

THE HALL OF BATTLES

An Escorial not of victory but of peace; Glory and disaster at sea: Lepanto and the Armada; The painting of the Hall of Battles

AN ESCORIAL NOT OF VICTORY BUT OF PEACE

Early descriptions of the palace-monastery refer to it as San Lorenzo de la Victoria,[1] but the friars persuaded the king that the title 'Royal' would be more appropriate than the warlike 'Victory'. The name therefore became San Lorenzo el Real. The entire concept of the Escorial – the monastery, the secluded environment, the concern for prayer and commemoration of the royal dead, the tranquillity of the gardens – betokened peace. For the king too it became a haven of retirement, where he could work unmolested as well as devote himself to his family. Unlike some later royal palaces in Europe, and several noble palaces that, like Blenheim in England, owed their origin to success in warfare, it excluded the notion of conflict from both its art and its environment. After his return to Spain in 1559, the king made it his firm objective to maintain peace with all those – principally the papacy, France and England – who might have reason to be hostile. It is an astonishing fact that in the quarter of a century after its construction began not a single painting in Philip's Escorial was dedicated to battles, information that serves to confirm that the king believed his monastery should be devoted to prayer, not strife. Time and again, from the very moment he succeeded to the crown, he repeated to diplomats of all nations that his first desire was peace.

It is all the more incongruous, therefore, that in the generations after Philip's death there was in Spain a continuous emphasis on the Escorial as an expression of success in war. It is not surprising that a leading modern authority deems the building to be 'a monument to the Habsburgs' defeat of their arch-enemy'.[2] This idea was backed up by stressing the warlike character of the so-called Hall of Battles. 'This gallery', affirms a Spanish web page on the Escorial, 'shows scenes from the most famous battles won by the armies of Spain.'[3] That notion of victory, we are confidently assured, goes back to the battle of St Quentin of 1557, and well beyond it. The whole building, a historian of the 1960s proclaimed (writing in the name of the head of state himself), was a celebration of 'that glorious and transcendental battle with which the Prudent King began his reign'. The Escorial was viewed by the same writer as a testimony to Spain's might, 'when Spanish arms were at the height of their expansion through the virgin lands of America, carrying out the most stupendous endeavour that any nation had ever attempted'.[4] The ideology of state imposed its vision on the past, and disfigured what really happened in Philip II's Escorial. It is a viewpoint that continues to survive, not only in tourist handbooks but also in learned monographs. An expert on the Escorial, for example, refers to 'the Hall of Battles, [as] a reflection of the military exploits and glories of the fleets and armies of the most powerful monarch of his day, which more than one ambassador and dignitary would contemplate with undisguised terror'.[5]

Whether or not transfixed by terror, the visitor today is left in no doubt about the role of military achievement, which is depicted on every surface of the immense space surrounding the main cloister staircase of the monastery. This surely, one is invited to acknowledge, is a building constructed in honour of victory. The impression is reinforced when one passes through the building in order to contemplate the beautifully painted surfaces of the walls in the Hall of Battles. The hall, 60 metres long, 6 metres wide and 8 metres high, backs onto the main body of the basilica and consists of a series of painted surfaces, continuous on one side but interrupted by nine windows on the other. The magnificent ceiling is decorated with beautifully executed motifs that accompany the eye all the way down the corridor to the wall at the end, also decorated by a military painting.[6]

More than in any other part of the monastery, however, what we know about the building and more especially the hall has been modified to serve the interests not simply of tourists but, even more assuredly, of national pride. In the centuries after the battle of St Quentin, many Spaniards were eager to back up the desired image of a great and powerful Spain that had conquered half the world, and in order to do this they were keen to emphasise the role of military victory.[7] This takes us to the heart of one of the greatest enigmas of the Escorial. Philip II has been presented by both his admirers and his critics – who on this point ironically coincide in their views – as a monarch in the throes of militaristic euphoria, who created San Lorenzo as a memorial to military achievement and then commissioned the Hall of Battles as a further testimony to success.[8] (This image of a warlike king, we may note, is often entertained in the same breath as the image of a king who was, specifically in the case of St Quentin, a military coward.)[9]

The first point to observe is that the warlike decorations over the cloister staircase had nothing to do with the founder of the Escorial. Visitors today who are allowed to ascend the main staircase of the monastery have no reason to complain of a lack of martial splendour, for there before them they will see the rich and elaborate ceilings covered with a celebration of the 'Glory of the Spanish Monarchy'. They may need to be reminded that the painting does not form part of Philip II's original scheme, and that it was executed as an addition one and a half centuries later (1693) by the Italian artist Luca Giordano, in the reign of Charles II. It was a time when Spain was losing all its battles on both land and sea and desperately needed a visual reminder of the age when it had appeared to rule the world. The glory depicted was a dream of the past. In order to flesh out that vision of a long-gone age of prowess, on the frieze of one wall Giordano also painted a triumphant depiction of the battle of

St Quentin. Giordano's creation was a gesture meant to hearten the Spanish government in the midst of its deepest imperial despair. The paintings therefore had nothing to do with the part that the original battle may have played in the evolution of Philip II's artistic ideas for the monastery-palace. Alexandre Dumas' reaction to the frieze in 1845 was unequivocal: 'God have mercy on King Charles II, who touched up the Escorial!'[10] The decoration by Giordano also includes a depiction of the battle of Lepanto. In 1870 the American diplomat John Milton Hay had no hesitation in censuring 'Giordano, the nimble Neapolitan, emptying his buckets of paint on the ceiling of the grand staircase, where St Lawrence and an army of martyrs go sailing with a fair wind into glory'.[11] Subsequent generations found it necessary to invent an age of military glory, but Philip II had no such thoughts.

In reality, the paintings on the staircase and in the hall are not only an exception but even a contradiction in the Escorial, because they are the only areas to have a clear warlike theme and are therefore at odds with the message of the rest of the building. The contradiction, one must emphasise, was not engendered by Philip. For the king, the passage that became the hall had originally no military significance and was nothing more than a corridor. It served as a means of access, and in Philip's lifetime was called simply the 'king's private gallery' or 'His Majesty's gallery'. The present name was given to the corridor nearly two centuries later, in 1764, when it seemed preferable to apply a description that accorded with the wall decorations. The king, by contrast, had at first no intention of introducing military themes into a building that was clearly religious, and his commissions to artists in the first thirty years after he returned to the peninsula – a long enough period for us to conclude that he knew what his intentions were – do not include any military paintings.

With all these facts at our disposal, however, some intriguing and vitally important questions arise. Though one may believe that Spain's military victories are commemorated in the hall, why is it that in fact *none* of Spain's land victories – except that of St Quentin, painted only at the end of Philip's life and not, as we know, a primarily 'Spanish' event – is commemorated? Why does not a single Spanish victory of the century preceding Philip II make its appearance? If there was one military event which older Spaniards of that time would have retained in their collective memory, it would have been the capture of Granada from the Muslims in 1492. Why does the hall ignore that crucial event, and dedicate itself almost entirely to an unknown interior battle of over two centuries before (1341)? Why are none of Charles V's famous victories, in all of which a significant part was played by Spanish troops, commemorated? Spain played a crucial role in the battle of Pavia (1525), when the king of France was taken prisoner and brought captive to Madrid, but only the Netherlanders seem to have celebrated the victory in their art, with a beautiful seven-piece set of tapestries presented by the States General to Charles in 1531. When Philip went to stay with Mary of Hungary at her palace in Binche in 1549, his bedroom was hung with the whole set.[12] In the same way, Philip had a direct link with Charles' greatest military victory outside Europe, the occupation of Tunis in 1535. He featured personally in the splendid tapestries of the event, which were given to him as a wedding present by the emperor in 1554, and taken personally to London by the weaver Willem de Pannemaker.[13] Yet neither Pavia nor Tunis features in the themes for celebration in the Escorial. The list of omissions is both startling and impressive. Perhaps the most significant military victory of the emperor in Europe was the 1547 battle of Mühlberg, won against the Protestants in Germany.[14] Many Castilian historians today insist on viewing it as a uniquely 'Spanish' victory (it was, of course, primarily a German rather than a Spanish event). If we can be persuaded to believe that it was indeed a Spanish victory, we may well ask: why does it not then appear in the hall?

It is equally baffling that none of the military actions of the reign of Philip II was commemorated by Spanish artists at the time of the event. Why are there no Spanish paintings of the actions of Spanish forces in Europe? As we have observed (Chapter 2), Spain's historians have relegated the battle of St Quentin to oblivion: in five centuries no Spanish artist has seen fit to produce a worthy canvas on the theme. Within the Escorial, the only public recognition of the 1557 victory was Giordano's fresco painted a century and a half after the event. In the preceding generations, the walls of the palace-monastery spoke exclusively of religion, not of war. Only towards the end of his life did Philip II decide to allow the event to be commemorated in the Hall of Battles. The following pages attempt to look more closely at this curious non-appearance of the victory in a building that was supposedly meant to celebrate it.

Court painters of the day were sometimes contracted as war correspondents to go to the scene of battle and record what happened, as Charles V did with the Flemish artists he took with him on the 1535 Tunis campaign (see Chapter 6). It has been suggested that, in the same way, Philip II sent the Dutch artist Van den Wijngaerde to accompany the naval expedition to the Peñón de Vélez in 1564 because he required a painting of the action for the Escorial.[15] The artist did indeed execute a number of interesting paintings of the naval manoeuvres, but there is (to my knowledge) no evidence that the king required the pieces for the Escorial, and none of them came to occupy any space in the monastery.

In pursuing an enquiry into the relation between warfare and the art in the Escorial, we would be justified in asking why the monastery, and with it the Hall of Battles, ignores what the public today might identify – Cervantes certainly did so – as the greatest victory of that time, the naval battle of Lepanto in 1571. (Cervantes had proclaimed it to be 'the greatest occasion that past or present ages have seen, or that future ones can hope to see'). It had taken place a full thirteen years before Philip II instructed his artists to paint the Hall of Battles, yet not a trace of it can be found in the hall, a circumstance on which we shall comment below. Many Italian artists celebrated the event, yet no Spaniard did so. What lay behind this uncanny refusal to revel in military glory?

The question of the depiction of warfare in the Escorial can be related, surely, to what we know of Philip's lack of enthusiasm for warfare. Charles V had always made sure that his son would be brought up as a soldier. As seen through the engravings done for Philip by the Dutch painter Heemskerck in 1566, Charles was the prototypical military hero, whose victories over the Lutherans in Germany were on a par with his triumphs over the papacy, over France and over the Turks at Vienna in 1529. Philip's entire training, his long familiarity with tourneys and games of war, his skill at hunting, meant that he could adapt easily to a military role. As a young man, his tastes centred on war and hunting. Well before his English marriage, he had an impressive collection of arquebuses, swords and bows. As we have seen, he had, for all that, never been in action, and unlike his father was not a devotee of warfare.[16] 'The emperor', commented the Venetian ambassador in 1556, 'was inclined to things of war, the king dislikes them. The former threw himself with ardour into great enterprises, the latter avoids them.'[17]

The attitude of the king to warfare was, however, rather more complex than the ambassador was suggesting. Philip had always accepted the need to be a soldier. There are two infallible pieces of evidence to demonstrate that he was aware of the relevance of war. First, he loved war games. At every stage of his early life, he revelled in the rites of chivalry, a taste that shines through the accounts of his Fortunate Journey to northern Europe. Second, he adored armour. During his visit to Augsburg in mid-century he purchased armour. His favourite portrait of himself was the full-size one done of him in armour by Titian which occupied the place of honour in his chamber in 1553,[18] together with one of his father. At least two of his formal portraits show him in armour. At the camp in St Quentin, he donned armour in order to receive the noble prisoners, and that is the guise in which Antonis Mor painted him. Armour symbolised status and power as well as personal dignity. The acceptance of warfare at a personal level, however, did not mean that Philip felt the urge to display his own masculinity or that of his country. It was obvious to observers that he had no martial inclinations; he never attempted to equal the achievements of the emperor. He could continue to venerate his father while in practice adopting a quite different approach to problems. Throughout his reign, he avoided recourse to war, believing firmly that it was never a solution.

When the time came for action at St Quentin, Philip was second to none in his enthusiasm for battle. He and the other young nobles in Brussels in 1557 were anxious to win their spurs in action.[19] He increased the war expenditure of the government more steeply than any other ruler in Spain's history, but at the same time he came to see that military solutions were never the most effective. Philip rejected the use of force against England for over twenty-five years, refused stubbornly to intervene in France for decades until intervention finally became inevitable, and avoided the military solutions proposed by his commanders in the Netherlands. Time and again, he insisted that military force was not the answer to disturbances. He gave way when the duke of Alba insisted that it was necessary, but emphasised to Alba's successor Requesens that moderation was the only course. Only after years of sufferance – Queen Elizabeth came to the throne in 1558 but it was not until thirty years later that the Great Armada sailed – did he decide that military action against England was unavoidable. And during those years he was the first to protest against the pope's ill-advised excommunication of the queen in 1570.

His troops invaded Portugal in 1580, because he and his advisers saw no other way of securing his claims to the crown of that country in the face of possible military intervention by England and France. Only after years of opposing the advice of his own ministers to intervene in the French civil wars did he reluctantly give in and send troops to support the Catholic cause. The most significant case of all was the Spanish presence in the New World, where he prohibited (in 1573) any further military expeditions. The king's permanent commitment to peace seldom paid off, for there were too many factors at work to make a real peace attainable. A good case, however, can be made for the argument that his armies did not undertake a single unprovoked act of aggression (that is, seizure of someone else's territory) during his reign. The only arguable exception to this statement occurred in 1570, when the army from Milan marched in and occupied the Italian coastal territory of Finale to prevent its strategic port falling into French hands. Like any head of state, however, Philip never ruled out recourse to force. His numerous military interventions were always carefully planned to ward off imminent threats, which meant that he was quite capable of planning, with complete sangfroid, actions that might have dire consequences in terms of bloodshed.

The victories at St Quentin and the Gravelines in mid-century, it seemed, marked the closing of an era of wars with France. If St Quentin was to be commemorated in the Escorial, it was as a God-given mercy, not as a military success (see Chapter 2). The annual day of the saint was always commemorated by the monks, but in religious and never in military terms. In any case, we should remember that Spaniards had few reasons for celebration in the period after St Quentin, when the country suffered unprecedented military and naval disasters not in northern Europe but in the Mediterranean. The biggest disaster, indeed the biggest military disaster of Spain's entire history until that date, was the defeat inflicted by the Turkish navy in 1560 at the island of Djerba (mentioned below). As a consequence, Philip committed Spain to a high level of vigilance in the Mediterranean.[20] The tide began to turn at the relief of Malta (1565), but the first significant military victory after St Quentin came only much later, at Lepanto. It is an incident to which we must turn, because the non-appearance of the battle of Lepanto in the Escorial of Philip II is no less strange than the non-appearance of the battle of St Quentin.

GLORY AND DISASTER AT SEA: LEPANTO AND THE ARMADA

The greatest naval battle of the century took place on the outer fringe of Christian Europe, but had profound repercussions throughout the continent and in the Mediterranean.[21] The naval campaign against the Muslim powers came about as a result of agreement between the Christian princes in the Mediterranean, led by the pope, over the strategy to be adopted. This Holy League supervised the arrangements for the fleet. It was agreed that the supreme commander would be Don Juan of Austria, the king of Spain's half brother. A massive Turkish fleet of over 300 galleys was ravaging the coastline of settlements in the eastern Mediterranean. In the west, Don Juan was determined – against the advice of veteran seamen – to test to the full the resources at his disposal. At the end of August 1571 he was in Messina, the appointed rendezvous for the ships of the Holy League. The assembled Christian fleet comprised over 200 galleys and well over 50,000 soldiers, supplied and paid for by the papacy, Venice and Spain. Although Philip II's treasury was the biggest single contributor to costs, the so-called 'Spanish' contribution was in reality largely Italian. Of the galleys supplied by Spain, four-fifths were built and paid for by the Italian states of the monarchy.

The fleet left Messina on 16 September and headed towards Corfu. There they were informed that the Turks were in the Gulf of Lepanto, off the coast of Greece. The two massive formations came upon each other on the morning of 7 October in the gulf. Calculations of the numbers of ships and men on each side vary widely, but it is likely that the Turks had some 230 ships and well over 50,000 men while the Christians had some 200 vessels, not all of which took part in the battle, and about 50,000 men. By the end of the day Don Juan's ships had won a decisive victory. The Turkish vice-admiral, Uluj Ali, escaped with about 30 galleys. All the others were captured or destroyed. The Turks suffered 30,000 casualties and 3,000 prisoners. Christian losses were by comparison small: 10 galleys, and some 8,000 men killed.

In the afternoon of 29 October 1571 a courier from Venice brought to the Venetian ambassador and to Philip, then in Madrid, reliable word of the victory at Lepanto. 'The king's joy at receiving the news was extraordinary', the ambassador reported. 'In that very moment he ordered a Te Deum sung.'[22] Over the next few days all Madrid exploded in an orgy of celebration. A solemn procession was held in which the king insisted on having the Venetian ambassador at his side. The fact that Philip had already heard the good news of the battle in Madrid refutes the commonly repeated story that he first learnt of it when he was in the Escorial. Further news came in the form of the first official confirmation by letter, which he received in the Escorial, probably on 20 November, from the governor of Milan, Luis de Requesens. Only afterwards, on 22 November, did a special envoy, Lope de Figueroa, bring confirmation from Don Juan. By then the king had known about the victory for over three weeks. One of his courtiers, fat, excited and breathless, burst in to say that a messenger had arrived from Don Juan. 'Calm down,' said the king. 'Let the messenger in, he will say it better.'[23] Philip quizzed Figueroa eagerly. 'For the first half-hour he did nothing but ask, "Is my brother well?" and all sorts of questions', the latter reported. The queen came in with her ladies and also questioned him. 'Thus I passed an hour in the most agreeable manner possible', Figueroa wrote to Don Juan.[24] Philip displayed 'great delight and joy',[25] ordered the prior to have a Te Deum sung, and went to his rooms highly contented.

Don Juan was given his full share of public glory. Philip wrote to him, 'I am pleased to a degree which it is impossible to exaggerate. . . . To you, after God, ought to be given, as I now give, the honour and thanks.'[26] The military hero of Spain, victor first of the campaign against rebel Muslims in the Alpujarras (1569–70), and now of Lepanto, Don Juan was fêted throughout the peninsula. The king continued to distrust him, but gave him all due honour for his successes. The recognition by Philip of Don Juan's triumph disproves the suggestion that he deliberately played down the prince's role, a suggestion that has sometimes been based on the apparently modest role assigned to the prince in the paintings of the event done by the artist Luca Cambiaso (discussed below).[27] The truth is that Cambiaso painted his canvases not for the king of Spain but specifically for the great Genoese admiral Doria. The Italians, who always claimed Lepanto to be an Italian victory, were not likely to concede primacy to a Spanish prince. If Don Juan does not stand out sufficiently in the canvases, the fault was not that of Philip II but rather of the Genoese patrons of the artist.

Lepanto was a victory for Christendom. But, as historians recognise, it was never simply a Spanish victory. Without the extensive resources of the Italians, Spain would have been powerless to act. Philip was perfectly aware of this and it explains his refusal to participate in the daydreaming in which less realistic men, such as Don Juan and Pope Pius V, indulged. They imagined a possible liberation of the Holy Land, and even of Constantinople. The legend of Lepanto would, however, live on. Philip clearly shared the enthusiasm generated by the victory, but he 'opted for the possible, not for the grandiose'.[28] We may imagine him in his monastery-palace in 1571, giving thanks to God for the amazing graces of that year. With God's blessing, everything had come together. The residential quarters at San Lorenzo were completed by early summer, and for the first time the monks, the king and the immediate court were able to take up residence in the Escorial. The first mass at the altar of the new church was celebrated in August, in honour of San Lorenzo.[29] Only two months later, in the same residence of the Escorial, Philip would receive formal news of Lepanto. And only two months after that, just before the year 1571 was out, he was blessed with the birth of the Infante Fernando, the first child of his new and beloved Queen Anna.

The great enigma is why, after so many triumphs, he failed to commemorate any of them in his new palace, where he had received the first official news. A scholar reminds us that the king 'commissioned only one work of art to commemorate the victory',[30] namely the work by Titian. It is true that in 1571 the monastery was still under construction, and the area where a painting might have been hung did not yet exist. The absence of a celebratory painting, however, affected not simply the Escorial but the whole of Spain. No Spanish artist painted the glory of Lepanto.[31] It is one of the great puzzles of the story. Were Spaniards unaware of the battle? We know they were not, for many cities held public celebrations, and Barcelona later enthroned Don Juan's large battle crucifix, known as 'The Christ of Lepanto', in the cathedral, where it may still be seen. In those months, a handful of Spanish publicists and writers published works praising the achievement; the poet of heroic verse Fernando de Herrera published a poem on the theme (1572), and another, Francisco de Aldana, wrote a sonnet greeting the victory as confirmation of King Philip's universal sway.[32] The excitement of 1571, nevertheless, led to no change in the king's artistic commissions for the Escorial or, indeed, for Spain.

It has been suggested that the king was reluctant to celebrate Lepanto because he realised that it had given a major boost to the participating Italian states.[33] There is no evidence whatsoever to back up this theory. However, it is true that in Italy, where the victory was with good reason considered Italian,[34] there were immediate masterly renderings of the battle by Paolo Veronese, Andrea Vicentino, Tintoretto and Titian. The Vatican, which financed a good part of the Christian outlay, ordered a celebratory wall fresco. Gian Andrea Doria commissioned six enormous tapestries for the Palazzo del Principe of the Doria family in Genoa. Designs were prepared by Lazzaro Calvi and Luca Cambiaso and the tapestries, woven in Brussels, reached Genoa in 1591. The cartoons by Cambiaso served at the same time as the basis for six paintings which he executed for Doria, who subsequently made a gift of them to Philip II's secretary Antonio Pérez (see below).

We come back to the enigma that not a single Spanish artist of standing painted the battle. Those who did so, as in the case of an (anonymous, with good reason, in view of its poor quality) oil painting in the Museo Casa de Cervantes in Valladolid, done fifty years after the battle, merely copied existing Italian canvases and added their own finishing touches.

Titian, who was then in Rome, made the only notable contribution on behalf of Spain. Philip commissioned him to produce a canvas in celebration of the naval victory and also of the birth of Prince Fernando. As in most such commissions, the king communicated an outline of what he wanted. Sanchez Coello, virtually Philip's artist-in-residence at this period, executed a sketch that he took personally to Titian to explain the king's wishes. Titian mentioned in a letter to Philip, written from Venice and dated 22 December 1574, that he had already started work on the painting of Lepanto and also on a Nativity, when he had heard from 'the painter who came here from Spain to see me the other day' with details of what the king wanted. The resulting canvas was completed in 1575, just before the artist's death from plague (and advanced old age, since he was eighty-eight years old!) in 1576. Whether due to the difficulty of envisioning the king's idea, or because of his own failing powers, Titian produced a canvas that some critics judge to be one of the artist's weakest and most maladroit pieces of work. Usually titled *Allegory of the Battle of*

Lepanto, the canvas brings together the naval victory (depicted only in the form of a subdued Turk) and the birth of Prince Fernando as testimony to the mercies conferred by heaven. The relationship between the events, however, is ill-defined, and the naval aspect of Lepanto – surely a fundamental consideration – is wholly absent. It is possible that the king did not want the military theme to have any key part in the composition, which we may suppose followed the guidelines he laid down in the letter taken to Titian by Sánchez Coello. The end result, however, is poor testimony to the public aspects of the rejoicing over Lepanto that took place in Spain.

At the same time, Titian brought out of storage a painting he had done forty years earlier (*c*.1534), retouched it for Philip, and gave it an appropriate name: it is the canvas we know as *Spain Succouring Religion*. In view of the doubtful relevance of the picture to its title, one may be forgiven for speculating whether Philip was really happy with this last offering from his favourite artist.

For over a decade after the naval victory, there was no artistic work produced on the theme in Spain. Like St Quentin, Lepanto went unacknowledged and uncommemorated.[35] A new twist to the story came in the 1580s with the arrest and trial of Philip's former secretary, Antonio Pérez. In the summer of 1584, just over a year after Philip's return from Lisbon, official charges were brought against the ex-secretary. The government had been slow to act, for a very compelling reason. Pérez was in possession of an alleged 'thirty cases' of the king's confidential papers. When it appeared that Pérez might flee, he was arrested in January 1585, ten days after the king had left for Saragossa. Pérez attempted to escape with the help of his friend cardinal Quiroga,[36] but was seized and imprisoned. A public sale of some of his confiscated property, in particular Pérez's fine collection of paintings, was held in 1585, on the basis of a full inventory drawn up in May that year. At least a hundred paintings featured in his collection.[37] The motive for the sale was the presumption that the paintings had been acquired through manifest corruption (which nobody doubted). Philip acquired a set of pictures from the collection: six large canvases depicting the battle of Lepanto, which Pérez had obtained from the Genoese admiral

Gian Andrea Doria.[38] This sale appears to explain how Philip came to possess the canvases,[39] which were deposited in the Escorial. But in what circumstances did the king purchase the paintings of Lepanto? It is significant that there is no record of any payment being made to the artist, who in any case died in the year that the auction was held. If money changed hands, it did not go to Cambiaso but to the beneficiaries of the sale.

The fact remains that all the best canvases of Lepanto that have survived are Italian, and it is likely that no Spanish artists of the time were proficient in painting sea battles. This presumption is confirmed by the detail that not a single significant Spanish naval expedition of the subsequent two hundred years was depicted by Spanish painters. Ships feature in several works of art, but only as incidental items in the background. Sea battles in the Channel, by contrast, were magisterially recorded (or remembered) by English or Dutch artists.[40] Not until the nineteenth century did Spanish artists begin to paint naval engagements. Just as all the significant land battles of the late sixteenth century were depicted for Spanish eyes by Flemish artists, so the significant naval encounters were depicted by Italians. If the king wished to commemorate the events of 1571, therefore, he had no option but to call in foreigners. Antonio Pérez had solved the problem by purchasing canvases, but the king wanted something different to decorate his walls.

We should not imagine that Philip was indifferent to the glory of battle. His correspondence, quoted above in Chapter 2, is testimony to his personal pride in the triumph of St Quentin. In the same way, he was aware of the need to record successful military enterprises. In 1560, barely a year after his return to the peninsula, the Turks inflicted on Spanish forces a crushing defeat at the island of Djerba.[41] The Christian commanders fled in their ships, but 10,000 men surrendered and were led in triumph a few days later through the streets of Constantinople. It was the biggest Spanish defeat in the country's military history. Some honour was regained in August 1564 when the newly appointed commander of Spain's Mediterranean fleet, García de Toledo, managed to put together an expedition which captured the ill-defended fortress of Vélez de la Gomera on the

North African coast. Philip had the foresight, as we have already observed, to send his Flemish artist Van den Wijngaerde to accompany the fleet. The result was a series of unique drawings depicting a Spanish victory at first hand. Yet this was by no means a new departure. Years before, in the Netherlands, Philip obtained from the same Van den Wijngaerde a superb drawing of the victory of St Quentin, the only authoritative depiction of the battle (Chapter 2), since the artist must have consulted military commanders when he executed his work. The thrill of victory was not absent from the king's soul, but it is certain that he did not consider the monastery a suitable place in which to demonstrate it.

The purchase of the Pérez paintings shows that Philip was grateful to have some visual record of Lepanto. However, he seems to have been unsure what to do with the large canvases, which obviously did not fit into his plans for decorating the walls. Eventually, they ended up stored in the Escorial, where they faced a highly uncertain future. At the close of the century they were hung on the walls of an empty ground-floor room where they remained until the eighteenth century, when they were moved. A modern historian of the Escorial[42] suggests that Philip may have contracted the canvases from Cambiaso, who came to work at the Escorial in October 1583 and continued employed there until his death in September 1585. He admits, however, that there is no record of payments being made to the artist for this item. The idea that the king should suddenly, twelve years after the famous victory, realise that it was worth memorialising in paint, and should then entrust the task to an artist who had no special qualification other than being on the spot, is both improbable and – as we know from the Antonio Pérez auction – erroneous. The king came into possession of the canvases in circumstances that bore no relation to his plans for the Escorial. Cambiaso was there to help with a wholly different matter, the decoration of the royal gallery. The six Lepanto canvases remained where they were, largely forgotten and in bad condition. In 1856 they were at last restored and rehung.

The indifference in the Escorial to commemorating military victories extended, logically, to Spain's greatest military defeat, that of the Great Armada that was sent against England in 1588. In June 1588 the king was informed that a Carmelite nun in Valladolid had cried out 'Victory! victory!' during a trance. She also promised good news. Two weeks later she sent a written message of hope to the king. Philip had scribbled on it: 'Please God it be as this paper says. We shall soon know.'[43] When the first reliable reports arrived in mid-August, their impact was profound. The messenger, on arriving at the Escorial, was received by the king's ministers Cristóbal de Moura and Juan Idiaquez.[44] The former volunteered to break the news to the king. Philip was working at his desk and broke off to ask if anything was known. Moura replied that the news of the Armada was bad. The emissary was brought in and delivered his message to the silent king. Philip then said (according to one version), 'I give thanks to God, whose generous hand has helped me with strength and troops, and will make it possible for me to raise another armada. It does not much matter if the flow of water is cut off, so long as its source is still running.' He turned to his desk, and resumed writing. The same day he ordered 50,000 crowns to be assigned to the relief of the wounded, and ordered the churches to give thanks for the safe return of the survivors.

The king's stoic response has since passed into the history books. But it was criticised by many courtiers, who disapproved of what seemed to them play-acting at such a grave moment.[45] In fact, the king was deeply shocked. He received the first detailed report in a letter from the duke of Parma in the Netherlands, dated 10 August, which arrived in Madrid on the 31st. 'His Majesty has felt the blow more than you would believe', Idiáquez wrote back to Parma that same day. Three days later he wrote, 'Although he felt the news very much at the beginning, he feels it more every day. . . . It hurts him immensely that he failed to render a great service to God, after doing more than you could have asked or imagined.'[46] In private Philip reflected somberly: 'I hope that God has not permitted as much harm as some fear; everything has been done in his service, and we must not stop praying.'[47] The fault was no one's. In the draft of the king's next letter to Parma, a secretary referred to 'the honour (*reputación*) of all, which is at stake'. Philip scored out the phrase and wrote in the margin: 'see if you can remove this, since in the affairs of God it is not a question of losing or gaining honour'.[48] The Venetian ambassador that week, observing the king closely, commented that he appeared to feel utterly alone.[49]

The full extent of the disaster took some time to sink in. Not until the third week of September did Medina Sidonia stagger into Santander with eight of his galleons. A further 27 battered ships made it into other northern ports. Possibly 60 of the 130 brave ships that had sailed out in May had made it home. But around 15,000, or five-sixths of the men on board, had perished. The impact on Castilians was devastating. It was, commented a monk of the Escorial, 'one of the most notable and unhappy disasters ever to have happened in Spain and one to weep over all one's life. . . . For many months there was nothing but tears and laments throughout Spain.'[50] With hindsight, little can be said in defence of the enterprise against England.[51] Neither the king nor anyone else was quite sure what it was meant to achieve. No concrete plans were ever drawn up, either military or political, on what was to be done should the invasion succeed. Those with most experience in war, namely Alba and Parma, always had doubts about it and opposed it. Forecasts of its failure which appeared in prophecies of the time very likely drew on a current of opinion circulating among members of the administration.

THE PAINTING OF THE HALL OF BATTLES

Five years before the Armada debacle, the king was thinking at last about portraying military events on the walls of his monastery. Twenty years had passed since the commencement of building, and now the last stone was about to be put into place. Why did he take so long to arrive at his decision? There appears to be no written evidence on the matter, and we are driven to speculate.

Possibly the first direct link to the decision to decorate the walls of the gallery was the occupation of Portugal and the death, just before that campaign, of the love of his life, Queen Anna. An epidemic of influenza was raging through most of the peninsula in the summer of 1580. The outbreak ravaged Madrid, where 'there are so many dead that no one takes note of them, and the deaths continue'.[52] The court, which was at that time in Extremadura, did not escape. Philip, Prince Diego and the Infanta Catalina were all laid low, but recovered, thanks in part to the efficiency of the family doctor, Dr Vallés. Queen Anna was not so fortunate. She was well into another pregnancy when the epidemic caught her. She suffered several days of fever, and had to be bled. Shortly before dawn on 26 October 1580, at the age of thirty-one, she died of the epidemic. The king was grief-stricken. His love for her had been very great,[53] and Anna's death haunted him during the crucial months of the campaign to secure Portugal against likely English and French intervention.

Philip was in Portugal from the end of 1580 to the spring of 1583. The Cortes of Tomar, which met in April 1581, were a historic occasion. They confirmed the union of the whole peninsula under one crown, swore fealty to the king and recognised Prince Diego as his successor. In return, Philip confirmed all the privileges and the independence of Portugal, on terms similar to those which had linked the other realms of the peninsula with Castile over a century before. Portuguese overseas possessions fell in line with events at home and accepted Philip. There was resistance only in the Atlantic islands of the Azores, where the Portuguese claimant to the throne, Prior Antonio, held out with the help of a French naval force. On 23 June 1582 a fleet consisting of 54 ships, 12 galleasses, 61 small vessels with 8,400 troops and 3,400 mariners sailed from Lisbon under the command of the marquis of Santa Cruz.[54] They inflicted a decisive defeat on the French fleet off the island of Terceira on 25–26 July. The fate of Portuguese captured from the opposing forces was drastic: all prisoners were treated as rebels, the nobles were decapitated, and soldiers and sailors aged over eighteen were hanged.[55] A further engagement took place in the summer of 1583, confirming Spain's control over the islands.

The victory of the Spanish fleet over the French at Terceira in the summer of 1582 was seen as a basic security 'for Flanders'.[56] Reflecting on the victory, which was won on the feast of St Anne,

26 July, Philip was convinced that the saint 'must be playing a big part in these events'. Behind the saint, however, there was his late wife Anna: 'I've always believed that the queen is playing a role in them'. The signs were good: 'it's a good start, but our business is not yet finished'.[57] Santa Cruz wrote to him after the Azores victory to propose an immediate naval attack on England. The king thanked him, and consulted Parma about the feasibility of the idea.

The occupation of Portugal took the king away from his attention to the Escorial. He did not return to Spain until spring 1583, and after his long absence was anxious to see what progress had been made on the building. The main purpose of his first visit, however, was piety. The day after arriving there he presided in San Lorenzo over solemn funeral honours for the late queen Anna.[58] Having returned from Portugal, he chose at last to relent from his apparent refusal to portray military actions on the walls of the Escorial. Over twenty years had passed since the laying of the foundation stone. He had sponsored many great campaigns, including the outstanding one of Lepanto, but had never accepted their commemoration in his palace-monastery. What, then, changed in 1583 to make Philip decide to issue commissions for the decoration of the gallery which till then had been an access passage of no special significance?

Philip had always avoided military triumphalism, so we need to find a specific reason why he should now give orders for commemorating events in the Azores.[59] The first and most relevant event to affect the king's unpainted gallery was the discovery in the castle of Segovia of an old painting rolled up like a carpet. When the item was unrolled, it turned out to be a deteriorated late medieval painting, 60 metres long, of a forgotten battle (the battle of Higueruela, near Granada, in the year 1431) between Moors and Christians. The news was given to the king, who immediately decided that the treasure should be preserved, not as it was – which would not have been feasible – but as a wall painting of similar length that faithfully copied the medieval details. It must have cost him very little effort to recall that he had just the required space available in the neglected and unpainted royal gallery of the

Escorial. The next task, to find suitable artists, was soon resolved. Since 1581 a team of Genoese fresco painters under the direction of 'il Bergamasco' (Giovanni Battista Castello) had been at work in the Escorial after spending several years (since 1567) decorating the palaces of the Alcázar and the Pardo.[60] Since they were already busy on work in the monastery, there was no hurry to issue the instructions, dated 1584, for the painting of the gallery. The instructions for painting the ceiling were issued by the king in December 1584, from El Pardo, and the work was finished by July 1585. Then, in January 1587, the painters began work on the battle of Higueruela. In February 1590 they were contracted to paint 'the War of St Quentin and the battle of Terceira'. In February 1591 this part, and indeed the whole work, was finished and paid for.

Why decide on the medieval theme? It is important to emphasise that the exercise was artistic, not militaristic or triumphalist. Had Philip really wished to celebrate the glories of the crown's battles against Islam he would have had an incredibly rich choice of possibilities. Why not, as we have had occasion to mention, the capture of Granada in 1492 by Ferdinand and Isabella (which Spanish artists only got round to painting four centuries later)? Why not the capture of Tunis in 1535 by Charles V (celebrated at the time by Italian artists, but not, it seems, by Spaniards)? Why not the relief of Malta in 1565? Why not, above all, the battle of Lepanto? All these campaigns had brought glory to the crown, all had furthered the reputation of Spain, most had occurred within living memory of Spaniards. Yet Philip chose to commemorate a wholly unknown medieval incident, involving very few soldiers, fought within the country and with no significant repercussions for anyone. It was, moreover, not a 'Spanish' victory, for Spain as a political entity had not yet existed; the Muslims in the battle were, indeed, as Spanish as their Christian adversaries.

The king's decision was, as the viewer today can judge, fully justified by the quality of the original scroll, which depicted faithfully and in fascinating detail a wide range of aspects of medieval battle. The Jesuit Juan de Mariana, who saw the finished product on the wall, was moved to claim that the incident at Higueruela was 'one of the most noble triumphs that generations of Spaniards can recall with satisfaction'.[61] It was a somewhat exaggerated burst of enthusiasm, since nobody alive in 1598, when Mariana wrote, could possibly have had any memory of a battle fought two centuries before. It serves, nevertheless, to remind us that Castile had little or no artistic record of its military past, and the unexpected depiction in glorious colour of a military event – any military event – was bound to stir emotions and a sense of pride. The depiction of Higueruela, moreover, had a special appeal. Before the era of film recording there was no satisfactory way of describing what really happened in battle. Witnesses might describe to the artist what they had seen, but for the most part painters resorted to stylised themes that came from their own imagination. They painted confrontation, death and triumph, using traditional postures.[62] The Higueruela scroll offered an exciting near-contemporary record that must have seemed a godsend to the painters who copied it.

Having occupied the complete wall of the gallery with the theme of the medieval battle, the king had to decide how to decorate the remaining surfaces. It is most likely that his decision was a matter that affected him personally and involved nobody else. The gallery was, we should remember, not open to the public and would not normally be seen by members of the court or even by the monks. There was no call, therefore, for a public theme meant to evoke public reactions of pride in military prowess. Instead, Philip chose to remember the mercies he personally had received from heaven. The wall at the end of the gallery, therefore, was devoted to the naval victory that his forces had won thanks to (he believed) the intercession of his late wife Anna. There was no intention of celebrating any triumph over Portugal, which in any case – and as he had always insisted – was not conquered by force. He had sent his troops into a country that had already chosen to accept him as king. Nor had there been any battles during the Portuguese campaign. The conflict in the distant Azores was a battle provoked directly by French intervention, and viewed at the Spanish court as a fight against France. It was a fitting theme, seen as an extension of the struggle against France that took place at St Quentin.

Nearly five years after the completion of the ceiling and three years after the completion of the Higueruela wall, Philip decided to fill the remaining space in the gallery with a celebration of the first and greatest of his mercies, that which he had received at the beginning of his reign and which had inspired the building of his palace-monastery. This was the campaign of St Quentin, in which he now allowed himself to be depicted, because he had been the recipient of the mercy. Once again, of course, it was no celebration of a 'Spanish' victory, for the troops were the Army of Flanders, not the army of Spain. Why did he leave it so late – over thirty years after the battle and just a short time before his death – to commemorate the event? It is one of the many truly enigmatic questions about the Escorial. The orders to paint the battle are, as we have mentioned, dated 1590, which means that the king was already seriously ill when the five frescos – four devoted to the battle and one to the taking of the town – were completed. The late decision to paint St Quentin brings back, inevitably, the question of Lepanto. In the case of the latter battle, one may explain its absence in the Hall of Battles by the fact that the king had, in 1585, already come into possession of the six large Cambiaso canvases. Possessing them made it unnecessary to repeat the theme in the Hall of Battles (although one could argue that the painters of the hall might have achieved a far more pleasing result than Cambiaso did with his wholly mediocre renderings).

Why, however, did St Quentin come back into Philip's mind, so briefly before his death, and when his health was seriously failing? There is no straightforward answer. One may suggest that since the battle, like that of the Azores, did not involve Spain directly and was fought in a far-off country, the Netherlands, the motives for the painting may have been personal rather than political. Indeed, the exact and fascinating rendering of the king's own camp in the battle makes it likely that he supplied personal information about details. Just as the victory in the Azores represented a divine mercy gained through Queen Anna, so St Quentin was a divine mercy to which he could at last look back with gratitude. Terceira and St Quentin were the only two military operations of his reign in which he could feel he had a personal role, and in both the king wished to record the hand of God, not the achievements of men nor even the glory of Spain.

A significant proportion of Philip II's correspondence has still not been examined by researchers.[63] When it is, we may be in a better position to understand how he arrived at his decisions about decorating sections of the Escorial. The generations that came after him chose to read events in their own, not always correct, way. They renamed the royal gallery, thereby wilfully changing the whole perspective from which we should view it. As a Hall of Battles, it makes no sense, for it commemorates very little of significance in Spain's military history. As a personal gallery of the king, however, it allows us to see yet more deeply into the soul of the monarch, as he made his way through it to the basilica and paused now and then to gaze upon the brilliant colours and give thanks to God for the divine mercies he had been privileged to receive.

CHAPTER 8

POWERHOUSE OF FAITH

The Escorial as symbol of Spain's religion; The priest-king of the Escorial?; Powerhouse of the Counter-Reformation?; Symbol of severity: the Escorial and the Inquisition; Symbol of superstition: the relics; The royal Bible at the Escorial

THE ESCORIAL AS SYMBOL OF SPAIN'S RELIGION

The overwhelming, gaunt lines of the monastery leave the viewer in no doubt of the building's immense spiritual power. An unbeliever has the option of pushing the idea away, but the feeling remains hauntingly present. The problem has always been how to identify that power. Does it represent the traditional spirit of Catholicism? Is it a reflection of the obsessions of the king? One of the most widely prevalent ideas about the structure is that it epitomises the religion of Spain. Its solid, challenging profile is seen as a mirror of Spain's religious orthodoxy, its firm confidence in God, the Church and the Inquisition. For many, the building expresses also a newer trend, the dynamism of the Counter-Reformation. On either view, it is seen as a rock-like fortress of faith and certainty, 'a visible bastion against the rising tide of heresy'.[1] In the seventeenth century, Baltasar Gracián in *El Criticón* saw it as 'a triumph of Catholic piety'. Such views are, within their context, logical. There is absolutely no doubt that the principal emphasis of the building is religious. The heart of the structure is the basilica; and

200

the chief human component is the monastery. Religion was the inspiration and the driving force.

There is, however, a huge gap between affirming the religious nature of the building and claiming that it epitomised Spain's spirituality. Few other similar structures in Europe have merited this description. Not even St Peter's in Rome has been identified with the spirituality of Italians. And if the Escorial somehow symbolised Spain's religion, what was that religion really like? Should we accept the opinions of Spaniards of that day? Or should we, perhaps, accept as more detached the opinion of foreigners?[2] Can we trust the view of a Protestant English ambassador in 1604 that 'the Spaniards universally are much inclined to religion, with immeasurable superstition'?[3] Or should we credit rather a Catholic, Francesco Guicciardini, Florentine ambassador to King Ferdinand, who described Spaniards as 'very religious in externals and outward show, but not so in fact'?[4] What was the religious context within which we should view the Escorial?

Spain's religion, as studies have demonstrated, was no different from that of the Europe of its day.[5] Religious practice and belief, especially in the rural and mountainous regions of Spain, were often little more than a veneer on popular custom. To deal with problems such as illness, epidemics and adverse weather, where the Church could offer no solution, people resorted to remedies that might be religious in appearance but contained aspects which the clergy denounced as superstition. Moreover, the ignorance of a high proportion of the clergy was universally recognised. In Santiago de Compostela in 1543 the bishop's officials reported that 'parishioners suffer greatly from the ignorance of their curates and rectors'; in Navarre in 1544 ignorant clergy 'cause great harm to the consciences of these poor people'. By the 1560s, when the king began to plan the Escorial and the first church reforms were initiated, the state of Spanish religion was far from being as exemplary as later writers have assumed. Indeed, the king himself recognised the problems and became a strong supporter of reform. Yet little improvement had been achieved twenty years later, when the Escorial was being completed. In no way, consequently, can the building be seen as the reflection of a solid and triumphant Catholicism in Spain. Was the Escorial, then, a reflection not of a firmly Catholic nation but rather of its king's own religious attitudes?

THE PRIEST-KING OF THE ESCORIAL?

It was the king, of course, who was the focal point of the religious character of San Lorenzo. In consequence, Philip's attention to religion from his eyrie in the Escorial has been interpreted at times as almost pontifical. Some have seen him as a Spanish pope, others as a sort of high priest. Recently, as we have noted above, it has been argued that 'the Escorial epitomized Philip's conception of his dual role as king and priest'.[6] It is an important claim, and merits some examination.

Did Philip ever express in words this 'conception' of being a priest-king? In effect, one searches in vain for a single word or action of the king, at any moment of his life, which can be construed to suggest that he saw himself as a 'priest', let alone a 'priest-king' along biblical or theocratic lines. In Christianity, the original priest-king was Christ, though the roots of the symbiosis of priest and king go back through the pages of the Bible to the beginnings of the Jewish people, when Abraham first encountered the king-priest Melchizedek (Genesis 14). From the Indus Valley to Knossos, from Egypt to pre-Aztec Mexico, the figure of the priest-king in ancient times combined both secular and sacred power. In medieval Europe writers were fascinated by the apparent existence in ancient Egypt of a Christian ruler, Prester John, who combined mystically in his person the roles of priest and king. No such phenomenon occurred in medieval or early modern Spain, where the priest-king did not exist either in reality or in legend. The Spanish monarchy relied for its support among the communities of the peninsula on no mystical rites or sacralising ceremonies of any sort (see above, Chapter 6). In France and England, there were ceremonies that identified the ruler with God and religion: the king was anointed with sacred oils, crowned with a sacred crown, swore a sacred oath. His person therefore became sacred, and he might even lay claim to priestly powers.

He was, in Shakespeare's words, 'the deputy elected by the Lord' (*Richard II*, III, ii, 54–7). In Spain, by contrast, there was no ceremony of coronation, and no possible convergence of the two functions of priest and ruler.

By extension, therefore, the king in the Escorial had no priestly role, and the Escorial itself was simply a monastery, with no pretensions to special authority. It was certainly not the seat of a priest-king. It had a special status, similar to that enjoyed by several church institutions in the Later Middle Ages, that gave it independence from Church and state. Both the monastery and its basilica were from the start placed under the direct control of the papacy, as an 'exempt jurisdiction' (exempt, that is, from control by any Spanish bishop), a privilege confirmed by papal bulls of 1578 and 1586. Throughout the king's reign the building and the basilica had the status of private property, and were not normally accessible for worship to the general public. This is a crucial fact that helps us to understand a great deal in the monastery's history.

The special position of the Escorial gave it – significantly – some autonomy not only from the Church but also from the crown, as we can see in a famous incident a century later. One of the notable religious relics of the Escorial was the sacred host (the Eucharist wafer), known as the 'Sagrada Forma', which apparently had its origins in the epoch of the revolt of the Netherlands. During civil strife in the town of Gorcum in 1572, the commander of the Sea Beggar rebels, Count Lumey van der Marck, ordered the execution of nineteen Catholic clergy. When the local church was being sacked by the rebel soldiers, the host miraculously withstood being trampled underfoot. It was saved by a Catholic soldier, and eventually taken to Vienna, from where it made its way to the Escorial in 1597 along with other relics imported by Philip II from the German lands. The next stage in its history occurred in 1677,[7] when government troops entered without the permission of the prior into the monastery in order to seize a prominent noble who had taken sanctuary there. The violent intrusion was denounced as a sacrilege, which the king, Charles II, was obliged to expiate in 1684 in a formal ceremony dedicating a special chapel to the Holy

Eucharist. At the king's command, the dedication was commemorated in Claudio Coello's riveting painting *La Sagrada Forma* (1690), which was placed in the sacristy of the basilica, and depicted the king on his knees before the altar, surrounded by dignitaries of the court.[8]

The image of the king on his knees, overt recognition of the sacred role of the priest standing before him, was a basic symbol in the Escorial. The Leoni tomb statuary before the high altar, in which Charles V and Philip II and their wives kneel in worship, confirms this. All the kneeling figures, including the emperor and the king, face the tabernacle on the altar. The imagery can also be seen in portraits of Philip II, most notably in the El Greco painting known as *The Dream of Philip II* (1579), preserved in the Escorial and, in a different version, in the National Gallery, London.[9] In all these works of art the king is always depicted on his knees before the priest. Never in his wildest dreams, and not even metaphorically, would Philip have thought of himself as a priest-like figure or allowed his own role to be confused with that of a minister of God.

Sigüenza's testimony on the matter is irrefutable and conclusive: 'in all the public rites carried out in the church, he showed such respect for and observed so scrupulously the obligation owed to the affairs and personnel of the Church, that he always put himself last in any ceremony'. Out of 'a hundred examples' known to him, the monk cited one: 'when new masses were celebrated, he used to kiss the hand of the celebrant, and did it as though he were just another worshipper'.[10] The 'new mass' was the name given to the first mass celebrated by a cleric who had just taken holy orders. We may well imagine the nervousness of a new young priest having his hand kissed by the king of Spain.

As a Catholic who believed himself a lesser being than the meanest priest, the king never felt that in religious matters he had a special relationship with God, and nothing he ever wrote indicates that he thought so. On the other hand, when it came to political matters, he certainly felt that his immense duties and responsibilities entitled him to call upon God for help in moments of distress – any believing Christian in his position would have presumed the same. However, it is improbable that he considered his objectives to be the same as God's, as suggested by a leading historian who interprets literally Philip's common affirmation about 'God's cause and mine, which are the same'.[11] The king, as seems more likely, was simply stating that his own cause did not diverge from that of God. This interpretation is clear, for example, from the way he applied the same phrase to his subordinates. When his secretary Mateo Vázquez wrote to him (in about 1575) that he was so ill he wished to die, the king chided him for expressing such a sentiment: 'There is no reason why you should wish for death; you must wish for life, in order to employ it *in God's service and in yours, for they are the same*' (my italics).[12] In other words, Vázquez should – as Philip did – place his hand in that of God. It was and is a common evangelical sentiment. By extension, the king felt that some of his policies were faithfully following the will of God, who logically had the duty of backing them up. Some heads of state of our own day would understand very clearly the issues involved.

POWERHOUSE OF THE COUNTER-REFORMATION?

Was the monastery, as many scholars have suggested, a symbol of the Counter-Reformation? Like other ill-defined historical terms, 'Counter-Reformation' – a term invented in the nineteenth century by German historians (*die Gegenreformation*) – has served as a label to fix on the Escorial and its historical period. Application of the term to Spain is particularly strange, because until a few years ago Spanish scholars denied that any Counter-Reformation had taken place in the country. They have traditionally believed that the Counter-Reformation (the sixteenth-century reform movement inspired from within the Catholic Church and directed in part against the Reformation) happened only outside Spain, not inside it; and until very recently no Spanish scholar was concerned to study the Spanish Counter-Reformation. It was consequently easy to accept the image of a firmly Catholic country where nothing changed over the centuries, an image that gave added force to the apparent solidity of the Escorial.

Despite the scant attention paid to the subject in the past, there is now no doubt that a substantial Counter-Reformation did occur in Spain,[13] though the Escorial did not necessarily symbolise it. No significant push for reform took place before the year 1565, when Philip II formally received the decrees of the Council of Trent and supervised the holding of provincial councils of the clergy. The date marks the beginning of a long process, lasting maybe a generation, that we may term Spain's Counter-Reformation. It follows that in the 1560s, when architects and engineers were working to construct the Escorial, there was little of a Counter-Reformation visible in the country and Spain was not yet a fortress of dogmatic faith or of religious certainty. The building, common sense tells us, could hardly reflect a profoundly religious environment that reformers were still labouring to create.

Yet the Escorial certainly benefited from new influences that were not native to Spain but brought in from outside. As we have noted above (Chapter 3), artistic and architectural ideas from the Netherlands and Italy were fundamental to the advance of Spain's culture, as were external religious influences, notably the ideas of the Dutch thinker Erasmus,[14] whose *Works* had formed part of Philip's reading. When the prince visited Rotterdam during his Fortunate Journey, he exchanged courtesies with the burgomasters at the foot of a statue of Erasmus, and the next day went to mass at the church beside Erasmus's birthplace.[15] Several of Philip's colleagues in the Netherlands – like Calvete de Estrella – were sympathisers. As it happened, the enthusiasm of Spaniards for Erasmus turned out to be a passing phase. Subsequently, they preferred to seek much of their religious inspiration in Italy. Italy, indeed, became the dynamo that helped to charge and renew Spain's Catholicism; Italian religious orders, especially the Jesuits,[16] and Italian religious customs and prayers, helped change the nature of Spain's everyday religion.[17] It was no coincidence that the Italian artists who decorated the Escorial also brought Italian influences with them.

Foremost among these influences was the Council of Trent, which played a key role in the development of the Escorial, not least because of the personal link between the council and the founder of the Escorial. Of much lesser significance was the link between Spain and the papacy at Rome. Recently it has been suggested that 'during the late 15th and early 16th century' the Spanish Church came under the direct control of Rome, and Spanish religious art 'would henceforth conform to a Roman model'.[18] It would be more plausible to say that Rome at no time managed to achieve significant control of Church or religion in Spain,[19] and was never able to dictate artistic norms. If Spanish clergy and the king looked towards Italy, it was not because of Rome but largely out of respect for the Council of Trent. One of the king's most intense convictions, expressed tirelessly both verbally and in print, was that the Council of Trent offered an answer to the religious problems of the day. To understand his deeply personal identification with this principle we have to go back many years to that epoch-making journey across the Alps in the winter of January 1549, and to the king's equally significant return journey two years later (see Chapter 1). Philip's unique achievement in being the only European prince to assist at the council (even the pope did not attend its sessions) inspired in him a certainty that he must identify himself with the cause of religious reform. This certainty, however, was not shared in equal measure by other rulers in Europe, nor even by the bishops and clergy in Spain.

Philip never ceased to insist that other Catholic states should take up the cause of reform. Acceptance of the spiritual authority of Trent, where his own bishops had made a powerful contribution, was, he felt, absolutely essential to any reform programme. After his return home from Germany in 1551, he waited in Barcelona for a few days expressly to greet the first Spanish bishops returning from the deliberations at Trent. Already in 1553, three years before he became king, he was instructing his government to adopt each of the decrees of the council as they emerged.[20] After his return to Spain as king, in 1560 he subjected the French ambassador to 'a long discourse on the need for general councils'.[21] He took pains to send the best possible men from Spain to the new sessions that began in 1561; they were by no means yes-men, and the king made little attempt to control them. Some of his nominees were accused by other Spaniards of supporting 'most improper measures',[22] meaning that they were too reformist. During the last stages of the Council of Trent in 1563, Philip in Spain handled a voluminous correspondence relating to its sessions through his special envoy the count of Luna. Philip reiterated his view that the council was 'the sole true remedy remaining to us'.[23] He even sent proposals for reforms in his own hand, hoping that the cardinals would discuss them. The Council of Trent closed at the end of 1563 and the pope issued its decrees formally in June 1564. Two weeks later, on 12 July, Philip in Madrid accepted the decrees as the law of Spain, the first European ruler to do so.

The ending of the sessions of Trent in 1563 had a very special significance for the Escorial, because the year coincided exactly with the laying of the first stone of the monastery, on 23 April 1563. Years later, Sigüenza looked back to the event and drew his own parallel:

> It took forty-six years to build the Temple of Jerusalem, and the Council of Trent took the same time, if we calculate from the beginning of the heresy of Martin Luther in 1517 to the end of the Council in 1563.[24]

For Sigüenza the analogy was between the Temple at Jerusalem, Solomon's temple, which was a work of God, and the doing of God's work in the council. However, the work of Solomon and the work of the fathers at Trent were also analogous to the construction of the great new monastery of the Jeronimite order, of which Sigüenza was both librarian and historian. He was eager to identify his monastery closely with the council but, as we shall see, matters were not so simple.

Can the Escorial be identified closely with the Counter-Reformation policy of Trent and of the king? Or, as a persistent clerical tradition (at its most vocal during the Franco regime) has continually asserted, were these the same thing, so that the Escorial expressed at one and the same time the unchanging faith of Spain and the progressive faith of Trent? In a commemorative volume issued in 1963, a priest claimed in virtually the same sentence that 'the Escorial is the material expression of the decrees of Trent', and 'the Escorial was born as a concrete expression of the Catholic nature of Spain'.[25] The deliberate fusion of the two concepts was, of course, an ideological exercise and as such had little to do with what really happened. The religion proposed by Trent was, as numerous recent studies have emphasised, substantially different from the old religion of Catholic Spain; and the projected Tridentine reforms were bitterly contested at all levels throughout the country. It would have been impossible for the Escorial to represent simultaneously the old Catholic Spain and the new tides of Trent.

The distinction – an important one – will concern us for a moment. Taking into account the context that inspired it and the mentality of the various individuals who worked to promote the building's interests, it seems correct to say that the Escorial had more in common with the new reforms than with medieval religion. There is absolutely no doubt that Philip's religious policy was forward-looking, even revolutionary, and by no means a mere imposition of traditional Catholicism. He gave full and enthusiastic support to the novelties introduced by Trent. Root and branch reform of all religious orders, the disciplining of all clergy, education of parish priests, reform of religious practice among both laity and clergy, abolition of the old mass and old rites, adoption of a new mass, a new prayer book, a new calendar, the training of missionaries and the establishment of schools: all of this constituted a formidable modernising programme which the king endeavoured to implement.[26] His attempts to reshape the religious orders were no less ruthless than the measures undertaken by reformers in the England of Henry VIII. Monasteries and convents all over Spain were occupied by soldiers and closed, monks and nuns expelled, property confiscated. Never a religious conservative, Philip embraced change with enthusiasm. He even contributed personally to textual amendments to the Spanish mass,[27] on one occasion proposing that a new phrase be introduced, 'as I have it in a missal that used to belong to my great-grandfather'.[28]

The Escorial was conceived and constructed exactly during the years that Philip was participating in the reform programme. It would therefore be fair to assume that some of the ideas at work in the monastery-palace were in step with the perspectives of Trent. Almost from the beginning the king established a seminary, which Trent had recommended as a useful instrument of education. The Letter of Foundation set up a theological college for 'a few boys, as in a seminary'. It began to function in 1567, with twenty-four boys 'of twelve years upward', and Sigüenza later stated that the college was meant to fulfil 'the directives of the Council of Trent'.[29] Virtually all the artistic and musical refinements that featured in the building were also based on Italian and Tridentine practice. For example, the space available for worship inside the basilica followed the norms being imposed in Italy, with emphasis on a central high altar visible from all points of the church. The fact that the public, as we have noted, did not normally have access for worship, did not affect the reality. Finally, the new forms of music recommended by Trent were introduced into the monastery and the church. An authoritative recent study points out: 'At the Escorial, music was an essential part of a coherent, minutely planned, highly developed, politically motivated Counter-Reformation strategy developed by the king himself'.[30]

The intentions and policy of the king are therefore not in doubt. The Escorial was intended to conform in every way – whether in its architecture or its art or its music or its norms of conduct – with the new Catholic approach that we call the Counter-Reformation. However, the reality did not always live up to expectations. For one thing, the monastery, even though it was directly inspired by the king, did not become a model for Spain. As an 'exempt' jurisdiction, administered separately from the rest of the Church in Spain, the Escorial did not have the authority to be, nor was it in a position to become, the centre for a pro-Trent policy drive. The king had a strong voice there, but all the other churches of Spain went their own way and paid no attention to what was being done in one isolated monastery, staffed by monks who had little effective role in the world outside their cloister walls. Moreover, close adherence to the rules and practice of the new reform movement seems not to have borne much cultural fruit. In music, for example, the Escorial was second to none in observing the new methods of composition and singing. Yet, it has been pointed out, 'all this money, all this opportunity, all this breeding, failed to produce one single musical composition which anyone in their right minds would wish to perform today. The strange thing is that the blight only seemed to affect music.'[31] In fact, music was not the only area affected, and it can reasonably be argued that in many other areas of culture there was no significant output from the new monastery. The Escorial drank in a multitude of influences, nearly all foreign in origin, but turned out very little. In that, it was a faithful mirror of Spain, which in religious and cultural matters likewise absorbed more than it gave.

In respect of Trent, perhaps the important negative development was the active opposition of the monks. The Jeronimites belonged by nature to a different age, and were essentially a contemplative order, their main duty being that of prayer. In Italy all the new religious orders that developed, most notable among them the Jesuits, put the contemplative life behind them and dedicated their energies instead to working actively in the world to convert people. The Jeronimites of the Escorial were, by contrast, uninterested in the new ideas emanating from Italy. Far from being a good example of support for the reforms of the Council of Trent, the monks of the Escorial actually opposed them. This was not exceptional, and coincided with a general trend of opposition to be found in most religious orders throughout Spain.[32] At a general chapter of the Jeronimite order held in 1567, shortly after the provincial councils of the Church had taken place in Spain, the eight representatives who constituted the chapter voted to reject the new breviary and missal of the Council of Trent. Their reasons were logical and by no means based on blind opposition to change. The two manuals were formally approved and issued by the papacy in 1568 and 1569 respectively, but the cathedrals and monasteries of Spain found that the new books contained unwelcome novelties, such as the abolition of customs, rituals and saints that were part of their traditional form of worship. The king had to tread carefully in dealing with rebellion within his own foundation. He had encountered similar problems in his other favourite religious foundation, the abbey of Montserrat in Catalonia,[33] and as in Montserrat he used the tactic of moving troublesome monks to other monasteries.

As it turned out, the Escorial's only positive role in relation to Trent was as a centre for distribution of reformed mass-books imported from the Netherlands, where they were printed by Christophe Plantin (see below, in this chapter). In July 1573 Philip II issued an order that only breviaries (prayer books) and missals (mass books) printed by Plantin and distributed by the Escorial could be used in the Castilian Church. (It is highly likely that he thought up this system of monopoly distribution in an effort to win the support of the recalcitrant clergy in his monastery.) The order was extended to the Church of the crown of Aragon in August,[34] and to America at the end of the year. Texts that were not produced by Plantin could not be printed, imported or sold.[35] A large bookshop for the sale of the new manuals was set up in the monastery of San Jerónimo in Madrid, with the monks receiving one-third of the takings. The shop continued to function with apparent success until the end of the eighteenth century. However, the monastery's monopoly provoked a storm of indignation throughout the Spanish Church, the Castilian clergy making an official protest to the king in 1575 and to the pope in 1613. Many bishops defied the monopoly by having their own mass-books printed more cheaply in Spain as well as in Italy. The conflict harmed the reform programme, and for up to a century more the clergy in very many parts of Spain refused to pray or say mass according to the texts sanctioned by Trent. In this sense, little of the Counter-Reformation entered Spain. San Lorenzo's pretensions to lead the reform programme were not merely dashed, but got in the way of changes that the king had hoped to introduce.

SYMBOL OF SEVERITY: THE ESCORIAL AND THE INQUISITION

The drive for reform was, of course, only one aspect of the religious question as it affected the Escorial. The stern and forbidding exterior of the monastery gives an unmistakable hint of the severity that some have identified as a key component of royal policy. Théophile Gautier's opinion of the basilica as the haunt of 'the gloomy Philip II, a king born to be a grand inquisitor',[36] expresses concisely a long-held view. The image of the king as inquisitor is normally backed up by allegations of Philip's supposed enthusiasm for the *autos de fe* of the Inquisition. A *Time* magazine article of 1963 said of the Escorial: 'many saw in the macabre plan of the monastery a visible proof of his will to burn alive all heretics from the Catholic faith'.[37] Once again, fiction is very much at work. Had the king been a devotee of *autos*, he would surely, in the very many months and years in which he lived in his beloved Escorial, have arranged for at least one wonderful *auto de fe* to be held there, for the edification of the people. None was ever held. The king in fact attended four *autos de fe* in Spain in his lifetime, or one every eighteen years – hardly the zeal of a fanatic.[38] At none of them did he witness any executions. His last attendance at an *auto* was in 1591; prior to that, he had not been present at one in Spain for almost thirty years (in 1564). Writing in 1591 to his daughter Catalina, duchess of Savoy, the king noted: 'Your sister will give you an account of an *auto de fe* of the Inquisition that we saw yesterday, you have never seen one'.[39] It is a telling detail: a Spanish princess eighteen years old, daughter of a presumably rabid fanatic, who had never in her lifetime witnessed an *auto*!

Protecting Spain against heresy was feasible, and Philip attempted it. Sealing it off from Europe was, by contrast, never his intention. Measures such as a censorship decree in 1558 and restrictions on those who wished to study abroad were, by their nature, limited in impact.[40] They applied only to the realms of Castile, and were in any case difficult to enforce. In practice, Castilians continued to enjoy the freedoms available to most Europeans: to publish outside the country, and to travel without hindrance. In the non-Castilian parts of Spain a free movement of books, persons and students continued to operate for most of the reign. Foreign scholars, technicians and artists took advantage of the free access in order to come and seek the patronage of the Spanish king.

Philip was acutely conscious of the threat to faith, to public order and to the monarchy itself, whether in Spain or elsewhere. It was therefore ironic that in the 1560s, after he returned finally to Spain, he was considered not a fanatic but actually lenient towards heretics. It is a perspective that easily escapes notice, yet it was sufficiently overt to excite the animosity of the pope, who did not cease to make his views felt through his nuncio in Madrid, the archbishop of Rossano. In the eyes of the pope, Philip was not only failing to act against heretics in his own kingdoms of the north, he was also refusing to take any action against the heretical queen of England. In the early months of 1566 Pope Pius V criticised Philip's tolerance of Calvinist preachers in the Netherlands and stated, 'it is difficult to believe that it is happening against his will, for that goes against what he has assured me several times'. The nuncio duly bore the pope's message to the king, who responded to the pontiff with the same vigour, retorting 'that in no way does he wish to be ruler over heretics'.[41] The king was at this date attempting to keep his promise to his aunt, the governor of the Netherlands Margaret of Parma, to allow her policy of toleration free rein for a period. It was, however, a difficult period, and the king became increasingly impatient with Margaret's failure to control events.[42] In a letter to his ambassador in Rome, Requesens, Philip repeated what he had been saying for months to the nuncio: 'you can assure His Holiness that rather than suffer the slightest harm to religion and the service of God, I shall give up all my estates and a hundred lives if I had them, for I do not wish to rule over heretics'.[43] It was his way of telling the pope that he did not wish his hand to be forced.

His aim, Philip kept reiterating, was not to wage a campaign against heresy but rather to crush rebellion. It was true, he wrote to his ambassador in Paris in 1568, that he had advised the rulers of France to crush their enemies, but 'my intention was always to warn them that their declared policy should be the punishment of rebellion and not of heresy, for with the first one can achieve the second. I have never written or said anything to them with any other implication.'[44] All his acts up to that date confirmed his words. For over ten years he had openly defended the Protestant regime of

Queen Elizabeth in England. The aristocratic 'rebels' whom the duke of Alba had just executed in Brussels were all Catholics, not Protestants; they died not for their faith but for alleged rebellion. Up until approximately the time of the Treaty of Cateau-Cambrésis in 1559, Philip had shared with other European rulers a relatively easy-going attitude to the question of differences in faith.

From the years that he began to plan the Escorial, however, the king's attitude hardened, not perhaps because of any alteration in his personal outlook but rather because of the terrible threat to Spain posed by Turkish aggression in the Mediterranean, nascent nationalism in the Netherlands, dynastic instability in France and naval belligerence on the part of English colonial adventurers. Behind much of this threat loomed the shadow of Protestant subversion and violence. The gaunt lines of San Lorenzo can therefore quite plausibly be read as a statement of unbending orthodoxy. However, like any reasonable statesman, Philip also found it possible to put up with heresy when expedient. His personal convictions, which brooked no compromise, did not stand in the way of accepting political necessity. Throughout his life, he did not change his attitude. During the last phase of his father's rule, from 1547 to 1556, Philip had lent tacit support to Charles' policy of compromise with the Lutheran princes in Germany, and had accepted without demur the need for the tolerant Interim issued by the emperor in 1548. During his visits to Germany and the Netherlands, and his fourteen months in England in mid-century, he gave ample evidence of his reluctance to interfere in matters of religion. The overriding preference always was for political stability. When he became king, however, for the first time he could take an independent stance on religion, and made clear to his diplomatic representatives that no concessions would be made to Lutherans, whether in Germany, France or the Netherlands.

Even so, political caution was always the first principle. The most aggressive of the military expeditions launched from the Escorial, the famous Armada directed against England in 1588, downplayed the theme of religion. The English government, anxious to stimulate patriotism, distributed propaganda claiming that Philip threatened the freedom of conscience of Englishmen. This was never a relevant issue. When Don Juan of Austria first suggested the idea of an invasion to the king in 1576, Philip thought about it and later sent Don Juan a lengthy memorandum.[45] Reading it, one can see that the king was virtually thinking aloud. The pros and cons of invasion are debated, the need for careful planning emphasised. The basis for any invasion, Philip stressed, must be support *within* the country: 'no kingdom, no matter how weak or small, can be won without the help of the kingdom itself'. An initial force of 4,000 infantry, supported by cavalry, would do the trick. Once the country was secured, there should above all be no repression of any sort: 'there must be no talk of "rebels" or "heretics"'. The king had learnt enough to recognise that there were different ways to achieve political stability. Two typical and important statements made by the king at key moments of his decision-making may be quoted here.[46] In 1573, when he replaced the duke of Alba with Luis de Requeséns as governor in the Netherlands, Philip ordered the latter to 'treat the people there with love and goodwill, because nothing is lost thereby'. In 1591, when the affair of Antonio Pérez provoked riots in the city of Saragossa, his first reaction was in favour of caution: 'if mild measures can serve to solve this, it is better than having to use force'. Historians wedded to the old Liberal legend decrying the king have scrupulously – and one may well ask why – refrained from citing these passages, with which they are undoubtedly familiar.

Even towards the end of Philip's life his willingness to compromise was evident. In Aranjuez in November 1589 the president of the Council of State of the Netherlands, Jean Richardot, put forward a plan for a peace agreement between the southern Netherlands and the northern provinces of Holland and Zeeland, then under Calvinist control even though the majority of their population was Catholic. The Spanish position was that 'if they [in Holland and Zeeland] for their part allow the public exercise of our faith, His Majesty will allow and tolerate the public exercise of their erroneous opinions in a few select towns'.[47] Holland and Zeeland had strong objections (which they never modified) to the proposal for toleration. Philip supported the proposal as a temporary measure on the grounds that 'it would be very good to achieve by this means all that is offered'.[48] The king was always willing to give way when reality dictated that he should. In this sense, he was by no means as immovable as the immense structure of the Escorial might seem to suggest.

SYMBOL OF SUPERSTITION: THE RELICS

To a modern eye, perhaps the most bizarre aspect of Philip's religion was his devotion to relics,[49] and numerous nineteenth-century historians delighted in citing his obsession with relics as proof of Philip's fanaticism. Some non-Catholic writers insist on the theme because it can be manipulated to depict the king as psychologically disturbed. The role of relics in the ideology of the Escorial was undeniably crucial. We may best begin by giving the total number of relics cited by the monk chroniclers. Philip's final collection amounted to over seven thousand items. Among them were 10 whole bodies, 144 heads, 306 arms and legs, thousands of bones of various parts of holy bodies, as well as hairs of Christ and the Virgin, and fragments of the True Cross and the crown of thorns. Each relic was usually encased in a rich setting, normally silver, for which reason the collection did not have the ghoulish aspect a listing of its contents might otherwise suggest.

When did the king begin collecting? The first mention of it is during the journey back from the Netherlands in 1550, when the prince was just twenty-three years old. We have seen how, after leaving the Netherlands, the royal party stopped at Aachen and then at Cologne, where the prince and nobles purchased several relics (Chapter 1). Cologne cathedral in particular boasted possession of the heads of the 11,000 virgins of the Three Wise Kings, and of those of numerous saints and martyrs. The prince's house steward Vicente Álvarez refused to be taken in by such superstition. 'All this business', he noted, 'made me suspect fraud, and the fear that instead of a saint's head I would be buying that of someone who was in hell. I prefer trusting in those who are in heaven rather than in bones.'[50] The prince, evidently, thought differently, for he immediately placed an order for some relics, a move that seems to have begun his lifelong devotion to the collection of the sacred remnants of saints. Thereafter he always considered Germany the ideal place to look for relics; he brought back from Augsburg relics that the cardinal of that city gave him. At the end of his life, in 1597, he was still financing searches for relics in Germany. The collecting went on until his dying day: in April 1598 four large boxes of relics arrived from Cologne.[51]

Though it is valid to believe (as Protestant reformers did during the Reformation) that relics were a form of superstition, we must bear in mind that they also had a vital social relevance. In medieval Europe, relics had an important political role because they were a symbol of divine power. In Catholic tradition all altars, to affirm their sacred character, contained bits and pieces of holy persons or of their clothing. Several sixteenth-century princes besides Philip were famous as collectors of relics, most notably the protector of Martin Luther, the elector of Saxony. The king was concerned primarily with the religious significance of the items he collected, but did not forget that they also had an important socio-political role, something he reflected in his plans for the Escorial. As noted earlier, as soon as the new church in the monastery was blessed in January 1568, he arranged for the deposit there of an arm of St Lawrence. The first substantial deposit of relics was made with all solemnity in April 1574[52] and represented a powerful boost to the spiritual authority of the new building. Philip's awareness of the political role of relics may be illustrated by three cases chosen at random.

The first notable example occurred in November 1565, when elaborate public ceremonies were put on at Toledo, in the king's presence, to celebrate the return of the presumed remains of the seventh-century bishop St Eugenius to his native see. The remains had apparently been taken to France when the Muslims occupied Toledo, and during his reign Charles V had requested their return. This was made possible only in 1564, after the marriage of Philip to a French princess. The second example comes from the 1570s, when the king sent Ambrosio de Morales to the northwest of the peninsula (see below), but desisted from seizing local relics because he was aware of their importance to local communities. The third example comes from 1581, after Philip entered Portugal as its new king. He took care to instruct the archbishop of Santiago de Compostela (in Spain) to send back to the cathedral at Braga (in Portugal) the relics of two popular saints in the cathedral's possession.[53] In each case the king was concerned that communities should enhance their religious identity through the ownership of revered sacred objects.

The search for relics was, in a sense, a duplication of the search for books (see Chapter 4), and often carried out by the same people, as witness the activity of his chaplain Ambrosio de Morales. In June 1572 the king sent Morales on a tour of the north-eastern provinces of Spain with instructions to look for three classes of item for the Escorial: books, relics and royal bodies. On his return, at the end of February 1573, 'I gave an account to His Majesty'. Although Morales accepted the king's view that bringing sacred relics to the Escorial would make them better known to a wider public, he had serious doubts as to whether many should be moved. The relics, he felt, 'belonged to their own territory', that is, they were an intimate part of their environment, where they should stay. Morales had experienced popular riots in villages in León when the inhabitants heard that he had come to take away their holy relics.[54] He came back with the sensible advice that the king should not, on the whole, remove relics from their sites since 'it would be unjust, cause great discontent in the territory, and might even provoke riots'.[55] The king was obviously convinced by the argument, because for the remaining quarter-century of his reign he tended to look for relics outside rather than inside Spain.

Relics were, we cannot doubt, affirmations of the community of saints, that is, the communication between all members, both living and dead, of the Church of God. They elevated the belief in this communication, which might sometimes take the form of miracles. In this sense, the collection was clearly meant to stress the part played by San Lorenzo in the process of contact between God and man. In previous times and in other places in Europe, Asia and Africa, specific relics of sacred persons had been used periodically as symbols of heavenly power in order to underwrite the authority of rulers. Philip was, as we have noted above, quite aware of the fact that relics are about power. Were they, however, about his own power? The vast royal collection gave to San Lorenzo an authority with which no church in Spain could compete, and it has been suggested that Philip collected the bits of saints in an attempt to reinforce his own 'somewhat precarious authority'.[56] The reality is that the king's authority was the least 'precarious' of any monarch's in Western Europe, and to bolster his already impressive power he did not need the aid of relics, which in any case were never used by him, at any time or in any place, as part of a public attempt to foster the cult of monarchy.[57] It is an interesting idea, therefore, but also wholly speculative, to suggest that Philip 'aspired to capture the sacred energy emanating from his relics to consolidate his own personal power'.[58]

Indeed, Philip received relics in part because others recognised his already impressive political power. As Rosemarie Mulcahy has shown, relics figured prominently among the presents that foreign princes and diplomats showered on the king of Spain.[59] Knowing that the king had a special interest in collecting sacred objects, public figures in the Catholic world who wished to improve their standing with the king continually sent him relics. The grand dukes of Tuscany, who always looked towards Spain for support against other princes and even against the papacy, were second to none in their attention to donating relics. In this way, Philip received items not only from northern Europe but from throughout the Catholic Mediterranean.

While firmly committed to the Catholic faith, Philip seems to have had little time for popular superstition. Among other examples, one may note how he scorned the traditional superstition among Spaniards about the day Tuesday (comparable to the English-speaking world's fear of Fridays). He frequently started journeys on a Tuesday in order to give the lie to the superstition.[60] His faith in relics, on the other hand, was unshakeable, though he accepted that the objects themselves were merely symbols and in that sense it did not matter if they were at times not genuine. He once stated: 'we don't lose our merit before God by revering his saints in bones, even if the bones are not theirs'.[61]

The declaration of faith was central to everything that the king undertook in his monastery-palace. As we have seen, the first major religious act in San Lorenzo was the inauguration of the basilica in the first week of August 1586, when the completed church was finally blessed. In previous months Philip had been superintending the move to San Lorenzo of a considerable number of paintings, largely religious in character, of which the works of Netherlandish artists, notably Michel de Coxcie, formed an important part.[62] They were the artistic contribution to the centrepiece of the building, the basilica. Its completion saw the end of two decades of construction, the culmination of the Escorial. The whole enterprise had been a success, and Philip did not conceal his great joy.[63] In a solemn and glittering ceremony, the sacrament was installed on the high altar. Such was the blaze of candles that 'it seemed as if one was in the presence of an unparalleled glory'.[64] The highest security measures were taken because the king ordered all the altars of the church to be covered with gold, silver, jewels and the most sacred of the relics. The ceremonies reached their climax with a high mass on 10 August, feast of St Lawrence.

The last solemn ceremony in the Escorial at which Philip assisted was the consecration of the basilica, on 30 August 1595. With one notable exception,[65] no modern historian attaches any importance to it, assuming no doubt that it was a standard procedure of those times, and of little interest to us in our secular age. Some do not even mention it, referring only to the religious ceremony put on to mark the completion of the basilica and its blessing, in 1586. Yet the ceremony in 1595 underscores a crucial fact about the place of the building in the king's Christian programme. The full service of consecration of a church (or dedication, the words are interchangeable in the Roman ritual) was early medieval in origin and signified that the building was to be reserved exclusively for religious purposes. The ceremony, whose essence was the anointing of twelve crosses on the inner walls of the church,[66] could only be performed by a bishop or a priest delegated by the pope, something expressly recommended by the Council of Trent in one of its sessions. Philip was convinced that it should be carried out in order to set the seal on the sacred status of the basilica.

Unfortunately, there was no written record of such a service having been performed in the churches or cathedrals of Spain so there was little to guide the clergy organising the event. Sigüenza confesses that it was a 'ceremony no longer in use in Spain',[67] a clear indication of the degree to which the country had lost touch with some of the basic rituals of the Church in Europe. The rite that was carried out in the Escorial in 1595, therefore, symbolised not only the opening of the first great church building to be founded in the country since medieval times, but also the acceptance of that building into the traditions and rituals of the reformed Catholic Church of Trent. Since, as we have commented above, the monastery was exempt from the jurisdiction of Spanish bishops, the prelate officiating at the ceremonies was the papal nuncio, Camillo Caetano, patriarch of Alexandria.

Sigüenza devotes four printed pages to a description of the ceremonial of that night. Several Spanish bishops were present, together with the chief ministers of the government. Because of his infirmities the king could not take an active part in the proceedings, so the principal role as spokesman for the building was taken by the heir to the throne, the Infante Philip. The king was caught up in the excitement of preparing for the occasion. On the previous night, he ordered torches (each wick set in a container of oil) to be placed in every accessible window throughout the building. There were torches beyond number; Sigüenza cites an estimate of five thousand. The entire structure suddenly glowed with light; the villagers came out to look at the display, and there were reports that the gleaming monastery could be seen for miles away. The king, confined to his specially designed chair, asked to be carried to the upper end of the cloister, near his apartment, in order to contemplate the wonder of the whole building ablaze with light.[68] The Infante rode up to the hills on his horse in order to see the sight from a distance.

In that single ceremony, Philip was confirming that the task was done. The monastery and church had been completed according to his desires and were now dedicated to the service of God. Everything had been done in fulfilment of the decrees of the Council of Trent, that august assembly at which he had assisted so very long ago, nearly half a century before.

THE ROYAL BIBLE AT THE ESCORIAL

As part of the religious enterprise initiated in the 1560s, to reform the Church, reform the liturgy and construct the Escorial, the king also dedicated his energies to produce a definitive modern edition of the Bible. The project was proposed to him by the printer Christophe Plantin, resident of Antwerp and therefore a subject of the king. In December 1566, a few months before the momentous military intervention by Alba's troops, he wrote to the king's secretary outlining a plan to print a new edition of the Bible in its five classical languages, Hebrew, Aramaic, Chaldean, Greek and Latin. The last great multi-language Bible had been printed in Spain in 1501, and Plantin was anxious to establish his reputation by publishing a significant work that would also guarantee his income. He had already been in touch with the duke of Saxony over finance, but was fortunate enough eventually to receive the backing of the king.[69] Philip did not give a positive response to Plantin until he had sight of the first proofs, and even then he took care to consult experts before making his decision. Finally, to make sure the Bible would be prepared in the way he desired, in 1568 he sent to Antwerp Spain's foremost Hebrew scholar, Benito Arias Montano, with detailed instructions about editing the volumes.[70] Montano set to work with a small team of expert linguists.

The first volume of the Bible came out in 1569, and seven further volumes were finished by 1573. Plantin printed a total of 1,213 copies of the entire work on four different types of paper, while 23 copies on special paper and on vellum were printed exclusively for the king. In addition to the eight folio volumes, there were volumes of commentaries and dictionaries. The largest polyglot Bible of the sixteenth century, it established Plantin's reputation and made him the most successful printer of his day. The printing was only one part of a careful business arrangement between the printer and the king that focused directly on the Escorial. As part of the agreement, the king ceded to the printer – as we have seen above – the monopoly for printing the new religious publications of the Counter-Reformation, whose distribution was entrusted to the monks of the Escorial.

Provisional approval for the Bible was secured from Rome in 1572 and 1576. There was, however, considerable criticism of the project in Spain. Writing from Rome in 1575, Montano complained of

> a great rumour which a certain León de Castro of Salamanca has raised in that university, to criticize and discredit the greatest work of letters that has ever been published in the world, the Royal Bible which His Majesty has for the benefit of Christendom ordered to be printed in Antwerp under my direction.

The following year Philip appointed Montano librarian of the Escorial. But the monastery did not cease to be the focus of clerical criticism, Montano complaining shortly after, in 1579, of 'men of letters who seek to find and note some error in my writings, making extraordinary efforts to do so'.[71] The conflict was primarily one between scholars, and the criticisms then levelled at the polyglot Bible are now considered to have been in part justified. Although the storm passed, Montano was the object of further, albeit indirect, attacks. In 1592 he was instrumental in bringing about a profound change in the spiritual life of José de Sigüenza, whose histories of the Jeronimite order and of the Escorial remain the fundamental sources for much of the information in this book. Montano, with his great learning and vast experience, based not only on books but also on his travels in Europe, had an enormous intellectual influence on Sigüenza. The changes were wholly spiritual in nature, and there is no evidence whatever to substantiate accounts according to which the Escorial, through these two men, became a hotbed of heresy.[72] In 1592 some of Sigüenza's malicious colleagues, motivated in part by anti-Semitic hostility to Montano's Hebraic studies, denounced Sigüenza to the Inquisition. In what was a brief three-month trial Sigüenza was completely exonerated.[73] Most of these conflicts, the products of personal spite and jealousy, went on without having any impact on the world outside. The vast and seemingly tranquil monument of the Escorial continued unfailingly to stir up fears and passions, but those who lived within its walls were capable of resisting unseemly pressures. Montano worked quietly putting the library in order, decorating its walls and ordering statues to embellish the exterior of the building. Sigüenza settled down to write his history. The great monastery, completed and consecrated, reposed in the Castilian hills, fulfilment of the dream of a king who had laboured for thirty years to bring it to perfection.

CHAPTER 9

INVENTING THE ESCORIAL

Why contemporaries criticised the Escorial of Philip II; Nineteenth-century ideology and the Escorial; The monastery-palace: art and power

Foreigners who visited Spain in the century after Philip II were invariably full of praise for the extraordinary structure that the king had built in the hills of the Guadarrama. One of the earliest reports came from the Englishman John Eliot, who stated in 1593 that the 'Esquireal' was

> the most magnificent palace of all Europe, ... and 'tis the fairest building that I ever saw in my life ... the most goodly, stateliest and sumptuous building that a man can imagine, a place enriched with great gardens, closes and orchards, and with the rarest fruits that a man can wish ... situated upon a pleasant river. ... A hundred times more magnificent than any in Italy. ... Surely a terrestrial paradise, such as promiseth Mahomet in his Alcoran.[1]

Another Englishman, in 1623, referred to it as 'so transcendently full of admiration that it is to be feared that they that enjoy the pleasures thereof will look for no other heaven'.[2] They were impartial reports and communicate some of the delight that the building could evoke in those days. However, precisely because they were visiting foreigners, the Englishmen did not see and could not have understood that the monastery stirred up rather less favourable reactions among many Spaniards who came into contact with it.

Even today, there is keen debate. For some, the building is the essence of Spain, and the Escorial a central achievement of Spanish culture. A short documentary film made under the Franco regime, *El Escorial, a Rock of Spain* (1964), set the seal on the process of presenting the building as a core element in the history of Spain's religion and civilisation. The film enjoyed the services of one of the most accomplished actors of that day, Fernando Rey. In the process of promotion, use was made of a little-known reference from a writer who in 1594 described the monastery as 'The Eighth Wonder of the World'.[3] At roughly the same time, the poet Luis de Góngora also used the description in one of his poems. The phrase, now part of the normal publicity associated with the monastery, does not take into account the fact that for a long time, and for many Spaniards, the Escorial was something strange and far from being a 'wonder'. In terms of architecture, this was not surprising. Nobody else in Spain built palaces (though some, like the dukes of Alba and of Mendoza, renovated theirs). Unlike Valois France and Elizabethan England, Spain in the late Renaissance had no new aristocratic castles, no Burghley House in Lincolnshire nor Chenonceau castle on the Loire.[4] The Escorial therefore stood out in splendid isolation, strange not only for its architecture but for its very existence. Despite what foreign commentators imagined at the time and what tourists today are led to believe, it was by no means a reflection of the Spain of its day. In some sense it may have been a symbol of the age, but it was also a novelty that many Spaniards found hard to understand.

It is all too easy to suppose that the Escorial was a direct point of reference for the people of the peninsula. For example, the preceding pages have repeatedly assumed that the monastery played a recognisable role in a unified political entity called 'Spain'. This could lead us into confusion. Spain was not a political unity, and in the rest of the peninsula outside Castile there was remarkable indifference to Philip's monastery-palace. Religion in Spain, as elsewhere in Europe, was still intensely local, each region having its own particular customs, monasteries and beliefs. The Catalans placed their confidence in the abbey at Montserrat, the Galicians in the shrine at Compostela. The Escorial meant little to them. Moreover, the king was not yet 'king of Spain',[5] so that the regions where his status was only that of 'count' or 'lord' did not pay much attention to the symbolism that the Escorial may have held for Castilians. Philip was well aware of the fact, and in the very years that he was constructing the Escorial he also made the gesture to Catalans of entirely rebuilding their basilica at Montserrat.[6]

The indifference that was the result of a lack of political and religious unity helps us to grasp why a writer in the mid-twentieth century should lament that 'the people of Spain have never understood' the Escorial.[7] In practice, the ordinary public were not the only ones who did not comprehend. Many among the elite in Castile seem not to have understood it either, for they ignored the real, historical Escorial and devoted their efforts instead to constructing round it a myth of national glory/shame that distorted both its reality and its functions. The monastery became a victim of ideology. We may consider the consequences of this at two vital points in history, the year 1836 and the year 1936.

In the early years of the nineteenth century the monks in San Lorenzo suffered various serious hardships, including the loss of many treasures to invading French troops. The most fundamental hardship began in the summer of 1835, when throughout Spain a wave of anticlerical violence, fomented in part by the government, drove thousands of clergy into exile. By September the majority of Spain's monasteries were closed and empty. The new prime minister, Mendizábal, introduced legislation that suppressed the religious orders in Spain and confiscated their property, a decree of 9 March 1836 ordering that 'all monasteries, convents, colleges, congregations and other religious houses or male religious institutes, be suppressed'. In 1836 the seminarists had to leave their quarters in the Escorial and by the end of 1837 all the Jeronimite monks had gone. The great building stood empty. Subsequent visitors (such as Théophile Gautier) saw from the outside only a gloomy, deserted hulk and hundreds of windows with shattered glass. When monks returned much later to the Escorial, they were from the Augustinian order.

A hundred years afterwards, the pattern repeated itself. The anti-clerical Second Republic that came to power in 1936 looked on impassively as monasteries were burnt to the ground and monks murdered. When the rebel army of General Franco neared the city of Madrid in November 1936, the government authorities – in particular, according to a Soviet official, the Communist activist Santiago Carrillo[8] – ordered all detained persons to be eliminated. In the words of the historian Frances Lannon, on 7 November the prisoners 'were deliberately massacred at Paracuellos de Jarama and Torrejón de Ardoz at the eastern approaches to the city, and their bodies dumped into mass graves. Between then and 4 December this outrage was repeated several times, and at least 2,000 victims died, including 68 Augustinian monks from the community at El Escorial.' She terms the massacre of the monks 'the worst atrocity on the Republican side during the war'.[9] Inevitably, the Franco regime that triumphed at the end of the civil war felt it had a duty to bestow special favours on the monastic community, which flour-ished during the twentieth century. Those two dates, 1836 and 1936, pinpoint the triumphs and tragedies of the monastery-palace of Philip II, and the fate it suffered repeatedly at the hands of its own people in Spain.

WHY CONTEMPORARIES CRITICISED
THE ESCORIAL OF PHILIP II

From the moment they adopted the mantle of imperial power in the late fifteenth century, Spaniards began to suffer from the hostility of those nations where their troops were active. This resentment, which numerous scholars have studied, was only one side of the wall of misunderstanding. From approximately the same period and well into the twenty-first century, many Spaniards also harboured a continuing resentment towards foreigners, their culture and their pretensions. Nowhere was this xenophobia more apparent than in their dislike of all their kings after the year 1516.[10] Ferdinand and Isabella were loved because they were Spanish. Charles V and his son were, in contrast, detested because they were foreign. 'God's body, signor ambassador,' the duke of Infantado exclaimed in 1568 to the Florentine envoy, when it appeared that because of Don Carlos' death the king might be succeeded by a German heir, 'Why do we always have to have foreign princes? You Venetians are fortunate indeed always to have your own native ruler!'[11] The Castilian elite detested the foreign ways introduced into Spain by Charles V, just as they were later to resent the French culture imported by the Bourbon dynasty in the year 1700. In much the same way they disliked and distrusted the Escorial. It is a crucial fact that is overlooked by many, who often think that only foreigners denigrated the monastery-palace of Philip II.[12]

Spaniards have always been the first to express disagreement with their own rulers and institutions, and they were not reticent with their views on the fifty-year reign of Philip II. In Castile there were signs of dissatisfaction from the very early years of the reign, in great measure because it was Castile that bore most of the brunt of taxation and military recruitment which the monarchy needed in order to maintain its imperial commitments. In 1564, as we have seen (Chapter 6), a correspondent could report from Madrid that he found 'everybody very discontented with His Majesty'. In the 1570s, tax levels in Castile began to rise and the Escorial was not exempt from experiencing the consequent social tension. The chroniclers of the monastery date precisely to the year 1577 the first appearance in the environs of San Lorenzo of a 'black dog' that began to howl in the night. Popular rumour connected the appearance of the dog to 'the groans of the towns' under the burden of taxes.[13] Open disagreement began to be voiced only in the 1580s, when the accumulation of problems at home and military disasters abroad served to fuel criticism.[14] The Escorial, a visible monument to the power and policies of the king, could not fail to be dragged into the arena of controversy. Every aspect of its creation (notably, of course, its cost), every way in which it could possibly symbolise the monarch who built it, was called into question by voices in

Madrid. The noted French scholar Alfred Morel-Fatio dated to this period an anonymous manuscript of which he found a copy in the National Library in Paris.[15] A biting satire directed against the Escorial, which the writer sneered at as 'escoria' ('slag', a reference to the residue from old mines in the area), the text proceeds to denounce, with evident exaggeration and hysteria, 'that harsh soil, that accursed village of the Escorial, a village without comfort, a wretched mountain, an unfriendly place, where everything is horrible, everything abominable'.

In this atmosphere, discordant voices such as that of a young visionary of Madrid, Lucrecia de Leon, revealed the existence of a real crisis of opinion over aspects of the king's policies. Aged twenty-two when arrested by the Inquisition in Madrid in 1590, Lucrecia was a seer whose prophecies and dreams stimulated a small aristocratic circle at court.[16] In her dreams, explained to the Inquisition during the months of the Armada crisis, she saw a Spain ravaged and invaded, a Philip too feeble to cope. In December 1587, eight months before the event, she saw the defeat of the Spanish fleet by the English. Subsequent dreams, as narrated to her confidants, presented an image of the kingdom that undoubtedly reflected concerns felt and expressed by very many. In a dream in the spring of 1590 she was told by one of her dream figures: 'Philip does not know, and if he knows he does not want to believe, that his enemies will soon be in his lands. He wants to spend his summers in the Escorial, but he should beware, it is not the time to retire there without fear'. 'Beware,' warned one of the figures, 'for this is the time of thunder.' Another dream a week later presented Philip as a tyrant who 'has destroyed the poor', and who would be punished by God through the agency of Elizabeth of England. Philip lived in his palace, 'his eyes bound and his ears shut', surrounded by a Spain in ruins: 'the hour has come to endure purgatory in Spain'.[17] The reflections were an unmistakable accusation that the king had shut himself up in the Escorial, and in doing so had cut himself off from his people.

Few were more conscious of the impact of the Armada than the monks of the Escorial. The king had enjoined them (and, of course, all the churches of the realm) to pray for its success, and when the enterprise ended in disaster they must have felt specially responsible for the failure to recruit God to their cause. Of all the laments made in those terrible days after the bad news of the Armada broke on the people, none was so anguished as that which arose from San Lorenzo. This breast-beating was considered inappropriate by others. In his biography of Philip II, written in the early seventeenth century but not published in full until the eighteenth, Luis Cabrera de Córdoba criticised the monks for their defeatist attitude. The disagreements over the Armada were only a small aspect of the many conflicts that provoked echoes in the Escorial. In the year 1591, when Philip was already seriously ill, disturbances broke out in the city of Saragossa.[18] Critics in Madrid felt that the king should move from the monastery and go and deal with the malcontents personally. The historian Antonio de Herrera was there to report:

> In Madrid, where news of these events arrived every minute, there were many opinions full of doubt and fear. Some lamented the troubles and misfortunes, while others who criticized the present government, which they condemned as shameful, rejoiced in the situation, which they blamed on the king, who in the midst of such dangers was wasting his time on matters of small importance, and they held that if he only bestirred himself everything would be settled.[19]

There is a highly significant coincidence between Antonio de Herrera's report and some other complaints of this period, though few seem to have directed their ire expressly at 'that accursed village of the Escorial', as the document we have mentioned above did.

There is a fundamental consideration that explains in great measure why the monastery was at the centre of so many complaints. When Sigüenza wrote his account in the first decade of the seventeenth century, he made every effort to outline and then respond to the different criticisms. A close examination of what he wrote suggests that a very simple explanation lies at the root of the controversy. The criticisms, it is certain, did not originate with the general public, nor indeed is there evidence that Castilians as a whole shared in them. Outside the capital – a situation common to other countries – few people had any idea of what was going on, nor would most Spaniards have known where or what the Escorial was. In every respect, the controversy was generated in Madrid by sections of the governing elite that feared to lose the unique grasp they had on the resources of the nation. Madrid, selected as seat of the royal court from 1561, was a fast-growing urban sprawl, living off the assets and produce of the surrounding countryside. By the end of the century, it was the only major town in Spain that could begin to compete in size with Seville. Some sections of the elite adored it because it was theirs. They had built their luxurious residences in it, and were the first to object when there were rumours that Philip II might move the seat of government to Lisbon. Others, by contrast, yearned to escape from it, and in the very decade that Sigüenza was writing his history the king's chief minister, the duke of Lerma, was actively planning to move the king, his court and his government out of Madrid.

The essential feature of the 'court' (that is, the government) in Madrid was the royal household. If the king was away, he took most of his household with him. This turned the Alcázar into an empty shell, populated only by its staff, some government officials and the household of any remaining member of the royal family. Only the presence of other royal persons helped to preserve the vitality of social life. In 1578 an ambassador observed that many nobles who came to Madrid in order to serve the king kept away because of the high costs of staying in a king-less city.[20] This situation in its turn affected the whole capital. Madrid during Philip's absences tended to become a den of vice where bored nobles, starved of the activity offered by the court's presence, dedicated themselves to gambling, womanising and night revels.[21]

Political opposition, in short, was at the root of all objections not only to the Escorial but to every alternative capital that might be proposed. Government ministers in Madrid always refused to accept that decisions could be made adequately outside of Madrid (a tendency that is still very much alive today). The first real evidence of this came in the two years 1580–2 when Philip decided to make Lisbon his working base. There were immediate fears that the king might settle in Lisbon, which was a far more attractive location, on the sea coast. Moreover, he was assured, 'the climate of Lisbon is ideal for Your Majesty'.[22] The reaction back home was by no means favourable. Ministers regretted the removal of the king's firm controlling hand. If the king were to leave, an observer felt, everything would collapse. 'His Majesty has only to leave Madrid for El Pardo, and the ministers of all the councils drag their feet and don't turn up at appointed hours or meetings.'[23] The pessimism was not misplaced. Mischief, disputes and violence grew up among the nobles, 'because with the king's long absences they have no reason to present themselves at the palace'.[24] Moreover, without the king to keep the peace between political factions, disputes broke out immediately. 'War and more war is what we have here,' commented the president of the royal council, Pazos, from Madrid. 'We are all up to our heads in it, though it is true that what you have there is real and what we have here is staged.'[25] The effects on the administration were highly detrimental. 'I admit', wrote Pazos, 'the importance of His Majesty's presence there, but one must also consider how necessary it is for business here.'[26]

The same tensions surfaced after the king's return from Portugal. Bureaucrats resented the king's absence if he travelled anywhere outside Castile. Their views were reflected in the comment of the French ambassador in the spring of 1585, when those in Madrid objected to the king leaving to spend almost a year in the crown of Aragon. 'The king is absent from Madrid nearly the whole year, he has few personnel with him, and he separates himself always from the body of the court. Whichever way you look here, there is only silence.'[27] In 1589, just after the Armada defeat, one of the king's officials, Juan de Silva, commented sardonically on the difference in outlook between administrators who worked in the Escorial and those who worked outside it: 'It is not surprising if there is tension between those in San Lorenzo and those outside, the buzz is so unmistakable that it deceives nobody.'[28] When De Silva went to

Madrid shortly after, he found a strange tension in the air: 'The air in Madrid makes me seasick even without stepping out of doors. The style and manner of business, friendship and love, is as strange to me as if I had been born in China.'

The most intense war in those later years was between Madrid and the Escorial. Because the king was most frequently in San Lorenzo, a group of ministers worked there. They lived in the village, which (as we have commented in Chapter 5) was conveniently referred to in inter-Escorial correspondence as 'downstairs' ('*abajo*') while the monastery was termed 'upstairs' ('*arriba*'). But another group, mainly those in finance, had to work in Madrid. The government in this way had two groups of ministers, who worked independently of, and sometimes against, each other. In August 1595 the president of the council of Finance, Poza, protested: 'here we try to turn stones into bread, there they turn bread into stones'.[29] While the rivalry was often good-humoured, the two groups of ministers even sending handwritten jokes to each other inside official documents, nevertheless the system of splitting up decision-making encouraged the growth of political opposition. Ministers working from the royal palace in Madrid resented having to wait for decisions from another palace. Criticisms of the Escorial's role in politics became inevitable.

The 'complaints' listed by Sigüenza, then, were not always complaints so much as a distinct political programme. The 'some' who formulated them around the year 1601, were stated by Sigüenza to be muttering:

> Why didn't the king place so beautiful a building in the centre of or near to a big city of Spain, where everybody would take pleasure in it, where children and adults could visit and it would be for all the people to see and enjoy, rather than in so remote a place, so rugged, cold, dry, ugly, inaccessible and unhealthy?[30]

The 'big city' was of course Madrid, outside of which nothing was deemed to exist, a belief to which administrators in Madrid would cling through the centuries. Sigüenza had a ready and witty defence. If the monastery was judged to be out in the wilderness, the same could be said of Spain's other great monasteries, at Montserrat and Guadalupe. And since those sites were commonly thought to be miracles, then the Escorial also was a miracle.

The second main criticism levelled at the time against the Escorial was its cost. Some modern commentators have suggested that the monastery was a grandiose ego trip on the part of the king, and that opposition to it came from progressive opinion that had a real social concern for the waste involved. That, as we shall see, was an opinion much cultivated among nineteenth-century writers who disliked the monarchy and by extension disliked all its trimmings, notably its palaces. But, the evidence shows, it was also an opinion held even at the time that the monastery was being built. The devil went around, says Sigüenza, 'stirring up the towns, making them believe that all the treasure of the kingdom was being spent here'.[31] Sigüenza dates this complaint to around 1577, which coincides with the changes that the king was proposing in the tax system in Castile. In 1575 the Cortes of Castile had assented to the enforcement of the principal public tax, the *alcabala*, at its full legal rate of 10 per cent. Many towns objected, and refused to collect the tax so that the government was forced to send in its own officials. There were protests, tensions and conflict. 'All Spain was tense, angry and in turmoil,' noted a monk of the Escorial.[32] In October 1577 a new *alcabala* was agreed, at a lower rate. One way or another, however, the tax burden rose. Government tax revenue in Castile in 1577 was about 50 per cent higher than in 1567. Naturally the increase was extremely unpopular. Opposition to taxes gave rise to periodic incidents, and satires aimed at the king were posted on the doors of the main public buildings of Toledo in July 1577. There is little doubt that the unpublished satire mentioned above, which equated the Escorial with *escoria* (slag), was connected with this period of criticism.

Since Sigüenza had access to all the documents concerning the administration of the building, he was in a position to rebut criticisms with statistics: 'I don't really claim to make any apology or defence of this house or its founder, but to dispel the ignorance of people who have been misled'. From early on, he pointed out, the king had been concerned about the possible cost. Philip had asked Herrera what the eventual cost might be, and when told around 1 million ducats he answered that it was too much. However, Philip said, he was less concerned with the actual cost than 'with the complaints of the kingdom, which spoke so openly about this building'.[33] The likely total cost of construction, as it turned out, would be over 5 million ducats, which with the addition of the price of luxury materials such as gold and silver for decoration raised the total cost to around 6.5 million ducats.[34] The most expensive part was evidently the basilica, which accounted for 1.5 million ducats. With these figures before him, Sigüenza proceeded to set out a number of arguments in defence of the expenditure, basing himself mainly on the statistic that the cost over thirty-eight years of construction came to little more than 160,000 ducats a year, a small sum (he felt) to spend for such great spiritual and cultural benefit.[35]

One may look at the question of costs in relation to timeless achievements such as Versailles or the Hermitage or the Taj Mahal, from various standpoints. In historical perspective, a monument may be viewed as priceless. On the other hand, any figures for building costs must inevitably fall far short of the real overall cost. One can point out that Sigüenza's figures refer only to bills paid and not to the total social cost. If one were to calculate not simply the nominal cost of building and decorating, which is what he includes, but also the secondary costs relating to personnel, transport and imported materials, it would be possible to raise the total figure substantially.

The third criticism, and the last to which we shall refer here, concerned the special privileges of the religious order placed in charge of the monastery. Of all countries in Europe, Spain was the one where contention among the religious orders was at its most extreme. It is a subject that can fill volumes, but has never been documented – and indeed does not merit documenting – because the themes involve base human passions of rivalry, enmity and personal ambition. The clergy quarrelled among themselves over lands, privileges, control of universities, positions of political power and precedence in public. Philip II tried to keep everyone happy by having, as spiritual advisers, clergy from different ends of the spectrum. But the problem was always intractable. There was, for example, widespread hostility from other clergy when he showed favour to the Jesuits during their early period in Spain in the 1550s. In the same way, most orders resented the special position that the Jeronimites occupied in the Escorial, resentment which reached its peak when the monks were granted a monopoly of the new mass books a decade later. Sigüenza mentions how there were moves, supported by some ministers of the king, to expel the Jeronimites from the monastery and put another religious order in their place:

> They tried to get the king to change his mind, and give this house to another order that would serve him better and act more openly. There were strong moves in this direction, from many who were in the circle of the king.[36]

In some measure, Spaniards did not understand the Escorial because it was strange, both in style and in location. Even Castilians might feel that it was not part of their world, a disaffection which explains why Sigüenza made strenuous efforts to demonstrate that the whole peninsula had participated in its creation.[37] He detailed the multitude of workers who had come from all parts of Spain in order to take part in the construction. Foreigners, too, were among the workforce: 'many came from Italy and Flanders'. The only people excluded as workers on the king's orders were 'unfree people or pagans', that is, slaves and non-Christians. Sigüenza insisted that the monastery was the work of Spaniards and, as such, an integral part of Spain. Spaniards of a later generation were not so sure.

NINETEENTH-CENTURY IDEOLOGY AND THE ESCORIAL

Modern perceptions of the Escorial took shape in the early nineteenth century, when observations by foreign travellers blended with opinions that Spanish political leaders were beginning to form about the building. In large measure, attacks against the concept of the Escorial were part of a campaign directed against Philip II as the personification of all that was bad in traditional Spain. The myth of Philip II as an evil ruler became an integral part of the refusal to understand the Escorial.[38] In the mid-twentieth century a priest and scholar concluded that 'the nineteenth century never understood the secret of the Escorial'.[39] Anti-Catholic and anti-clerical visions converged in the mind of visitors who approached the vast walls of the monastery and gave themselves over to philosophical reflection. One of the first to do so was the French writer Chateaubriand, who passed that way shortly before 1808:

> I travelled through Hesperia before the French invasion, I found the Spaniards still protected by their ancient way of life. The Escorial revealed to me, in a single site and a single set of buildings, Castilian severity: a barracks for coenobites, built by Philip II in the shape of a martyr's grid, in remembrance of one of our disasters, the Escorial was built on rocky ground among gloomy barrens. It contained royal tombs, filled or to be filled; a library on which the spiders had set their seal; and masterpieces by Raphael mouldering away in an empty sacristy. Its eleven hundred and forty windows, three quarters of them broken, opened on silent reaches of earth and sky: the Court and the Jeronimites, gathered there formerly, expressed their epoch and their distaste for their epoch.
>
> Near that redoubtable edifice, like an aspect of the Inquisition driven into the desert, was a park scattered with broom and a village whose smoke-stained buildings revealed the ancient passage of man. This Versailles of the barrens was only inhabited during intermittent royal visits. I saw a redwing, thrush of the heath, perched on the roof at dawn. Nothing could be more imposing than that sombre religious architecture, invincible in its faith, noble in its expression, taciturn in its history; an irresistible force drew my eyes to the sacred pilasters, stone hermits carrying religion on their heads.
>
> Farewell, monasteries, which I have gazed at in the valleys of the Sierra Nevada, and on the coast of Murcia! There, to the tolling of a bell which soon will chime no more, under crumbling archways, among voiceless tombs, the shade-less dead; in empty refectories, and abandoned courtyards where Bruno has left behind his silence, Francis his sandals, Dominic his torch, Charles

his crown, Ignatius his sword, Rancé his hair-shirt; there, at the altar of a dying faith, one became accustomed to despising time and life: if one still dreamed of the passions there, your solitude lent them something which well suited the vanity of dreams.

Among these funereal buildings, one saw the shade of a man in black pass, that of Philip II, their creator.[40]

Few other travellers were capable of such expressive prose. In 1830 Richard Ford limited himself to a wholly unsympathetic sketch of the building: 'Cold as the grey eye and granite heart of its founder, this monument of fear and superstition would have been out of keeping amid the flowers and sunshine of a happy valley.'[41] It was an unvaryingly negative picture and one that during the nineteenth century was shared by most visitors, whether Spanish or foreign. The American naval officer Alexander Slidell Mackenzie, who spoke fluent Spanish and visited the site on two occasions (the first, in winter), commented in *A Year in Spain* (1831) that it was 'dreary'. 'Its bleak situation upon the mountain exposes it to the cold and furious winds. There are no trees, no rivulets, no fountains, no cultivation, no industry, nothing in short but monks, masses and granite.'[42] He at least saw monks. When Théophile Gautier passed that way in 1840, he was able to see only the grey hulk of a monastery emptied of its residents by the anti-clerical legislation of 1835. He resorted to imagination because he was unable to view what had been the everyday reality: 'I came away from this desert of granite with an extraordinary sensation of satisfaction and relief. I was delivered from that architectural nightmare which I thought would never end.'[43] The monastery cast its long shadow over the nineteenth century, when politicians vied with one another to demonstrate that they stood for the future of the country while the Escorial stood for its past. Not surprisingly, liberals and anti-clericals objected to a structure that, they claimed, had cost millions which would have been better spent on progressive causes, and represented religious beliefs which were now deemed reactionary and anti-quated. In the 1880s the historian Felipe Picatoste accordingly referred to the monastery as 'a madness and an insult to the poverty of the people'.[44]

Astonishingly, no defence was forthcoming from upholders of tradition. The great Catholic polymath Marcelino Menéndez Pelayo in his *History of Aesthetic Ideas* considered the Escorial incomprehensible – 'a colossal Sphinx' – and incapable of exciting enthusiasm because of its 'dry character, empty of poetry'. In the same vein, the leading conservative historian of the day, Antonio Cánovas del Castillo, could summon up only enough fervour to identify the monastery with the personality of its creator: 'that pale mountain of stone, uniform, monotonous, joyless, huge, built for eternity, was a true reflection of the soul of Philip II'.[45] These grudging tributes to the Escorial and to the king who built it, from intellectuals who should have been the first to shower praise on the so-called 'Eighth Wonder', were grim evidence of how far the building had fallen in the estimation of Spaniards. During his years as a professor at Salamanca, Miguel de Unamuno used to make occasional trips out into the countryside in order to find material for his newspaper essays. One such trip in 1912 took him to the village and monastery of the Escorial. In a weak essay that says nothing at all about the monastery, into which he appears not to have entered, Unamuno commented on how Spaniards viewed the historic structure: 'Nearly all who visit the Escorial go with blinkers, and political and religious prejudices, in one sense or another; they go less as pilgrims of art, than as progressives or traditionalists, Catholics or Freethinkers. They go in search of the shadow of Philip II, a man little known and even less understood, and if they do not find it they invent it.'[46]

The negative views of the king continued to flourish well into the twentieth century. In a discussion of the Escorial, the *Encyclopaedia Britannica* stated that 'Philip II was morbid and melancholic, a religious fanatic', a succinct, hostile presentation of both the building and its creator. It is apparent that the Escorial has seldom been judged simply on its own merits, but rather as a reflection of the personage who created it, a fact that makes it even clearer that we should first seek to understand Philip II before evaluating his masterpiece. Unfortunately, commentators have habitually imposed their opinion rather than attempted to understand their subject. The way they did it can be seen through one example.

When we enter the library of the Escorial, we may gaze upon the cheerless and moving portrait of the king aged about sixty-two painted by Juan Pantoja de la Cruz.[47] The unforgiving eye of Richard Ford prompted his comment:

> Here we see him in the flesh and spirit, with his wan, dejected look, marked with the melancholy taint of his grandmother, and his bigot, grey eye, cold as frozen drops of morning dew.[48]

The alleged 'melancholy taint' is a reference to the plight of Queen Juana the Mad. With the combination of madness and bigotry, the classic view of Philip favoured by Protestant historians was complete. What, however, did those next to the king see?

Still in mourning for his wife Anna (after her death in 1580 he invariably wore black), and saddened at being deprived of the companionship of his youngest daughter Catalina,[49] the king had every reason to be dejected. His unhappiness was one of the reasons that drew him to the religious environment of San Lorenzo. Ford's nineteenth-century perspective on the king, however, bears comparison with the sixteenth-century one of the Sieur de Longlée, who during his years as French representative in Madrid would certainly have known the artist, and was in a position to observe the king dispassionately at the very time that Pantoja was beginning his portrait. It was Armada year, 1588, just before the naval disaster. Longlée explained the king's person, his problems and his love of the Escorial:

> The king is diligent in work and all matters pass through his hands. As though he were only forty years old, he trusts no one else to manage. He does not fail to spend time in devotion; and at other hours, as he has always done and depending on the weather, he goes out in a carriage with his children, or goes walking, or hunting or to see a deer hunted, or even sometimes goes fishing. He retires to bed late, as has been his custom in all the time that I have served here, and there is as yet no rumour of him wishing to

unburden himself of business or of the government of these states. He gives audiences, and does not conceal himself at all, though it is true that he doesn't like too many of them, and though he might postpone them he does not refuse them. He has always taken pleasure in being away from Madrid, because he loves his buildings, his gardens, the country air, purer than that of the towns, and is more able to dispatch his affairs at leisure and be less pressurized by people.

As is his custom, he will pass this summer in the residences he has six or seven leagues from here [Longlée was writing from Madrid]. It is normal to lose weight at the age His Majesty has, but in truth he is rather thin, and in the coming years his age will make this show even more. Madame the Infanta [Isabel] normally keeps him company, but she does not enter in any way into affairs, even though His Catholic Majesty is delighted that she has an understanding of most of it, which she manages because she is continually with him.[50]

Shortly afterwards, in 1590, the very year of Pantoja's painting, the Flemish courtier Jehan Lhermite gave a pen sketch of the king, 'in his sixty-third year, very subject to gout, his hair white and balding, but in good physical condition, his mind lively and his memory even better than ever'.[51] Lhermite's balanced view hides nothing. And the king himself sought to hide nothing, since he permitted the portrait to be hung in his library.

THE MONASTERY-PALACE: ART AND POWER

After this historical journey through the endless cold stone-paved corridors of the Escorial, we may feel justified in asking whether Philip II actually achieved anything substantial with the mammoth construction on which he expended so much energy and money. Was any of it worth the effort?

In other princely courts of Western Europe, the public display of art and entertainment was consciously aimed at garnering support for those who wielded authority. Rituals, processions, festivals were part of a political process intended to enhance the standing of the monarchy.[52] In the same way, the Catholic Church (and, inevitably, the papacy) began to employ music and art in a conscious effort to assert its spiritual power. In sixteenth-century France, there were 'court festivals, with teams of artists, poets and musicians' to promote the status of the king.[53] Little of this happened in Philip II's Spain.[54] The king was, as we have already pointed out, probably the leading patron of art and culture in Europe; he spared no expense to acquire the experts in every field. But little of that art was made to serve the interests of his political authority.

Ironically, the Escorial, at first sight the most conspicuous symbol of royal power, never served as a theatre to showcase the monarchy: no specific rituals or royal celebrations were ever held there, other than those connected with the monastery. Its enormous contribution to art was made almost furtively, without the admiration or the participation of the public. Even diplomats, well placed to appreciate the culture of San Lorenzo, paid its artistic embellishments little attention in their reports, and some – notably the Venetians – treated the building as an aberration. A telling instance of this lack of an audience for the Escorial was the most striking ceremony ever held within its walls, the consecration of the basilica in 1595 (Chapter 8), which was witnessed only by an assembly of clergy and courtiers. The public had to watch with wonderment from outside, and content themselves with the sight, at every window, of the glittering of thousands of oil lamps that etched out against the night the gaunt outlines of the building.

As an artistic exercise the Escorial was a stupendous achievement, surpassed shortly afterwards only by the newly emerging St Peter's in Rome. Nowhere else in Europe did a sixteenth-century monarch make such a grandiose statement of belief in the possibilities of architecture, sacred art, book learning and the reality (as expressed through relics) of the communion of saints. The collection of paintings and manuscripts (including scientific manuscripts such as those of Dr Hernández) was without equal. As we have noted (Chapter 3), 'artists contributed enormously to the grandeur and standing of the king'. The selection of tapestries had no precedent in Spanish history. As a collector but also as a creator, Philip can rightly lay claim to be a prodigy – his intellect soared above those of most of his contemporaries. He did not need to take inspiration from some mythical Solomon in order to develop his ideas and aspirations. If we may draw a tentative conclusion from all this, it is that the king – unlike some rulers of his day, including his father the emperor – did not make use of art to express his power; rather, he used his power to give expression to art.

As an exercise in political power, on the other hand, Philip II's Escorial was certainly ambiguous and consistently misunderstood. Outsiders, and subsequent scholars and politicians, judged the building by its immensity and reacted accordingly. They felt that the king was making claims for personal, religious and political hegemony. As we have argued above, there is no tangible basis for any of these charges. In Versailles a century later, the king of France encouraged the development of an environment that would elevate his own person. Philip, by contrast, was concerned only to magnify the glory of God. His paintings and relics were an attempt to enhance the dignity and spiritual power of the monastery, not of the monarchy. By constructing on so grand a scale, however, the king provoked questions that came to be directed both against himself and against his foundation. In that sense, if there was a message of power emanating from the Escorial, it may be considered a failure. As in the ceremony of 1595 to which we have referred, the public were left outside, excluded from the theatre. They failed to identify themselves with it, and the consequences were evident in the centuries that followed.

One way or the other, and particularly so for some Spaniards who were intent on visualising it as a unique emblem of their hopes and fears, throughout its history the Escorial took on forms and meanings that its founder could never have imagined. It became an unexplained, mysterious phenomenon, constructed along occult lines, a den of superstition and tenebrous plots,[55] in which nevertheless many claimed to be able to make out the lineaments of the authentic spirit of the nation. Observers read what they wished into its gaunt profile. Few, however, were as detached as the Czech writer Karel Čapek, who came upon the monastery at nightfall one summer at the opening of the twentieth century. We take our leave with his words:

In the brown, stony slope there is a miraculous sight: dark green gardens, avenues of dark cypresses, a dense and gloomy park; a huge, stark and lordly cube with four bristling turrets; a monumental solitude, a hermitage with a thousand haughty windows: El Escorial. The cloister of the Spanish kings. A castle of sorrow and pride above the parched countryside.[56]

ABBREVIATIONS

AGS	Archivo General de Simancas, Valladolid
AGS: CR	AGS, section Casas Reales
AGS: E	AGS, section Estado
AGS: E/K	AGS, section Estado, serie K
AHN Inq	Archivo Histórico Nacional, Madrid, section Inquisición
BCR	Biblioteca Casanatense, Rome
BL	British Library, London, manuscript room
BL Add.	BL Additional MS
BL Eg.	BL Egerton MS
BNac	Biblioteca Nacional, Madrid, manuscript room
BP	Biblioteca del Palacio Real, Madrid
BZ	Biblioteca Zábalburu, Madrid, manuscript collection
CODOIN	Colección de Documentos Inéditos para la Historia de España
CSP Foreign	Calendar of State Papers, Foreign
CSPV	Calendar of State Papers, Venetian
Favre	Collection Favre, Bibliothèque Publique et Universitaire, Geneva
HHSA	Haus-, Hof-, und Staatsarchiv, Vienna
IVDJ	Instituto de Valencia de Don Juan, Madrid
MZA: RAD	Moravský Zemský Archiv, Brno: Rodinný Archiv Ditrichšteinu

NOTES

PREFACE

1. *Time*, 27 Sept. 1963.
2. Carlos M. Eire, *From Madrid to Purgatory. The art and craft of dying in sixteenth-century Spain*, Cambridge 1995, p. 261.
3. In his book, which offers an excellent brief survey of the Escorial, Eire is not of course suggesting that there was a mystical code inspiring those who built the Escorial (Eire, pp. 258–82); he is referring rather to the dynamic relationship between a building and those confronted by it.
4. Miguel de Unamuno, *Andanzas y Visiones españolas*, Madrid 1988, p. 83.
5. Spelt in this way by the king, and also in this book. The modern Spanish habit of writing 'San Lorenzo de El Escorial' has, I believe, no contemporary support.

CHAPTER 1: GENESIS

1. 'No kings of Spain ever took on a similar project': Bustamante García, p. 31.
2. They did, however, build or endow churches and monasteries, notably the beautiful Gothic-Flemish monastery of San Juan de los Reyes in Toledo.
3. 'Spain' at this date was, like Italy and Germany, not a unified country but an amalgam of autonomous territories sharing a common ruler.
4. Note by king, 28 Dec. 1574, BZ 144 f. 39.
5. W.S. Maltby, *The Black Legend in England*, Durham, North Carolina, 1971, gives a perspective of English opinion on the subject. Among other surveys of how Europeans viewed Spaniards, see Hillgarth, *The Mirror of Spain*.
6. For nineteenth-century Spanish views of Philip as a foreigner, see Kamen 2008, pp. 49–50.
7. Braudel, II, 904.

8. Maximilian, born in the same year as Philip, was the son of Charles V's younger brother Ferdinand, who later became emperor as Ferdinand I. Maximilian succeeded his father as emperor (1564–76). See Paula S. Fichtner, *Emperor Maximilian II*, New Haven and London 2001.

9. The Catalan humanist Calvet, in the original correspondence by him that I have seen, wrote and signed his name as 'Calvet'; the form 'Calvete' seems to have been used by Castilians, who found it easier to pronounce his name this way. To avoid confusion, I shall use the incorrect form 'Calvete' in this book.

10. Calvete de Estrella, p. 5. There were also a number of other vessels for transporting servants and horses.

11. Letter of 30 Nov. to his father, printed in CSP, England and Spain, IX, 318 (the original letter is in the archive at Simancas); and of 1 Dec. 1548 to Lope Hurtado de Mendoza, in BZ 114 f. 63. The letters were written by his secretary Gonzalo Pérez.

12. Charles took steps to reinforce Philip's authority by having him invested as duke of Milan in a private ceremony at Guadalajara on 16 September 1546.

13. Brown 1986, p. 30.

14. Cf. *Los Leoni*.

15. The relevance of friendship between Philip and Protestants is touched on below in Chapter 8.

16. Álvarez, p. 56.

17. Venetian envoy Soranzo, in 1565: Alberi, ser.I, vol. 5, p. 112.

18. Calvete de Estrella, p. 52.

19. It is interesting that a luxurious volume published by the Spanish government to commemorate the fourth centenary of the death of Philip II, *Jardín y Naturaleza*, is illustrated throughout with pictures of French, Italian and English palaces and gardens, but no Spanish ones apart from the royal palace at Madrid.

20. The gardens for which the castle was later most famed, laid out by the French engineer Salomon de Caus, were not commenced until the first decade of the seventeenth century.

21. Álvarez, p. 70.

22. Philip to Gonzaga, Heidelberg, 8 Mar. 1549, AGS: E leg.645 f. 30.

23. Álvarez, p. 77.

24. Eleanor of Habsburg, born in Louvain, was queen of France by virtue of her marriage to Francis I, who died in 1547.

25. Cited in Gachard 1854, *Introduction*, p. 18.

26. Álvarez, p. 79.

27. Cited Forneron, I, 11, from Venetian ambassador.

28. On Binche, see Calvete de Estrella, pp. 182–205.

29. Álvarez, p. 112.

30. Calvete de Estrella, p. 281.

31. Letters in autograph from Philip to Maximilian, July–Nov. 1549, HHSA Spanien, Hofkorrespondenz, karton 1, mappe 3, ff. 143–4.

32. Álvarez, p. 120.

33. Álvarez, p. 120.
34. Philip to Maximilian, autograph from Cologne, HHSA Spanien, Hofkorrespondenz, karton 1, mappe 3, f. 161.
35. Merriman, III, 406.
36. Bishop of Arras to Margaret of Hungary, 13 Oct. 1550, CSP, England and Spain, X, 156.
37. Álvarez, pp. 131–2.
38. Philip to Juan Hurtado de Mendoza, Augsburg, 12 Sept. 1550, AGS: E leg.645 f. 81.
39. AGS: E leg.645 f. 87.
40. Mark A. Meadow, 'Hans Jacob Fugger and the Origins of the Wunderkammer', in Pamela H. Smith and Paula Findlen, eds, *Merchants and Marvels: Commerce, Science and Art in Early Modern Europe*, New York 2002, p. 194. It should also be remembered that the host of the prince in Bavaria, Albrecht V, was a humanist and bibliophile who, shortly after the prince's visit, founded the Bavarian State Library.
41. Braudel, II, 915.
42. Antoine's father, Nicolas Perrenot, Cardinal Granvelle, had died in August 1550. Antoine replaced him as chief adviser to Charles V.
43. There were three documents: a contract between Maximilian and Philip, an undertaking by Philip, and an undertaking by Maximilian.
44. Philip's movements are attested by the Netherlands chronicler who documented all the emperor's movements and now accompanied the prince back to Spain; Jean de Vandenesse, in Gachard 1882, IV.
45. In French, 'La feste Dieu'; Gachard 1882, IV, 4.
46. For the dome in late medieval church architecture, see Wolfgang Born, 'The Introduction of the Bulbous Dome into Gothic Architecture and Its Subsequent Development', *Speculum*, vol. 19, no. 2 (Apr. 1944), pp. 208–21. For the later changes, see Henry-Russell Hitchcock, 'The Schmuzers and the Rococo Transformation of Mediaeval Churches in Bavaria', *Art Bulletin*, vol. 48, no. 2 (June 1966), pp. 159–76.
47. All the prince's movements come from Gachard 1882, IV, 4.
48. Constancio Gutiérrez, *Trento: un concilio para la unión (1550–1552)*, 3 vols. Madrid 1981, III, 398.
49. Gachard 1882, IV, 5.
50. AGS: E leg.646 f. 226.
51. Soriano, in Alberi, ser.I, vol. 3. Cf. the comments of Merriman, III, 366, who like others accepts the Venetian view.
52. Morán and Checa, p. 77.
53. See the report on her made by Francisco de Borja to Philip in 1554: *Monumenta Historica Societatis Iesu: Borgia*, Madrid 1908, III, 161.
54. Philip to Maximilian, 16 Sept. 1551, HHSA Spanien, Hofkorrespondenz, karton 1, mappe 4 f. 23.
55. Philip to Maximilian, 25 Sept. 1551, HHSA Spanien, Hofkorrespondenz, karton 1, mappe 4 f. 27.
56. Vandenesse, in Gachard 1882, IV, 7.

57. Philip to Maximilian, 29 Sept. 1551, HHSA Spanien, Hofkorrespondenz, karton 1, mappe 4 f. 29.
58. Philip to Maximilian, 2 Jan. 1552, HHSA Spanien, Hofkorrespondenz, karton 1, mappe 4 f. 39.
59. Philip to Maximilian, 5 Apr. 1552, HHSA Spanien, Hofkorrespondenz, karton 1, mappe 4 f. 44.
60. John Elder, *The Copie of a letter sent in to Scotlande*, London 1554.
61. Muñoz, p. 99. The Venetian ambassador claimed that she spoke Spanish fluently (CSPV, VI, ii, p. 1055), but the testimony of Muñoz is more reliable. It is noteworthy that Elizabeth also spoke some Spanish.
62. Details in G. Constant, 'Le mariage de Marie Tudor et de Philippe II', *Revue d'Histoire Diplomatique*, 26 (1912), pp. 244–60.
63. Philip to Juana, 2 and 18 Sept. 1554, AGS: E leg. 808 ff. 38, 40.
64. Cf. D.M. Loades, 'Philip II and the government of England', p. 190, in C. Cross et al., eds, *Law and Government under the Tudors*, Cambridge 1988.
65. Cited in Kamen, 'Toleration and dissent', p. 14, in *Crisis and Change in Early Modern Spain*, Aldershot 1993.
66. Castro did not live to take up his post. He accompanied Philip to Flanders, and died in Brussels in 1558.
67. Gachard 1854, *Introduction*, 80–103.
68. Gachard 1854, *Introduction*, 98, demonstrates that Philip spoke his few words in French.
69. Sébastien de l'Aubespine, bishop of Limoges, to King François II, Ghent, 27 July 1559, in Paris, pp. 49–54.
70. Checa, p. 87.
71. A good overview is J.K. Steppe, 'Mécénat espagnol et art flamand au XVIe siècle', in *Splendeurs d'Espagne et les villes belges 1500–1700*, 2 vols. Brussels 1985, I, 247–82.
72. Brown 1986, p. 17.
73. Paris, p. 64.
74. Although Philip never became a linguist, his travels enabled him to improve his command of languages, and he grew competent at reading French and Italian.
75. 'Spanish culture in the sixteenth century drew for the most part on Italian influences, and to a lesser extent on Northern influences': Joan-Ramon Triadó, 'La Cultura', *Historia de España Planeta*, Madrid 1988, vol. 5, *El Siglo de Oro*.
76. Max J. Friedlander, *Antonis Mor and His Contemporaries*, Leiden 1975.
77. Gachard 1867, p. vii.
78. Philip to Charles, Vlissingen, 22 Aug. 1559, CODOIN, II, 548.
79. Challoner to Cecil, 27 Aug. 1559, CSP, Foreign 1558–9, p. 503.

CHAPTER 2: THE BATTLE

1. Several modern accounts repeat erroneously that the battle was fought on the 'birthday' of the saint. In Christian usage, the day of commemoration

was always that of the ascent into heaven, i.e. the day of death, and in the case of St Lawrence the day of his martyrdom.

2. There may be political motives for this refusal to study Spain's battles. A Spanish historian comments: 'the history of war in the early modern period has not, in our country, attained the level it deserves, on one hand because of the ideological contempt towards the subject felt by certain historians, on the other because of the very few contributions made to the theme': Antonio Espino López, 'La historiografía hispana sobre la guerra en la época de los Austrias. Un balance, 1991–2000', *Manuscrits* (Barcelona) 21, 2003.

3. Cabrera de Córdoba, 1st part, book 4, chaps 5 to 9.

4. Carlos Martinez de Campos, *Espana belica: el siglo XVI*, 2 vols. Madrid 1966, vol. II, chap. 1.

5. Henri Forneron, *Histoire de Philippe II*, 4 vols. Paris 1880, and Sir Charles Oman, *A History of the Art of War in the Sixteenth Century*, London 1937.

6. E. García-Hernán and Davide Maffi, eds, *Guerra y Sociedad en la Monarquía Hispánica. Política, estrategia y cultura en la Europa moderna (1500–1700)*, 2 vols. Madrid 2006.

7. William H. Prescott, *History of the Reign of Philip the Second*, 2 vols. Boston 1855–6, vol. 1, chap. 7.

8. *La Guerre de 1557 en Picardie*, ed. E. Lemaire, E. Fleury, É. Theillier et al., Saint Quentin 1896 (Société des Sciences, Arts, Belles-Lettres et Agriculture de Saint-Quentin).

9. CSPV, VI, ii, 1,179.

10. CSPV, VI, ii, 1,063.

11. 'All sinew, little flesh . . . born to command': Cabrera de Córdoba, I, 166.

12. King to Savoy, 26 July 1557, AGS: E/K 1490 no. 40.

13. The account that follows is based largely on Philip's original (and, until recently, unknown) military despatches, in BL Add.28264. A briefer version appears in my *Philip of Spain*, chapter 2. In English the standard accounts are by late nineteenth-century American historians, who evince an unconcealed prejudice against Philip II. For example, a highly entertaining but thoroughly hostile account of Philip at St Quentin is given by Motley (see note 34 below), pp. 89–99. In Merriman, IV, 11, Philip is caricatured as scribbling letters instead of going out personally to do battle, a defamatory picture that seems to have been borrowed from Henri Forneron's *Histoire*, I, 92. Astonishingly, no Spanish historians have shown any interest in the battle, with the result that there are no researched accounts of it in Spanish.

14. King to Savoy, Brussels, 20 July 1557, AGS: E/K 1490 no. 41.

15. King to Savoy, Brussels, 26 July 1557, AGS: E/K 1490 no. 40.

16. BL Add.28264 ff. 10–12. This bundle of documents consists of original despatches, of which some exist in copy in AGS: E/K 1490.

17. BL Add.28264 f. 17.

18. BL Add.28264 f. 19.

19. From Cambrai, 8 Aug., BL Add.28264 f. 19.

20. My italics: BL Add.28264 ff. 26–7. There is a copy of this letter in AGS Estado K 1490 no. 57, with slight variations of wording.
21. Savoy to king, 8 Aug. 1557, AGS: E/K 1490 no. 65.
22. Savoy to Eraso, 8 Aug. 1557, AGS: E/K 1490 no. 67b.
23. Ambroise Paré, *Journeys in Diverse Places*, trans. Stephen Paget, vol. 38, part 2. New York 1909–14.
24. The notion that Philip's handwriting was almost illegible is without foundation. When he was relaxed his script was perfectly formed and easy to read. When, however, time pressed (as was usually the case when he had to go through administrative correspondence), his hand often became difficult to decipher.
25. Philip to Charles, 11 Aug. 1557, AGS: E/K 1490 no. 72.
26. Venetian ambassador Suriano, Brussels, 11 Aug. 1557, CSPV, VI, ii, 1,244.
27. *La Guerre de 1557 en Picardie*, p. lii.
28. The analysis that follows is based on the excellent data in *La Guerre de 1557 en Picardie*, p. 237, document 70.
29. His remark to the Venetian ambassador Suriano: CSPV, VI, ii, 1,348.
30. Who died that week, of gout, aged only fifty-one.
31. Report by Suriano, 17 Aug. 1557, Brussels, CSPV, VI, ii, 1,345.
32. CSPV, VI, ii, 1,345.
33. Suriano to Senate, 24 Oct. 1557, CSPV, VI, ii, 1,354. Suriano's letters make clear that the retreat after St Quentin was a decision imposed by the council.
34. John L. Motley, *The Rise of the Dutch Republic* (published in the nineteenth century in several editions, but now conveniently available as an e-book), London 1912 edn, p. 96: 'The pusillanimity of Philip prevented him from seizing the golden fruits of his triumph.' Motley admits, however, that the alleged 'rage' of Charles on learning of the decision not to advance on Paris is not confirmed by the emperor's correspondence.
35. Philip to Savoy, Brussels, 21 Oct. 1557, AGS: E/K 1490 f. 98.
36. Philip to Ferdinand, 29 Aug. 1557, San Quentin, CODOIN, II, 493–6.
37. Bedford to William Cecil, quoted in *La Guerre de 1557 en Picardie*, p. 324. Philip, according to his own letters, ordered the evacuation of women and children from the town in order to save them from the soldiers. Motley, p. 97, presents this as an act of cruelty.
38. Cabrera de Córdoba, first part, book 4, chaps 7 to 9.
39. Philip to Juana, 2 Sept. 1557, AGS: E/K 1490 no. 82b.
40. Stephanie Breuer, *Alonso Sánchez Coello y el retrato en la corte de Felipe II*, Madrid 1990, item 1 in the catalogue.
41. Braudel, II, 942 notes it as 'a turning point in western history'.
42. BL Add.28264 ff. 41–4.
43. The celebrations were interrupted by a terrible accident, the mortal wounding of Henry II of France in a joust on 30 June. Just before he died a few days later, the king gave orders for celebrating the wedding between Marguerite and the duke of Savoy.

44. I myself have not seen the painting. If the king treasured such an item, it would have been not only because of the presumed intimate connection of the Shroud with the historical Christ, but also because the painting was a link with his now absent favourite daughter.

CHAPTER 3: FOUNDATION

1. Cited in Álvarez Turienzo, p. 35.
2. Sigüenza, II, 407.
3. Cromwell commented in a letter to the Speaker of the House of Commons about his victory at the battle of Worcester (1651): 'the dimensions of this mercy are above my thoughts. It is, for aught I know, a crowning mercy.'
4. Philip to Juana, 2 Sept. 1557, AGS: E/K 1490 no. 82b.
5. Gautier, p. 101.
6. Sigüenza, II, 404.
7. Sigüenza, II, 423.
8. Rivera, p. 62.
9. He arrived safely by ship from Naples, but a subsequent vessel, carrying his wife, children and books, capsized and all on board were lost.
10. Richard L. Kagan, ed., *Spanish Cities of the Golden Age. The Views of Anton van den Wyngaerde*, Berkeley 1989, pp. 120–2.
11. Quevedo, p. 6.
12. Quevedo, p. 6.
13. Rivera, p. 294.
14. John W. Bernhardt, ed., *Itinerant Kingship and Royal Monasteries in Early Medieval Germany*, Cambridge 2002, p. 291.
15. E. Michael Gerli, Samuel G. Armistead, *Medieval Iberia: an Encyclopaedia*, London 2003, p. 2.
16. Fernando Chueca Goitia, *Casas Reales en Monasterios y Conventos Españoles*, Bilbao 1983.
17. Report by Francisco de Luzón, AGS: CR leg.247 f. 30.
18. Incident reported by an attendant of the emperor to Jean Lhermite: Lhermite, I, 101.
19. Checa, p. 34.
20. I have used the excellent English edition of *On Architecture*, 2 vols. New Haven and London 1996, translated from Italian and edited by Vaughan Hart and Peter Hicks. The section on domes features here in vol. I, pp. 101–3.
21. Cited in Álvarez Turienzo, p. 195.
22. The architect will be referred to in this book simply as Juan Bautista, since his real surname is uncertain.
23. In an article of 1985, Catherine Wilkinson, 'Planning a style for the Escorial: an architectural treatise for Philip of Spain', *Journal of the Society of Architectural Historians*, March 1985, vol. XLIV, no. 1, argues that 'in 1559 Philip II suddenly altered his style of architectural patronage' by

inviting in foreigners and Italians. This does not seem plausible, since he seems to have been actively in contact with the books and persons of Italian architects since at least 1548.

24. Alfonso Rodríguez, 'En torno a Felipe II y la arquitectura', in *Real Monasterio-Palacio de El Escorial*, p. 125.

25. A notable exception was the Mendoza family. For a perspective on the nobles as a whole, see Luis Gil Fernández, *Panorama social del humanismo español (1500–1800)*, Madrid 1981, pp. 299–327. In the sixteenth century, thanks to the third duke, the Alba family also achieved a high level of culture: see Henry Kamen, *The Duke of Alba*, New Haven and London 2007.

26. Ambassador Khevenhüller, cited in Friedrich Edelmayer, 'Aspectos del trabajo de los embajadores de la casa de Austria en la segunda mitad del siglo XVI', *Pedralbes*, 9, 1989, p. 47.

27. Cf. Kamen 1993, pp. 391–3.

28. His instructions to import quantities of writing paper are on record in the archive of Simancas.

29. Cf. the useful discussion in A. Alvar Ezquerra, *Felipe II, la Corte y Madrid en 1591*, Madrid 1985.

30. For what follows, Rivera, pp. 198–243.

31. Perhaps the best survey of the Alcázar is *El Real Alcázar de Madrid. Dos siglos de arquitectura y coleccionismo en la Corte de los Reyes de España*, Madrid 1994. This well-illustrated study has expert contributions by specialists.

32. Rivera, pp. 215–16.

33. Carl Justi, 'Felipe II como amante de las bellas artes', in W. Maurenbrecher, M. Philippson and Carl Justi, *Estudios sobre Felipe II*, Madrid 1887, p. 242.

34. Rivera, p. 276.

35. BL Add. 28350 ff. 19–26, 32.

36. Checa, pp. 63–4.

37. Cited in Checa, p. 63.

38. AGS: CR leg.247.

39. Reproduced in *Spanish Cities of the Golden Age*, p. 120.

40. Kubler, p. 42.

41. In Gregorio Marañón's study *Antonio Pérez* (first published Madrid 1948), which has since been issued in several editions in both Spanish and English.

42. Bustamante García, p. 20.

43. These themes are touched on in my *Philip of Spain*.

44. In M.J. Rodríguez Salgado, *The Changing Face of Empire. Charles V, Philip II and Habsburg Authority, 1551–1559*, Cambridge 1988.

45. Letters of Isabel to Lope Hurtado de Mendoza, 14 June and 7 July 1532, BZ 114 ff. 108, 111.

46. King to Ladrada, 9 Mar. 1572, BL Add. 28354 f. 362.

47. AGS: E leg.60 f. 56.

48. On the role of prayer, see the excellent details in Eire, *passim*.

49. For her role, see the various references in Kamen 1997.
50. The most reliable account of Juana is by her contemporary Juan Carrillo OFM, *Relacion Historica de la Real Fundacion del Monasterio de las Descalças de Sta Clara de la villa de Madrid*, Madrid 1616.
51. Cabrera de Córdoba, II, 212.
52. Cabrera de Córdoba, II, 6.
53. Mary of Hungary was born in Mechelen in 1505 and died in 1558 in Valladolid. She was married when young to the king of Hungary-Bohemia and later appointed regent of the Netherlands by her brother the emperor Charles V, with whom she retired to Spain in 1556. There is an incredibly appealing portrait of the young queen, aged eighteen, painted by the artist Hans Krell and now held in the Bayerische Staatsgemäldesammlungen, München [Munich]-Staatsgalerie Bamberg.
54. Morales, p. 11.
55. William Stirling-Maxwell, *Don John of Austria*, 2 vols, London 1883, is the only scholarly biography.
56. Sigüenza, II, 454.
57. Juan Hernández Ferrero, 'Orígenes históricos del Monasterio de El Escorial', in *Real Monasterio-Palacio de El Escorial*, p. 16.
58. Serlio, *On Architecture* (1996 edn, cited above), I, 101–3.
59. Howarth, p. 153.
60. Cf. Catherine Wilkinson Zerner, 'Body and Soul in the Basílica of the Escorial', *Fenway Court*, XXVIII, 'The Word made Image', Boston 1998, pp. 70–5.
61. Longlée, 29 June 1586, in Mousset, p. 275.
62. Fernando Bouza Alvarez, ed., *Cartas de Felipe II a sus hijas*. Madrid 1988, p. 111.
63. Sigüenza, II, 471.
64. Sigüenza, II, 470.
65. 'Copia auctentica de la traslacion que se hizo de los cuerpos reales' to the 'boveda debaxo del altar mayor de San Lorenzo', AGS: E leg.156 f. 17.
66. 'In order to avoid suffering,' says a monk, he did not come: Sepúlveda, p. 30.
67. 'He did not wish to be present at the reburial': CODOIN, VII, 410.
68. Mariana, II, 554.
69. BL Add. 28350 f. 101v.
70. Virginia Tovar, 'El arquitecto Juan Gómez de Mora y su relación con lo "escurialense" ', in *Real Monasterio-Palacio de El Escorial*, p. 198.
71. Cf. Kamen 1997, pp. 182, 201, among many other references.
72. Philip to Ruy Gómez, 19 Feb. 1559, in Weiss, V, 491.
73. An exception is the fine volume by J. Miguel Morán Turina and Fernando Checa Cremades, *Las Casas del Rey. Siglos XVI y XVII*, Madrid 1986, especially pp. 103–25.
74. *Jardín y Naturaleza*. The only acceptable part of this unfortunate volume is the small section on 'Las Influencias. Los jardines que el rey conocio', which deals with gardens in the Netherlands, England and Austria, but

without any attempt to identify the link between Philip and those gardens.

75. Joaquin Romero, 'Los jardines en el Escorial', in *El Escorial 1563–1963*, II, p. 684.
76. Cf Kamen 1997, p. 184.
77. Cf. Elisabeth Woodhouse, 'Spirit of the Elizabethan Garden', *Garden History*, vol. 27, no. 1, summer 1999, p. 14.
78. Iñiguez Almech, p. 165.
79. Aurora Rabanal, 'Felipe II y los jardines', in *Felipe II y el Arte*, p. 404.
80. Iñiguez Almech, p. 203.
81. BZ 146 f. 35.
82. Rivera, p. 251.
83. Cited in Manuel Danvila y Collado, *El poder civil en España*, 6 vols, Madrid 1885–6, II, 389.
84. 'Memorial de algunas cosas particulares', AGS: CR leg.247 f. 60.
85. AGS: CR leg.247 f. 49.
86. Sigüenza, II, 441.
87. Wilkinson, p. 95.
88. Pedro Navascués Palacio, 'El Patio y templete de los Evangelistas de El Escorial', in *Real Monasterio-Palacio de El Escorial*, pp. 69–72.
89. Howells, *Familiar Spanish Travels*, New York 1913, p. 104.
90. For what follows, Rivera, pp. 123–83.
91. Lhermite calculated that in the 1590s Aranjuez had 222,695 trees: Lhermite, II, 108.
92. Cf. Wilkinson, pp. 140–4.
93. Hoyo to king, 1562, BZ 146 f. 11.
94. Kubler, p. 70. For the Solomon thesis, the article by A. Martínez Ripoll, in *IV Centenario del Monasterio: La Biblioteca*, Madrid 1986, pp. 53–73.
95. Aranjuez, Apr. 1567, in Iñiguez Almech, p. 201.
96. BL Add. 28350 f. 100.
97. Cf. Wilkinson, p. 84. Herrera's publication in 1589 of drawings of the building served to forever associate his name with its construction: see Juan de Herrera, *Svmario y breve declaració de los diseños y estampas de la Fabrica de san Lorencio el Real del Escurial*, Madrid 1589.
98. Cf. Wilkinson, p. 103, who argues that the design which eventually prevailed was by Herrera.
99. Cf. Checa, pp. 231–2, discussing the allegedly 'secretive' aspect of the layout.
100. AGS: CR leg.247.
101. Sigüenza, II, 451.
102. Sigüenza, II, 450.
103. Mulcahy, p. 33.
104. See, in general, Checa, pp. 134–61.
105. Badoero, in Gachard 1944, p. 39.
106. Jane C. Nash, *Veiled Images. Titian's mythological paintings for Philip II*, Philadelphia 1985, is interesting, but posits an unacceptable tension between Titian's pagan themes and Philip's allegedly ultra-severe religion.

107. Lhermite, I, 98.
108. Sigüenza, II, 635–9.
109. J.K. Steppe, 'Mécénat espagnol et art flamand au XVIe siècle', in *Splendeurs d'Espagne et les villes belges 1500–1700*, 2 vols. Brussels 1985, I, 272.
110. Checa, p. 137.
111. Annie Cloulas, 'Les choix esthétiques de Philippe II: Flandre ou Italie', *Actas XXIII Congreso Internacional de Historia del Arte*, 3 vols. Granada 1977, II, 236–41.
112. I have been unable to consult Stephanie Breuer, *Alonso Sánchez Coello*, Munich 1984. However, her introduction to *Alonso Sánchez Coello y el retrato* is definitive.
113. On El Greco at this period, see Jonathan Brown, 'El Greco y Toledo', in *El Greco de Toledo*, Madrid 1982.
114. Wilkinson, p. 67f.
115. Wilkinson, p. 138.
116. Cloulas suggests that Philip had a choice between 'Flanders or Italy', but it seems reasonable to conclude that the 'or' should be 'and'.
117. Carl Justi, 'Felipe II como amante de las bellas artes', in *Estudios sobre Felipe II*, Madrid 1887, p. 269. Justi's essay was written in 1885; the book I have cited is normally catalogued under the name of G. Maurenbrecher; the original was in German.
118. Details from Michael Cooper, *The Japanese Mission to Europe, 1582–1590: The Journey of Four Samurai Boys through Portugal, Spain and Italy*, Folkestone 2005.
119. Eta Harich Schneider, 'Renaissance Europe through Japanese Eyes: Record of a Strange Triumphal Journey', *Early Music*, vol. 1, no. 1 (Jan. 1973), pp. 19–25.
120. Further fascinating details are in the book by Cooper. Of the four young Japanese, one Jesuit later ceased to be a Christian and got married, one died young, one was driven into exile and one died a martyr.

CHAPTER 4: THE MAGIC TEMPLE OF WISDOM

1. Popular books on the Escorial in Spanish in recent decades have opted almost wholly for fantasy, from imaginative novels to accounts of the alleged magic, mystery and diabolism concealed in the depths of the building.
2. For example, a webpage by a Dutch scholar from Delft, Marinus Gout, states that Philip II 'instructed the Jesuit Villalpandus to make a comprehensive study of King Solomon's Temple with the intention to erect a building in which the unity of church and state could be realized in the 16th century. This building had to become the centre of government for the whole empire of King Philip II.' The whole statement is undocumented fantasy.

3. 'Si l'idée de reproduire le temple de Salomon ne préexista pas à la construction de l'Escorial, il est certain que sa forme définitive chercha à en évoquer l'image': Edouard-Laurent, p. 19.

4. Taylor, in Select Bibliography.

5. Cornelia von der Osten Sacken, *San Lorenzo el Real de El Escorial: Studien zur Baugeschichte und Ikonologie*, Mittenwald 1979. The book was translated into Spanish in 1984.

6. Much of what follows is based on the Introduction to the brilliant Catalogue of the Museum of the History of Science, Broad Street, Oxford, for the exhibition *The Garden, the Ark, the Tower, the Temple: biblical metaphors of knowledge in early modern Europe* (1998), with text by Jim Bennett and Scott Mandelbrote.

7. King Solomon was supposed to be the author of several sacred books of the Bible which the early Church accepted but that were later excluded from the official canon of the Bible. In addition a so-called 'Testament of Solomon', or 'Book of Solomon', which circulated in manuscript from the fifteenth century in Europe, had a specifically occult character.

8. Samantha Kelly, *The New Solomon: Robert of Naples (1309–1343) and Fourteenth-century Kingship*, London 2003.

9. Maurice Lee, *Great Britain's Solomon: James VI and I in his Three Kingdoms*, Urbana, Illinois 1990.

10. Howarth, pp. 82–4.

11. Cf. the useful outline of Montano's work in Hänsel, noted in the Select Bibliography.

12. Ehsan Ahmed, 'Wisdom and Absolute Power in Guillaume Budé's *Institution du Prince*', *Romanic Review*, March 2005.

13. James Cracraft and Daniel Rowland, eds, *Architectures of Russian Identity, 1500 to the Present*, Ithaca, NY 2003, p. 45. For a popular presentation of the figure of Solomon in Russian history and mythology, see the webpage (in Russian) http://sergmoro.narod.ru/part1.html.

14. Muñoz, p. 135.

15. Daniel B. Rowland, 'Moscow – The Third Rome or the New Israel?', *Russian Review*, vol. 55, no. 4 (Oct. 1996), pp. 591–614.

16. 'David, aged and full of days, chose his son Solomon as king.'

17. Calvete de Estrella, pp. 127, 284.

18. Calvete de Estrella, p. 65.

19. Vilá y Tomás, p. 292.

20. Calvete de Estrella, p. 211.

21. 'I have set no limits to his power.'

22. Calvete de Estrella, p. 84.

23. Calvete de Estrella, pp. 90, 158.

24. Felipe de La Torre, *Institución de un rey christiano, colegiada principalmente de la Santa Escritura y de Sagradas Doctores*, Antwerp 1556.

25. Philip to Emperor Ferdinand, London, 18 May 1557, in CODOIN, II, 476.

26. Some years later, De Heere turned Calvinist and fled to England, where he became a prominent portrait painter.

27. Sigüenza, II, 414.
28. Sigüenza, II, 440.
29. 'Die wichtigste Zeit für Arias' künstlerische Aktivitäten bildteten sicherlich die knapp sechs Jahre in den Niederlanden', Hänsel, p. 203.
30. Kamen 2003, p. 211.
31. Quoted in Alvarez Turienzo, p. 198.
32. Bustamante García, pp. 636–9; Hänsel, p. 163.
33. Sigüenza, II, 215.
34. Sharpe, p. 872 n.115.
35. Cf. Vaughan Hart, *Art and Magic in the Court of the Stuarts*, London 1994, p. 69.
36. H. Rosenau, *Vision of the Temple: the image of the Temple of Jerusalem in Judaism and Christianity*, London 1979.
37. Ludwig Heinrich Heydenreich, *Architecture in Italy 1400–1500*, New Haven and London 1996, p. 105.
38. The relevance of the Milan hospital was first, I think, suggested by Secundino Zuazo, 'Los orígenes arquitectónicos del Real Monasterio de San Lorenzo de El Escorial', pp. 105–54, discurso leído en el acto de su recepción pública. Real Academia de Bellas Artes de San Fernando, Madrid, 1953.
39. Taylor in Select Bibliography.
40. J.B. Bury points out that 'a notable contrast between the architectural compositions of Juan Bautista and those of his contemporaries and successors at the Escorial is his predilection for the cubic figure and spaces based on multiples of cubes': *Burlington Magazine*, vol. 137, no. 1106, May 1995.
41. Frances A. Yates, *Giordano Bruno and the Hermetic Tradition*, London 1964, reprinted Chicago 1991, is the best outline of the cult of Hermetism.
42. Taylor, I, 89.
43. Taylor, I, 85.
44. Taylor, I, 94.
45. Taylor, I, 90. Sigüenza's statement was that the plan by Herrera 'imitó mucho a la del mismo Salomón': Sigüenza, II, 440.
46. Sigüenza, II, 662.
47. Juan Rafael de la Cuadra Blanco, 'The origins of Solomonism of the Escorial in the Netherlands', in Wim de Groot, *The Seventh Window*, Hilversum 2005, p. 169.
48. The list of speculations in the essay by Juan Rafael de la Cuadra Blanco is too extensive to detail here. I have made every effort to accept any credible suggestion, but it is obvious that Cuadra Blanco's thesis rests wholly on hypothesis and is unsupported by virtually any solid fact. Only one fact seems, as the author states, wholly 'indisputable': when living in Brussels in 1558, Philip II had a dog called Solomon (p. 173). My scepticism over Cuadra Blanco's arguments does not detract from admiration for his meticulous pursuit of the 'Solomon' theme and its connections with Philip II. His accumulation of data can be consulted on his webpage: http://www.delacuadra.net/escorial/.

49. Cuadra Blanco, 'The origins of Solomonism', p. 173.
50. Cabrera de Córdoba, I, 246, refers to a votive mass for Charles on 28 November.
51. The street ceremonies, in which the higher aristocracy of Europe participated, included a sermon preached in the cathedral in honour of the dead emperor.
52. Cuadra Blanco suggests that Philip hit on the idea that day because he was listening to the sermon, given by a notable Flanders cleric who made a reference to King Solomon. Since the sermon was given in French, a language which Philip did not understand at that period (even his father, let us remember, spoke to him in Castilian and not in French), it is highly unlikely that the king would have grasped anything the preacher said.
53. The Escorial is brought into play, for example, by the historian Jorge Cañizares-Esguerra in an impossibly wide-ranging argument in favour of 'Atlantic history'; see e.g. his 'Entangled Histories: Borderland Historiographies in New Clothes?', in *American Historical Review*, vol. 112, no. 3, June 2007.
54. An exception is the contribution by Osten Sacken. The most persistent speculations have come from Juan Rafael de la Cuadra Blanco, 'El Escorial y el Templo de Salomón', in *Anales de Arquitectura*, no. 7, Valladolid (1996). See above, note 47.
55. The Siliceo letters that follow are cited from J.M. March, *Niñez y Juventud de Felipe II*. 2 vols. Madrid 1941, I, 68–78, unless otherwise stated.
56. In my *Philip of Spain* I commented ungenerously on Philip's abilities. Ten years later, I feel that there is good reason to revise my previous judgements.
57. For the state of Latin among Spain's elite, see Luis Gil Fernández, *Panorama social del humanismo español (1500–1800)*, Madrid 1981.
58. Juan Huarte de San Juan, *Examen de Ingenios para las ciencias*, Seville 1594, f. 110v.
59. Angel González Palencia, *Gonzalo Pérez*, 2 vols. Madrid 1946, I, 108.
60. Antolín, p. 341.
61. AGS: CR leg.78.
62. Perhaps the only notable private library in Spain at the time was that of Columbus's son, Fernando Colón, in Seville.
63. Juan Páez de Castro, *Memoria a Felipe II sobre la utilidad de juntar una buena biblioteca*, Junta de Castilla y León, n.p. 2003, pp. 61–2.
64. Torre, *Institución de un Rey Christiano*, p. 24.
65. Cf. Lazure, p. 73.
66. King to Álava, 24 Dec. 1568, in Rodríguez and Rodríguez, no. 143.
67. Rodríguez and Rodríguez, no. 132.
68. King to Álava, 17 Dec. 1567, in Rodríguez and Rodríguez, no. 77.
69. The studies on the library are very numerous. Among recent essays, see François Géal, 'Supervivencias humanísticas en la España tridentina de finales del siglo XVI: el caso de la Biblioteca escurialense', *CRITICON*, 78, 2000, pp. 5–28.
70. Antolin, p. 367.
71. BL Eg 2047 f. 296.

72. BL Eg 2047 f. 302.
73. Gil Fernández, pp. 710–15. Hesiod describes Chaos in his poem *Theogony*.
74. Sigüenza, II, 437.
75. Morales, p. 214.
76. Philip encouraged the collection of state papers into a central repository in the old castle of Simancas, near Valladolid. The deposit had been begun by Francisco de los Cobos, but Philip as regent in 1545 took the first official steps to store papers. In 1578 he approved the construction of a building designed by Juan de Herrera.
77. Zayas to Álava, Madrid, 10 Sept. 1568, in Rodríguez and Rodríguez, no. 113.
78. Baudouin (1520–73) had been active in religious debates in the Netherlands.
79. Rodríguez and Rodríguez, doc. 51.
80. Quiroga to Philip II, 23 Sept. 1577, BL Eg 1506 f. 67v.
81. Very many years ago, I requested in the British Museum a book that turned out to be in the secret deposit. I was summoned personally to the librarian, and carefully grilled on my motives for wishing to read this prohibited work. François Géal, 'La notion d'enfer de la bibliothèque dans l'Espagne des XVIe et XVIIe siècles', *Bulletin du bibliophile*, no. 2, Paris 2004, pp. 271–300, gives some brief information on the theme.
82. AHN Inq leg.4470[1] no. 4; leg.4517[1] no. 1. Cf. also J. Pardo Tomás, *Ciencia y Censura. La Inquisición Española y los libros científicos en los siglos XVI y XVII*, Madrid 1991, pp. 289–91.
83. Sigüenza, II, 441, appears to state that Queen Anna's visit took place in June 1576.
84. The Austrian archdukes Albert and Wenzel, younger brothers of Anna, had come to Spain with her.
85. San Gerónimo, *Memorias*, CODOIN, VII, 126–8.
86. Luis García Ballester, *Los Moriscos y la Medicina*, Barcelona 1984, p. 39.
87. García Ballester, *Los Moriscos*, p. 54.
88. To Francés de Álava, Escorial, 28 May 1567, in Rodríguez and Rodríguez, no. 51.
89. Jeremy Lawrence, ' "Une bibliothèque foro complète pour un grand seigneur": Gondomar's manuscripts and the Renaissance idea of the library', *Bulletin of Spanish Studies*, vol. 81, nos 7–8, 2004, p. 1,089.
90. Mariana, 'Del rey y de la institución real', *Obras*, vol. 2, p. 553.
91. Antolín, p. 400.
92. Antolín, p. 402.
93. Jaime Moll, 'Problemas bibliográficas del libro del Siglo de Oro', *Boletín de la Real Academia Española*, 59, 1979; also his 'Valoración de la industria editorial española del siglo XVI', in *Livre et lecture en Espagne et en France sous l'Ancien Régime*, Paris 1981.
94. Cf. Andrew Pettegree, 'Centre and Periphery in the European Book World', *Transaction of the Royal Historical Society*, XVIII, 2008.
95. For a perspective on humanism and learning in Spain at this time, an excellent survey is Gil Fernández, *Panorama social del humanismo español*.

96. H. de Vries de Heekelingen, *Correspondance de Bonaventura Vulcanius pendant son séjour à Cologne, Genève et Bâle (1573–1577)*, The Hague 1923, p. 28:

In Hispania omnibus maximum fit studiorum detrimentum. Inter aulicos summa con miseria degitur. Compluti nullus fere est profitendi locus cum utilitate conjunctus, ne milli suas habent cathedras, quas vocant, neque iis nisi Hispanos praeficiunt. Praterea aestate summa hic per totos quinque menses solitudo est. Salamantiae vigent leges, sordet medicina, sordent literae.

De Smit (rendered in Latin as Vulcanius) left Spain for Belgium in 1570 in the company of the duke of Medinaceli. He died in 1614, professor of Greek at Leiden.

97. What follows is drawn mainly from the excellent essay by Goodman, pp. 3–19.
98. Note by king on letter from Pero Nuñez to Mateo Vázquez, 19 Aug. 1579, in Gaspar Muro, *Vida de la princesa de Éboli*, Madrid 1877, appendix 62.
99. Francisco Rodríguez Marín, *Felipe II y la alquimia*, Madrid 1927, p. 21.
100. To Zúñiga, 29 Aug. 1574, BL Add. 28357 vol. 1 f. 41.
101. The horns and other animal bones are listed in the inventory of his goods sold in 1603: Favre, 37 ff. 123–31.
102. Goodman, pp. 233–8.
103. Paula de Vos, 'The Science of Spices: Empiricism and Economic Botany in the Early Spanish Empire', *Journal of World History*, vol. 17, no. 4, 399–427. This author states, at p. 423, that in the 1580s 'two million pounds of ginger reached Seville annually', but I seriously doubt whether this is true. Moreover, as Robert W. Allen and Ken Albala point out in their *Food in Early Modern Europe*, Westport, Connecticut, 2003, p. 46: 'fresh ginger would never have lasted on the lengthy voyage from India'. Who consumed the ginger? Certainly not the Spaniards. The medicinal uses of ginger were important, but if the ginger did not arrive fresh, how was it processed?
104. Paula de Vos, 'The Science of Spices', p. 425.
105. Cf. Braudel, II, 762, for other perspectives.
106. J. A. Maravall, *Antiguos y modernos. La idea de progreso en el desarrollo inicial de una sociedad*, Madrid 1966.
107. Richard L. Kagan, ed., *Spanish Cities of the Golden Age. The views of Anton van den Wyngaerde*, Berkeley 1989. In the same years Joris Hoefnagel also prepared a series of sketches of Spanish towns for a work he published in 1572.
108. Ambrosio de Morales, *Las antiguedades de las ciudades de España*, Alcalá 1575, p. 4.
109. Hernández to Philip II, 30 Apr. 1572, in Varey, *Mexican Treasury*, p. 49.
110. Varey, *Mexican Treasury*, pp. 52, 55, 62.
111. Varey, *Mexican Treasury*, p. 4.

112. For the various foreign publications of fragments of the work, see in particular the chapter by J. M. López Piñero and J. Pardo Tomás, in Simon Varey et al., *Searching for the Secrets*.

CHAPTER 5: THE PRISONER OF THE ESCORIAL

1. Edward Grierson, *The Fatal Inheritance*, London 1969, p. 146.
2. Ford, III, 1205.
3. Norman Davies, *Europe: a history*, Oxford 1996, p. 534.
4. Mulcahy, p. 31.
5. Mariana, II, 550.
6. See the diagram of their travels in Henry Kamen, *Spain 1469–1714. A Society of Conflict*, 3rd edn, New York 2005.
7. Challoner to Queen Elizabeth I, 3 Aug. 1559, CSP, Foreign 1558–9, 503.
8. Feria to Granvelle, 7 Sep. 1560, BP MS.II/2291 ff. 205–8.
9. Philip to Granvelle, Toledo, 27 Dec. 1559, in Weiss, V, 672.
10. Fernando Checa, 'Monarchic Liturgies and the Hidden King', in Allan Ellenius, ed., *Iconography, Propaganda and Legitimation*, Oxford 1998, p. 98. Checa, of course, is fully aware of the fact that Philip was seen in more corners of Spain than any other Spanish ruler after Ferdinand and Isabella, and was therefore the least 'hidden' of the Habsburg kings. This has not deterred other researchers from claiming, with no evidence of any sort, that Philip II hid himself. With respect to the Escorial, a recent Spanish scholar claims that the king was 'a monarch who hid himself inside this building' (J.M. Matilla, in *El Linaje del Emperador*, Cáceres 2000, p. 94).
11. Alberi, serie I, vol. 5, p. 357.
12. Contarini, *Relazione*, in Alberi, serie I, vol. 5, p. 422.
13. Gautier, p. 104.
14. Antonio Ballesteros, in his *Síntesis de Historia de Espana*, Barcelona 1986, p. 299.
15. Cf. Carmelo Lisón Tolosana, *La imagen del rey. Monarquía, realeza y poder ritual en la Casa de los Austrias*. Madrid 1991, p. 85: 'his expression glacial, dressed always in black, walking slowly and solemnly'. It would be interesting to discover where the author obtained this wholly fictitious image.
16. Previously attributed to Sánchez Coello.
17. Gachard 1944, p. 121.
18. In Spain, until recently widows habitually wore black for the remainder of their lives. In small villages a generation ago, everyone seemed to be permanently dressed in black.
19. Juan de Mal Lara, *Recebimiento que hizo la muy noble y muy leal Ciudad de Sevilla*. Seville 1570, p. 47.
20. Juan de Varaona, *Viaje de Felipe II a Inglaterra en 1554*, in CODOIN, I, Madrid 1842, p. 572.
21. Secretary Courtewille, cited in Gachard 1867, p. 51.
22. Venetian ambassador Soranzo, cited in Gachard 1867, p. 99.

23. Henrique Cock, *Relación del viaje hecho por Felipe II en 1585*, ed. A. Morel-Fatio and A. Rodríguez Villa. Madrid 1876, p. 226.
24. Longlée to Henry III, 31 Jan. 1586, in Mousset, p. 217.
25. Cock, *Relación del viaje*, p. 253.
26. Longlée to Catherine de' Medicis, 8 Feb. 1586, in Mousset, p. 226.
27. The splendid John L. Motley, in his classic *The Rise of the Dutch Republic*, London 1912 edn, pp. 75–6, refers to Philip as 'deficient in manly energy, pedant, bigot, cold, mediocre, grossly licentious'.
28. Some of the Venetian ambassadors, who had a barely concealed dislike of the king and of things Spanish, are the principal source for the claim (accepted unquestioningly by Gachard, for example) that 'the king has little liking for festivities and spectacles. In his youth he sometimes took part in jousts and tourneys, but less out of taste for it than in order to satisfy opinion': Gachard 1867, p. 203. Ambassador Morosini, one of the more inventive of them, stated that Philip 'governs these peoples in Castile with an iron rod', and is the source for the phrase: 'they say proverbially in Spain that from the king's smile to his dagger there is no distance'; both cited in Gachard 1867, pp. 221, 227. It is important to treat the Venetian reports with great caution. Apart from their anti-Spanish prejudices, they contradict themselves, and sometimes even copy each other without attribution.
29. Pierre de Bourdeille, abbé de Brantôme, *Oeuvres complètes*, Paris 1866, XII, 91: 'il s'y fit de très beaux tournois et combatz à cheval et à pied, sur tout à Binche, chez la reyne d'Hongrie, où il ne se fit jamais partie, fust à pied, fust à cheval, que le roy d'Espaigne n'en fust et ne fist la sienne, où il acquist tousjours la réputation des mieux faisans et combattans, et de force et d'adresse, monstrant tousjours les armes si belles en la main qu'il emportoit toulsjours le prix. Aussi estoit-il de fort bonne grâce, beau et agréable, blond, et qui s'habilloit fort bien, comme j'ay veu'.
30. Both occasions are dealt with in my biography, *Philip of Spain*.
31. This is the image given in Gregorio Marañón, *Antonio Pérez*, 2 vols. Madrid 1958, I, 44–7, and followed thereafter by many historians.
32. Pérez de Herrera, in Cabrera de Córdoba, IV, 359.
33. Gachard 1944, p. 112.
34. Bustamante García, p. 675.
35. J. Zarco Cuevas, *Ideales y normas de gobierno de Felipe II*, Escorial 1927, p. 48. The document purports to be the king's 'testament' but no available evidence corroborates this.
36. For meetings of the Cortes, in 1563–4 and 1585–6, as well as for other reasons; and to Aragon alone in 1592.
37. For a detailed treatment of all the travels, see my *Philip of Spain*.
38. HHSA, Spanien, Varia, karton 2, n.
39. HHSA, Spanien, Varia, karton 2, s, f. 34.
40. HHSA Spanien, Varia, karton 2, s, ff. 34, 43.
41. Gachard 1867, p. 335.
42. Kubler, p. 109, states incorrectly that the king slept for the first time in San Lorenzo in 1571. He is also mistaken when stating (p. 126) that the king did not stay at San Lorenzo between 1571 and 1575.

43. BL Add.28354 f. 392.
44. In 1585, for instance: MZA: RAD, K 9/24, 'Relacion . . . para . . . Dietristan', Feb. 1585.
45. Sigüenza, II, 434.
46. King to chamberlain, 10 July 1572: BL Add. 28354 f. 422. The queen's chamberlain at this date was Antonio de la Cueva, marquis of Ladrada.
47. BL Add.28354 f. 414.
48. King to Vázquez, San Lorenzo, 13 July 1577, IVDJ, 53, carpeta 6, f. 39.
49. Cabrera de Córdoba, II, 198.
50. Memo from committee of ministers, Toledo, 11 June 1591, BZ 186 f. 6.
51. Diary of secretary Antonio Gracián, BL Add.28355 f. 30v. The king worked at his papers all Christmas Day and the day after, but the courier could not take the papers out because of a massive winter storm.
52. BL Add.28354 f. 370.
53. King to marquis of Ladrada, 2 Oct. 1572, BL Add. 28354 f. 490.
54. Sigüenza, II, 441.
55. Sigüenza, II, 465.
56. Gachard 1867, p. 63.
57. San Gerónimo, *Memorias*, CODOIN, VII, 369.
58. HHSA, Spanien, Varia, karton 3, c, f. 26.
59. Mousset, p. 59, letter of 21 Apr. 1584.
60. Details from Sepúlveda, p. 29.
61. San Gerónimo, *Memorias*, CODOIN, VII, 385, 394.
62. HHSA, Spanien, Varia, karton 3, c, f. 37a.
63. Ambassador Zane, 8 Mar. 1586, CSPV, VIII, 145.
64. Fernando Bouza Álvarez, *Cartas de Felipe II a sus hijas*, Madrid 1988, p. 107.
65. Longlée to Catherine de' Medicis, 12 May 1586, in Mousset, p. 261.
66. Sigüenza, II, 474.
67. Sigüenza, II, 479.
68. Sepúlveda, p. 117, in Zarco Cuevas, IV.
69. Quevedo, p. 75.
70. Lhermite, I, 257.
71. Sepúlveda, p. 170, in Zarco Cuevas, IV.
72. Lhermite, I, 292.
73. In 1581: BZ 142 f. 63.
74. This is explained in the 'Avisos de la Corte', in HHSA, Spanien, Varia, karton 2, p, f. 30.
75. Ambassador Soranzo, 1565, Alberi, serie I, vol. 5, p. 113.
76. HHSA, Spanien, Varia, karton 3, c, f. 21.
77. They were informed by the Catalan cleric Miquel Giginta, who happened to travel with the Frenchman on a journey from Madrid to Barcelona: Giginta to Mateo Vázquez, 11 Jan. 1583, IVDJ, 21 ff. 148–57.
78. 'Espejo que se propone', BL Eg. 330 ff. 4–20.
79. For Lafuente's quotation and its context, see Kamen 2008, chap. 5.

CHAPTER 6: A BRACE OF EAGLES: IMAGES OF
POWER AND MONARCHY

1. Dumas, *Adventures in Spain*, quoted in Cable, p. 139.
2. Jean-Frédéric Schaub, *La France espagnole. Les raciness hispaniques de l'abso-lutisme français*, Paris 2003, p. 31. There were many antecedents for this idea, perhaps the first being the publication by an exiled French Protestant, Quesnot de la Chesnée, of *Parallèle de Philippe II et Louis XIV sur le renverse-ment de la Monarchie Universelle*, Cologne 1709.
3. Henri Hauser, *La prepondérance espagnole (1559–1660)*, Paris 1933.
4. Cf. Schaub, *La France espagnole*, pp. 63–4.
5. Braudel, *Mediterranean*. Braudel's work was first published in 1949.
6. The best survey of Philip's decision-making is Hugo de Schepper, 'Ensayo sobre el modelo del proceso de decisión política en los Países Bajos de Felipe II', *Tussen twee culturen*, Nijmegen 1991, pp. 173–98.
7. His correspondence on the question, written mostly from the Escorial, is in AGS: E leg.168.
8. Édouard-Laurent, p. 9.
9. Marie Tanner, *The Last Descendant of Aeneas: the Hapsburgs and the mythic image of the emperor*, New Haven, Connecticut 1993, p. 133.
10. Roy Strong, *Splendour at Court. Renaissance spectacle and illusion*, London 1973, pp. 101–9, 133–40.
11. Specifically, during Prince Philip's Fortunate Journey to the Netherlands (see Chapter 1 above), and during the queen of Spain's visit to the French royal family at Bayonne in 1565 (see my *Philip of Spain*, p. 103).
12. The published literature on each point is substantial, but this book is not the place to elaborate on the theme.
13. For France, there is an enormous historical literature on the origins of the theory and practice of absolutism. A good starting point is the study by Roland Mousnier, *The Assassination of Henry IV. The tyrannicide problem and the consolidation of the French Absolute Monarchy in the early seventeenth century*, London 1973.
14. Notably the Jesuit Juan de Mariana, whose study *On the King* was written during the reign of Philip II and published in the year of the king's death.
15. Jerónimo Castillo de Bobadilla, *Política para Corregidores*, 2 vols. Madrid 1597, especially vol. I, pp. 584–6.
16. The idea that Philip wanted the crown is repeated by writers who appear not to have studied any of the documents. For example, one states: 'Son système de représentation révèle, durant tout son règne, sa détermination à s'investir de la fonction impériale', Édouard-Laurent, p. 9. This statement is, to say the least, wholly fictional.
17. Cf. his instruction to Luis de Venegas, 26 Aug. 1555, cited in Maurenbrecher, Philippson and Justi, *Estudios sobre Felipe II*, p. 78.
18. King to count of Luna, 28 Jan. 1562, CODOIN, XCVIII, 287.
19. King to Luna, 4 July 1562, CODOIN, XCVIII, 344.
20. J.H. Elliott, *Imperial Spain 1469–1716*, Harmondsworth 1970, p. 253.

21. Wilkinson, p. 115.
22. Wilkinson, pp. 115, 136.
23. Destroyed in the 1755 earthquake.
24. I take the simile from Wilkinson, p. 77.
25. One author, however, believes that 'Philip's interest in formulating an imperial vocabulary that would argue the providential rule of the Habsburgs is expressed clearly in the building and decoration of the Torreão': Barbara von Barghahn, *Age of Gold, Age of Iron. Renaissance Spain and symbols of monarchy*, 2 vols. New York 1985, I, 99.
26. See the informative volume on *El Real Alcázar de Madrid. Dos siglos de arquitectura y coleccionismo en la Corte de los Reyes de España*, Madrid 1994.
27. Bouza, p. 22.
28. 'Pocos príncipes del siglo XVI estuvieron tan atentos como Felipe II a los términos en que se producía la difusión de la imagen monárquica', Bouza, p. 138. The care of the king in this respect was exclusively to soften image-making, not enhance it.
29. Cf. Kamen 1997, pp. 169–75.
30. The important fact that the intense image publicity in the Netherlands was wholly unrelated to Spain is too often overlooked. For example, in a good unpublished thesis on 'Epica e Imperio. Imitación virgiliana y propaganda política en la épica española del siglo XVI' (thesis for the Department of Philology, Autonomous University of Barcelona, 2001), Lara Vilá y Tomás calls our attention (pp. 277–8) to significant engravings by Hieronimus Wierix, but omits to relate them to the context of the country where they were published, namely the Netherlands. She relates them instead to a country where they were neither published nor seen – Spain.
31. Sarah Schroth, 'Veneration and Beauty. Messages in the Image of the King in the Sixteenth and Seventeenth Centuries', in Chiyo Ishikawa, ed., *Spain in the Age of Exploration 1492–1819*, Lincoln, Nebraska 2004.
32. Maria Kusche, 'El retrato cortesano en el reinado de Felipe II', in *Felipe II y el arte de su tiempo*, Madrid 1998, p. 350.
33. Cf. Jorzick, p. 197.
34. The Golden Fleece itself was, of course, a symbol of power, but to my knowledge no scholar has analysed the contexts in which Philip II employed it as such. In the Escorial the Fleece had no role whatsoever; all Philip's Fleece ceremonies were held in other palaces, principally the Alcázar of Madrid. For some treatment of the theme, see Joan Feliu Franch, 'El Toisón de Oro y la alquimia en la corte de Felipe II. De brazo armado de Dios a rey pastor', in Victor Minguez, ed., *Visiones de la monarquía hispánica*, Castellón de la Plana 2007, pp. 285–318.
35. Cf. Jorzick, p. 198.
36. Information quoted, without attribution, in Gérard Sabatier and Sylvène Edouard, *Les monarchies de France et d'Espagne (1556–1715)*, Paris 2001, p. 184.
37. 'There is a relative absence of representations of the king's image', and 'an almost total absence of prints made by Spanish artists': José Manuel

Matilla, 'El grabado de la casa de Austria: la imagen del rey, la difusión de la idea dinástica y la memoria de los hechos imperiales', in *El Linaje del Emperador*, Cáceres 2000, p. 94.

38. Barghahn, *Age of Gold, Age of Iron*, I, 93; Lara Vilá y Tomás, 'Epica e Imperio', p. 282. Lara Vilá also (pp. 289–90) extends the metaphor of the sun to the Escorial, which she identifies (on very slim evidence) as a solar image.

39. Jorzick, pp. 218–19.

40. *La tres admirable et triumphante entrée du tres hault et tres puissant Prince Philipe*, Antwerp 1550. Philip's triumph in the city lasted five days. On this motto, cf. Jorzick, p. 222. 'Nec spe nec metu' can be traced back to a speech by Cicero; it was also used by more than one Italian noble family (the Gonzaga, the Este).

41. Cf. Jorzick, pp. 224–6.

42. Alfonso Rodriguez de Ceballos, 'Felipe II y la escultura', in *Felipe II y el Arte*, p. 434.

43. Parker 1998 states (p. 5) that it became 'the official logo of the monarchy'. He has been followed by British historians, one of whom claims in a review of Parker's book that Philip, 'long before James Bond, used the motto *Non Sufficit Orbis* – the World is not Enough'. In fact, the motto had been used previously, e.g. by King Francis II of France (husband at one time of Mary of Scots and, as such, king of Scotland), and was never an official device of Philip II. In any case, the device found by English seamen in Santo Domingo in 1586 was made, according to the English writer George Puttenham three years later in his *The Art of Poesie* (1589), 'peraduenture without King *Philips* knowledge' (p. 88).

44. Cf. Rainer Wohlfeil, 'Las Alegorias de la paz de la fachada occidental del palacio de Carlos V', *Cuadernos de la Alhambra*, vols 31–2 (1995–6), Granada 1998.

45. A work by Victor Minguez, *Los reyes solares. Iconografía astral de la monarquía Hispánica*, Alicante 2001, argues that Philip II, and with him all the kings of Spain, were Sun Kings.

46. Schroth, 'Veneration and Beauty', p. 113, cited above, suggests that the 'symbolism of armor has been largely overlooked by art historians'. This may be true, but its alleged symbolism has also, in the case of Philip II, been exaggerated.

47. Braden Frieder, *Chivalry and the Perfect Prince. Tournaments, art, and armor at the Spanish Habsburg court*, Kirksville, Missouri 2009, pp. 163–7 gives a good description of the armour purchased and used by the prince during the Fortunate Journey.

48. Stephen V. Grancsay, 'A helmet made for Philip II of Spain', *Metropolitan Museum of Art Bulletin*, New Series, vol. 13, no. 9, May 1955.

49. Grancsay, 'A helmet', p. 272.

50. Curiously, peninsular scholars have neglected the role of tapestries when they consider the public imagery of Philip II. By contrast, Belgian scholars are more responsive to the theme. An exhibition of tapestries made for the

emperor and the king was held at St Peter's Abbey in Ghent, from November 2008 to March 2009. Titled 'Flemish Tapestries for the dukes of Burgundy, Emperor Charles V and King Philip II', it was coordinated by Fernando Checa, of the University of Madrid.

51. Cf. Hendrik J. Horn, *Jan Cornelisz Vermeyen. Painter of Charles V and his conquest of Tunis. Paintings, etchings, drawings, cartoons and tapestries*, Doornspijk 1989, 2 vols.

52. I owe some of the ideas in what follows to the stimulating volume by Lisa Jardine and Jerry Brotton, *Global Interests*, noted in the Select Bibliography.

53. Iain Buchanan, 'The tapestries acquired by King Philip II in the Netherlands in 1549–50 and 1555–59: new documentation', *Gazette des Beaux-Arts*, vol. 134, Oct. 1999, p. 133.

54. My reading of the tapestry, which may be mistaken, is that the boy depicted is Prince Philip, then aged eight years. However, Hendrik J. Horn, in his *Jan Cornelisz Vermeyen*, suggests that the boy is somebody else.

55. Delmarcel, p. 156.

56. Alberto de Nobili, *La triomphale entrata del Serenissimo Prence dispagna nell'inclita città di Milano*, Milan 1548.

57. The themes are dealt with in the commemorative exhibition volume by Lothar Altringer et al., *Emperor Charles V (1500–1558): Europe's power and weakness*, Milan 2000.

58. Jardine and Brotton, p. 126: Alba ordered 'a smaller set of the Tunis series in the 1550s; a composite tapestry of the Tunis victory, dated to 1568; and an imposing series entitled "Victories of the Duke of Alba", woven in the Low Countries in the 1560s'.

59. For this incident, see my *Alba*, pp. 118–19.

60. All figures from Delmarcel, p. 157.

61. Cf. Jardine and Brotton, p. 135.

62. *Henry II on Horseback* by the Atelier of François Clouet (1536–72), of *c.*1547, at Upton House.

63. A recent discussion is Karen Hearn, 'Elizabeth I and the Spanish Armada: a Painting and its afterlife', *Transactions of the Royal Historical Society* (2004), 6th Series, 14, pp. 123–40, which accepts, in line with other recent research, that the painting was done after the queen's death.

64. The black-and-white print, showing Philip on a steed with (apparently) a branch in his hand, is captioned in Flemish and describes its subject as 'prince of Spain'.

65. The Vatican archives, Archivio Segreto Vaticano, *A.A.*, *Arm. I–XVIII*, 522, contain an impressive seal of prince Philip (1555), 111 millimetres in diameter and made of solid gold.

66. For example, there is an equestrian drawing, as well as a reproduction of two ceremonial arches, in Juan de Mal Lara, *Recibimiento* (cited at n. 68 below), at the end of the publication.

67. *The Copie of a letter sent in to Scotlande*, by John Elder, London 1554.

68. See the appendix to Juan de Mal Lara, *Recibimiento que hizo la muy noble y muy leal Ciudad de Seville*, Seville 1570.
69. Longlée to King Henri III, 6 Mar. 1586, in Mousset, p. 237.
70. Enrique Cock, *Jornada de Tarazona hecha por Felipe II en 1592*, ed. Alfredo Morel-Fatio and Antonio Rodriguez Villa, Madrid 1879, p. 74.
71. Lhermite, I, 200.
72. Rosemarie Mulcahy, 'Two letters by Alonso Sánchez Coello', *Burlington Magazine*, vol. 126, Dec. 1984, p. 777.
73. William Cohen, 'Symbols of Power: Statues in Nineteenth-Century Provincial France', *Comparative Studies in Society and History*, vol. 31, no. 3 (July 1989).
74. Diego Villalta, 'Tratado de estatuas antiguas', cited in Alfonso Rodriguez G. de Ceballos, 'Felipe II y la escultura', in *Felipe II y el Arte*, p. 433.
75. Strada, II, 734–5.
76. The kings are Jehosaphat, Hezekiah, David, Solomon, Josiah and Menasseh.
77. Parker, p. 97.
78. 'Al rey no le gustaba la escultura': *Los Leoni*, p. 24. Arias Montano seems to have had an obsession with erecting statues. He was also the man responsible for the idea of erecting a statue to Alba in Antwerp. This was confirmed in information given to Cardinal Granvelle, see Luis Morales Oliver, *Arias Montano y la política de Felipe II en Flandes*, Madrid 1927, p. 144.
79. Tanner, *Last Descendant*, p. 132. Tanner positions these words strategically next to an illustration of the statue.
80. *Los Leoni*, pp. 128–9.
81. Cf. the comments in Kamen 2008, p. 34.
82. Wilkinson, p. 104.
83. Brown 1989, p. 25.
84. See Parker 1998, in Select Bibliography.
85. Parker also links the two figures in his essay, 'The place of Tudor England in the Messianic Vision of Philip II of Spain', *Transactions of the Royal Historical Society* (2002), 12.
86. Bouza, p. 13.
87. Ambassador Lippomano, 6 May 1587, CSPV, VIII, 272, 277.
88. Venetian ambassador Gritti, from Rome, 19 Mar. 1588, CSPV, VIII, 345.
89. Count of Portalegre to Esteban de Ibarra, 9 Dec. 1589: BCR MS.2417 f. 60.
90. March 1601, in CODOIN, XLIII, 570.
91. Don Juan de Silva to the marquis de Velada, 8 Nov. 1597, BNac, MS.6198 f. 32v.
92. David Armitage, 'The Elizabethan Idea of Empire', *Transactions of the Royal Historical Society*, 14 (2004), pp. 269–77. One should not omit to mention the recent British film *Elizabeth: the Age of Gold* (2007), which draws a contrast between a heroic Elizabeth and a diabolic Philip.
93. Armitage, p. 275.

94. Parker 1998.
95. In what follows, I avoid what would have been an interesting but excessively lengthy exercise, a detailed comparison of the two monarchs based on both English and Spanish sources. Instead, my brief observations concentrate only on Philip II.
96. Armitage, p. 275.
97. The stimulating presentation of 'Elizabethan imperialism' by Frances Yates in *Astraea. The Imperial Theme*, pp. 38–59, is perfectly valid within the cultural context she is describing, but cannot be applied to the political sphere.
98. A wide-ranging survey of the various Spanish myths about imperial power may be found in Kamen 2008, chap. 4, which also looks in more detail at the subject of Philip II as an imperialist.
99. Calvete de Estrella, p. 47. The Latin text means: 'I have placed no limits to his empire either in time or in space'.
100. See, for example, Yona Pinson, 'Imperial Ideology in the Triumphal Entry into Lille of Charles V and the Crown Prince (1549)', *Assaph. Studies in Art History*, no. 6, 2001.
101. Calvete de Estrella, pp. 84, 90.
102. Calvete de Estrella, pp. 115–16. The Latin means: 'Abraham gave Isaac all that he possessed', and 'I appoint him heir over all the peoples of the earth'.
103. See, for example, the essay by Teresa Ferrer Valls, 'Las fiestas públicas en la monarquía de Felipe II y Felipe III', online article (http://www.uv.es/entresiglos/teresa/pdfs/fiestaspub.PDF).
104. Armitage, p. 275.
105. Cf. Jean Barbey, *Être roi. Le roi et son gouvernement en France de Clovis à Louis XVI*, Paris 1992, p. 150.
106. Luis Sánchez Agesta, 'El poderío real absoluto' en el testamento de 1554', in *Carlos V (1500–1558)*, pp. 439–60. Cf. also José Antonio Maravall's views on absolutism: J. A. Maravall, *Estado moderno y mentalidad social*, 2 vols. Madrid 1972, I, 279–84.
107. Maravall, *Estado moderno*, I, 253.
108. The word 'majesty' can be found in use in both Castile and Catalonia (see Maravall, *Estado moderno* I, 255–6), but seldom as an official title.
109. Felipe de la Torre, *Institución de un Rey Christiano*, Antwerp 1556. Torre's book is concerned with education, not power.
110. Kamen 1997, p. 225.
111. Cf. the comments in my *Imagining Spain*, chap. 4.
112. These crucial aspects have never been adequately studied in the case of Philip, but will not be touched on here.
113. See the important and fundamental study by Teofilo Ruiz, 'Unsacred Monarchy. The Kings of Castile in the Late Middle Ages', reprinted in his *The City and the Realm: Burgos and Castile 1080–1492*, Aldershot 1992, chap. XIII.
114. Spain is notably absent from the essays edited by János Bak, *Coronations. Mediaeval and Early Modern monarchic ritual*, Berkeley 1990.

115. The cult of Elizabeth was a serious propaganda exercise, assiduously participated in by the court and carried out by its agents. There is an excellent summary of its extent in Roy Strong, *The Cult of Elizabeth. Elizabethan portraiture and pageantry*, Berkeley 1977.
116. 'Avisos de la Corte de España', report of Oct. 1564 to archduke Maximilian, HHSA Spanien, Varia, Karton 2, 1564, ff. 13–14.
117. Richard C. McCoy, *Alterations of State. Sacred Kingship in the English Reformation*, New York 2002, p. 59.
118. Armitage, p. 276.
119. Cf. my *Imagining Spain*, chap.4.
120. Anthony Pagden, *Lords of All the World. Ideologies of Empire in Spain, Britain and France c.1500–c.1800*, New Haven and London 1995, p. 49.
121. Cf. the quotation from Vázquez de Menchaca in Pagden, *Lords of All the World*, p. 58.
122. See my *Alba*, p. 153.
123. A recent French thesis gives information on aspects of Spanish espionage in France shortly after the reign of Philip II, but admits that the details uncovered are 'une partie minime de la réalité clandestine': Alain Hugon, *Au service du Roi Catholique. 'Honorables ambassadeurs' et 'Divins espions'. Representátion diplomatique et service secret dans les relations hispano-françaises de 1598 à 1635*, Madrid 2004, p. 159.
124. Among the many studies in English, see John M. Archer, *Sovereignty and Intelligence. Spying and Court Culture in the English Renaissance*, Stanford 1993; Alan Haynes, *Invisible Power. The Elizabethan Secret Services 1570–1603*, Stroud 1992.
125. For magnificences, cf. Yates, *Astraea*, p. 149.
126. Strong 1995, II, 123.
127. See Chapter 9, below, about the authorship of this painting.
128. Strong 1995, II, 5.
129. Strong 1977, p. 49.

CHAPTER 7: THE HALL OF BATTLES

1. Cf. Kubler, p. 34.
2. Parker, p. 97.
3. www8.madrid.org/gema/goc/131/12/267/
4. Anonymous historian, writing in the name of General Franco, in *El Escorial*, I, 3.
5. Agustín Bustamante García, 'La arquitectura de Felipe II', in *Felipe II y el Arte*, p. 504.
6. Jonathan Brown, *La Sala de Batallas de El Escorial*, Salamanca 1998, is a brief look at aspects of the Hall.
7. A recent Spanish popular work manages to list fourteen names of 'the great battles of Spanish history', but of these four are famous defeats (among them Trafalgar), five are actions in which Spaniards played only a minor role (including St Quentin), and two were actions within Spain

(Las Navas de Tolosa and Bailén). Juan Eslava Galán, *Grandes batallas de la Historia de España*, Madrid 1994, p. 11. There was obviously a need to give St Quentin a significant historical role.

8. See e.g. Édouard-Laurent: 'La construction du modèle de vertus, dont l'Escorial fut la vitrine, se place dans un contexte de volonté iréniste. L'irénisme, dans le système de représentation de Philippe II, se profile derrière la puissante image du roi de guerre'. In fact, there are no images of·a warlike king in the Escorial, and by the same token there are no images of a peaceful king either.

9. Cf. the reference above, in Chapter 2, to Merriman's presentation of Philip II as afraid to invade France after the victory at St Quentin.

10. *Adventures in Spain*, in Cable, p. 139.

11. *Castilian Days* (1871), in Cable, p. 141.

12. Cf. Thomas P. Campbell, *Tapestry in the Renaissance: Art and Magnificence*, New York 2002, p. 321.

13. Delmarcel, p. 155.

14. Cf. the details on Mühlberg in my *The Duke of Alba*, New Haven and London 2004, pp. 32–3.

15. *Spanish Cities of the Golden Age*, p. 228.

16. CSPV, VI, ii, 1063.

17. Gachard 1944, pp. 38, 93.

18. AGS: CR leg.78 no. 38, 'los retratos q Su Alteça tiene en su camara'. The portrait of Philip is now in the Prado.

19. All evidence for the statements that follow can be found in my biography, *Philip of Spain*.

20. Cf. the excellent article by Philip Williams, 'The Strategy of Galley Warfare in the Mediterranean (1560–1620)', in *Guerra y Sociedad*, I, 891–920, a work cited above in Chapter 2, note 6.

21. The literature on Lepanto is immense. A recent summary is Capponi 2006. The classic background study is Braudel's *Mediterranean*.

22. Gachard 1944, p. 118. Philip's alleged impassivity on hearing the news is part of the curious mythology fabricated around him. As the documents show, he rejoiced.

23. Cabrera de Córdoba, II, 121.

24. W. Stirling Maxwell, *Don John of Austria*, 2 vols. London 1883, I, 450.

25. *Memorias de fray Juan de San Gerónimo*, in CODOIN, VII, 82.

26. Stirling-Maxwell, *Don John of Austria*, I, 461.

27. For example, F. Javier Campos y Fernández de Sevilla, 'Cervantes, Lepanto y El Escorial', *Actas del IV Congreso Internacional de la Asociación de Cervantistas*, Palma 2001, p. 19.

28. Braudel, II, 1,128.

29. Sigüenza, II, 425.

30. Capponi, p. 294.

31. A recent French historian, Bartolomé Bennassar, writing about Lepanto, comments that paintings of the battle were 'innumerable', but every painting he mentions (*Don Juan de Austria*, Madrid 2000, pp. 205–10) was painted in Italy, none in Spain.

32. Cf. Vilá y Tomás, p. 296.
33. Capponi, p. 294.
34. There are very many studies of the impact on Italy; see, for example, Cecilia Gibellini, *L'immagine di Lepanto. La celebrazione della vittoria nella letteratura e nell'arte veneziana del Cinquecento*, Venice 2008.
35. Even today, paintings about Lepanto originate in Italy. As I write, in November 2008, the art museum El Prado is hosting an exhibition of a large pictorial frieze on the theme of Lepanto, done by the American artist Cy Twombly for the Venice Biennale in 2001.
36. 'It is he who backs them [Pérez and his wife] and has always done': MZA: RAD, G.140, karton 9, sign. 12a, 'Relacion . . . para . . . Dietristan'. Quiroga owed his nomination as archbishop of Toledo to Pérez's influence with the king.
37. Cf. Morán and Checa, p. 157.
38. Angela Delaforce, 'The Collection of Antonio Perez, Secretary of State to Philip II', *Burlington Magazine*, vol. 124, no. 957 (Dec. 1982), pp. 742–53.
39. Capponi, p. 294, states that 'The six large canvases of the battle by Luca Cambiaso, now in the Escorial, were probably gifts of Giovanni Andrea Doria to the royal secretary Antonio Pérez, acquired by the king at a later date.'
40. Among the very many artists one may single out Reinier Nooms, whose work is displayed in the National Maritime Museum, Greenwich.
41. The name Djerba was difficult for Castilians to pronounce and was subsequently rendered in Spanish as 'Gelves', a confusion of names that continues to muddle students of history.
42. Bustamante García, 'La arquitectura de Felipe II'.
43. Favre, 31 ff. 169, 293.
44. I have followed the version given by Famiano Strada, *Guerras de Flandes*, 7 vols. Antwerp 1748, V, 1,190, as being the most likely. But neither this nor any other version of Philip's response is verifiable.
45. Strada, V, 1,191.
46. Gachard 1848–79, II, lxxvi.
47. On a letter from Vázquez to king, 4 Sept. 1588, IVDJ, 51 f. 190.
48. Gachard 1848–79, II, lxxvii.
49. Lippomano to Senate, 6 Sept. 1588, CSPV, VIII, 386.
50. Sepúlveda, p. 59.
51. It is interesting to note that a handful of Castilian historians now suggest (one of the professors contributing to the volume mentioned above in Chapter 2, note 6, follows this line) that the Armada was really a victory for Spain, and that English historians have deliberately falsified the facts.
52. President Pazos to Mateo Vázquez, 19 Sept. 1580, IVDJ, 21 f. 803.
53. Cabrera de Córdoba, II, 616.
54. Figures from the account sent by ambassador Zane, Madrid, 23 July 1582, in CSPV, VIII, 39.
55. Printed account of the battle in CSPV, VIII, 41.

56. Mateo Vázquez to king, 22 Aug. 1583, IVDJ, 51 f. 105.
57. Comments of king on letter of Vázquez to king, 22 Aug. 1583, IVDJ 51 f. 105.
58. San Gerónimo, *Memorias*, 364.
59. The account that follows is my own suggestion for the way the decisions were made. Detailed research in the correspondence of the king would almost certainly unearth facts that would enable us to arrive at a more exact explanation of the circumstances outlined here.
60. Cf. Mulcahy, p. 36.
61. Mariana, II, 554.
62. Peter Paret, *Imagined Battles. Reflections of War in European Art*, Chapel Hill, N.C. 1997; John Hale, *Artists and Warfare in the Renaissance*, New Haven and London 1990.
63. The British Library, the Biblioteca Zabalburu and the Instituto de Valencia de Don Juan in Madrid possess the three main collections of Philip's correspondence that may continue to reveal surprises.

CHAPTER 8: POWERHOUSE OF FAITH

1. Parker 1998, p. 97.
2. For a discussion of this point, see Hillgarth, chap. 3.
3. Hillgarth, p. 131.
4. Guicciardini, 'Relazione di Spagna', *Opere*, Bari 1929–36, vol. X, p. 131.
5. For a discussion of views about religion, as well as references to recent studies on the question, see Kamen 2008, chap. 3.
6. Parker 1998, p. 97. Parker states that 'Philip certainly viewed himself as *rex et sacerdos*' (p. 96), but gives no documentary reference for the statement or for Philip ever having used the phrase. Surely, if he 'viewed himself' in this way, he would have said so. It would be interesting to see whether historians can unearth evidence on the subject.
7. Just two years, as it happened, after the official beatification of the Gorcum martyrs by the pope in Rome in November 1675.
8. Edward J. Sullivan, 'Politics and Propaganda in the *Sagrada Forma* by Claudio Coello', *Art Bulletin*, vol. 67, no. 2 (June 1985), gives the best discussion of the matter. The relic of the Sagrada Forma, preserved in a monstrance, is still put on display for the faithful in the Escorial once or twice a year in late autumn.
9. The painting was renamed *Allegory of the Holy League* by Anthony Blunt in 1940, but most authorities prefer the title *Adoration of the Name of Jesus*, which probably accords better with the historical context.
10. Sigüenza, II, 442.
11. Parker 1998, p. 75.
12. King to Vázquez, n.d., IVDJ envío 53, carpeta 7, f. 67.
13. Among the very few studies on it, three are basic: Kamen 1993; Sara T. Nalle, *God in La Mancha. Religion, Reform and the People of Cuenca 1500–1650*, Baltimore 1992 (e-book); and Allyson M. Poska, *Regulating*

the People. The Catholic Reformation in Seventeenth-century Spain, Boston 1998.

14. The seminal study is Marcel Bataillon, *Erasme et l'Espagne,* Paris 1937.
15. Calvete de Estrella, p. 281.
16. It is a common misapprehension to present the Jesuits as a Spanish order. The missionaries who entered Spain were indeed Spaniards, because they had to speak the language, but the order was based in and directed from Rome.
17. For the Italian component of the Counter-Reformation in Spain, see Kamen 1993.
18. Lynette M.F. Bosch, 'Image and devotion in late fifteenth- and early sixteenth-century Spanish painting', *Fenway Court* 28 (1998), p. 41.
19. The Spanish Church, thanks to the unique authority exercised over it by the crown, was for all practical purposes autonomous (i.e. outside papal control).
20. Order to Council of State, Apr. 1553, AGS: E leg.98 f. 156. The importance of this order needs emphasising. Many historians present an inexplicably fallacious image, of a king opposed to the decrees of Trent.
21. L'Aubespine to Francis II, 16 Sept. 1560, in Paris, p. 551.
22. Martín de Córdoba, bishop of Tortosa, to marquis of Pescara, Trent, 26 May 1562, CODOIN, IX, 217.
23. King to Luna, 12 May 1563, CODOIN, XCVIII, 438.
24. Sigüenza, II, 414.
25. Fr Gabriel del Estal, in *El Escorial 1563–1963,* p. 467.
26. For details of Philip's religious modernisation programme, see Kamen 1993.
27. Changes he proposed for the form of the mass in 1575 occupy four sides of paper: IVDJ, 53, carpeta 7, f. 51.
28. 'Advertimientos de mano de Su Md', dated 1571, AGS: E leg.583 ff. 258–60. The great-grandfather was, of course, Ferdinand the Catholic.
29. Sigüenza, II, 420.
30. Noone, p. 9.
31. The comment is by Peter Phillips, reviewing Noone's book in *Musical Times,* autumn 1998.
32. Timothy J. Schmitz, 'The Spanish Hieronymites and the Reformed Texts of the Council of Trent', *Sixteenth-Century Journal,* vol. 37, no. 2 (2006).
33. See Kamen 1993, pp. 154–5.
34. It is relevant to point out that the so-called 'Spanish' Church was made up of two autonomous Churches, one in Castile (where the metropolitan see was Toledo) and one in Aragon (where the metropolitan see was Tarragona).
35. Christian Péligry, 'El monasterio de San Lorenzo de el Escorial y la difusión de los libros litúrgicos en España (1573–1615)', *Primeras Jornadas de Bibliografía,* Madrid 1977.
36. Gautier, p. 104.
37. *Time,* 27 Sept. 1963.

38. The *autos* were those of 25 February 1550 in Toledo, 8 October 1559 in Valladolid, 5 March 1564 in Barcelona and 25 February 1591 in Toledo. He also attended one in Lisbon on 1 April 1582.

39. King to Catalina, Toledo, 10 June 1591, in Erika Spivakovsky, *Felipe II. Epistolario familiar. Cartas a su hija, la infanta doña Catalina (1585–1596)*, Madrid 1975, p. 127.

40. On this and related issues the evidence is absolutely clear; see references in Henry Kamen, *The Spanish Inquisition. A Historical Revision*, New Haven and London 1993, and in Kamen 2008.

41. Archbishop to Cardinal Alessandrino, Madrid, 26 Oct. 1566, BNac MS8246 f. 176, 'Registro di Lettere di Monsign Arcivescovo di Rossano'.

42. Kamen 1997, pp. 112–14.

43. Luciano Serrano, *Correspondencia diplomática entre España y la Santa Sede*, 4 vols. Madrid 1914, II, xxxix.

44. To Francés de Álava, 14 Oct. 1568, in Rodríguez and Rodríguez, no. 126.

45. Philip to Don Juan, Nov. 1576, AGS: E leg.570 f. 88.

46. The sources of the statements may be found in Kamen 1997.

47. 'Lo que pareció sobre los quarto papeles que dio a Su Majestad el presidente Richardot por orden del Duque de Parma. En Aranjuez a 11 de noviembre 1589', AGS: E leg.2855.

48. The proposal was referred to the pope, who refused to condone it.

49. The article by Guy Lazure (Select Bibliography) has a useful discussion.

50. Álvarez, p. 121.

51. Sigüenza, II, 500.

52. Sigüenza, II, 431.

53. They were returned from Santiago to Braga: Favre, vol. 29, f. 132.

54. Morales, pp. 204–5.

55. Ambrosio de Morales, *Viaje por orden del rey Phelipe II a los reynos de Leon y Galicia y Asturias*, Madrid 1765, p. 207.

56. The words of Lazure, p. 64.

57. Many rulers, of course, used relics for political purposes. The question is whether Philip did so. In one case history, concerning early medieval Anglo-Saxon kings in England, a scholar demonstrates that the kings used relics in three ways: collecting them in order to increase their own prestige and symbolise their status; employing them in the process of government; and patronising specific relic-cults in order to extend political influence: D. W. Rollason, 'Relic-cults as an instrument of royal policy *c*.900–*c*.1050', *Anglo-Saxon England*, vol. 15 (1986), pp. 91–103. Only the first of these three practices can be applied to Philip II.

58. Lazure, p. 66.

59. Mulcahy, p. 71 et passim.

60. Balthasar Porreño, *Dichos y hechos del rey D. Felipe II*, Madrid 1942, p. 94.

61. Cited in Lazure, p. 60.

62. Cf. Checa, pp. 408, 417.

63. Cabrera de Córdoba, II, 198: 'gozando lo que tanto deseaba'.

64. Sigüenza, II, 467.

65. The exception is Eire, pp. 258–9.
66. *The Catholic Encyclopedia*, 15 vols. New York 1908, vol. IV, p. 281, item: 'consecration'.
67. Sigüenza, II, 485.
68. Subsequently, a monk claimed that the king was taken up the mountainside in his chair so that he could view the sight from his so-called favourite vantage point, the Silla del Rey, but in light of Philip's state of health this seems unlikely, and Sigüenza makes no mention of it.
69. The best brief summary of the origins of the Bible is given by Angel Sáenz-Badillos, 'La Biblia Regia', in *Felipe II en la Biblioteca Nacional*, Madrid 1998.
70. B. Rekers, *Benito Arias Montano*, Leiden 1972, chap. 3. This interesting study has several important factual errors.
71. CODOIN, vol. 41, pp. 316, 387.
72. The argument is presented in Rekers, *Benito Arias Montano*.
73. Gregorio de Andrés, *Proceso inquisitorial del Padre Sigüenza*, Madrid 1975.

CHAPTER 9: INVENTING THE ESCORIAL

1. Cited in Hillgarth, p. 95.
2. Hillgarth, p. 97.
3. The author was Juan Alonso de Almela, the work the 'Descripción de la Octava Maravilla del Mundo', a manuscript of 1594 that was not published until 1962.
4. Most Spanish *castillos*, now either in ruins or transformed into hotels, were defensive structures medieval in origin, and some (like the castle in Segovia) were subsequently made into residences. A few later noble residences, like the palace of the Infantados in Guadalajara, were fifteenth-century in origin.
5. Though Philip II occasionally used the form 'king of Spain' for convenience, the phrase never constituted an official title. The first king of a politically united Spain was Philip V, in the early eighteenth century.
6. For details of this interesting and often forgotten project, see Kamen 1993, p. 154.
7. Álvarez Turienzo, p. 208.
8. The Comintern agent in Madrid Georgi Dimitrov reported to Voroshilov in the Kremlin: 'When the Fascists were nearing Madrid, Carrillo, who was in control at the time, gave the order to shoot the arrested Fascist functionaries': Ronald Radosh, Mary Radosh Habeck and Grigory Sevostianov, *Spain Betrayed: The Soviet Union in the Spanish Civil War*, New Haven and London 2001, p. 223, document 46.
9. Frances Lannon, *The Spanish Civil War, 1936–1939*, London 2002, p. 48.
10. For a survey of this xenophobic hostility towards the monarchy, see Kamen 2008.
11. Letter of Florentine ambassador, Madrid, 31 July 1568, quoted in Gachard 1867, p. 481.

12. Kubler, for example (chap.1), gives importance principally to denigration by foreigners.
13. Quevedo, p. 49.
14. For criticisms of the king, see Kamen 1997, chap. 12.
15. The document is printed in full in an appendix to Kubler's study of the Escorial. The copy that I consulted is in the National Library in Madrid.
16. Richard Kagan, *Lucrecia's Dreams. Politics and Prophecy in Sixteenth-century Spain*, Berkeley 1990, p. 127. See also Maria Jordan, 'Real Dreams, Created Dreams: The Prophetic Tradition in the Dreams of Lucrecia de León' (Ph.D. thesis, University of Minnesota, 1998).
17. 'Sueños desde fin de Março de 1588 hasta 18 de abril 1590', AHN Inq leg.3712² exped. 2, pieza 4, ff. 25, 27, 33, 38.
18. The disturbances were provoked by supporters of Antonio Pérez, the king's former secretary, who had escaped to Saragossa.
19. Antonio de Herrera, *Historia General del Mundo, del tiempo del Señor Rey don Felipe II el Prudente, desde el año de 1559 hasta el de 1598*, 3 vols. Madrid 1601–12, III, 291.
20. Ambassador Badoero, in Alberi, ser. I, vol. 5, p. 277.
21. Cabrera de Córdoba, III, 205.
22. Unsigned memoir, printed in CODOIN, VI, 452.
23. The Jesuit Ribadeneira, cited in Fernando Bouza, 'Portugal en la monarquía hispánica (1580–1640)', unpublished doctoral thesis, Complutensian University, Madrid, 1987, p. 101.
24. Cabrera de Córdoba, II, 205.
25. President Antonio Mauriño de Pazos to Vázquez, Madrid, 9 June 1580, IVDJ, 21 f. 782.
26. President to Vázquez, Madrid, 10 Mar. 1582, IVDJ, 21 f. 875.
27. Despatch by Longlée, 23 Apr. 1585, in Mousset, p. 130.
28. BCR MS.2417 f. 37.
29. Consulta by Poza, 1 Aug. 1595, BL Add.28377 ff. 72–3.
30. Sigüenza, II, 409.
31. Sigüenza, II, 443. The reference to the 'towns' is because the towns of Castile were the principal payers of taxes.
32. San Gerónimo, *Memorias*, 155.
33. Sigüenza, II, 439.
34. Sigüenza, II, 653, 656.
35. In parenthesis, one may comment that 160,000 ducats was by no means a small sum, even by the standards of the time.
36. Sigüenza, II, 443.
37. Sigüenza, II, 679.
38. For an outline of these myths, see Kamen 2008.
39. Álvarez Turienzo, p. 208.
40. *Chateaubriand's Memoirs (Mémoires d'outre-tombe)*, vol. 20, in the internet translation by A.S. Kline, 2006.
41. Ford, III, 1,206.

42. A.S. Mackenzie, *A Year in Spain, by a Young American*, 2 vols. London 1832, II, 410. Washington Irving, then in London, described it as 'quite the fashionable book of the day'.
43. Gautier, p. 107.
44. Quoted in Álvarez Turienzo, p. 199.
45. Both Menéndez Pelayo and Cánovas, quoted in Álvarez Turienzo, p. 199.
46. Miguel de Unamuno, *Andanzas y Visiones españolas*, Madrid 1988, p. 83.
47. It has recently been suggested that the portrait is not by Pantoja but by Sánchez Coello: Maria Kusche, 'El retrato cortesano', cited above in chap. 6, note 32.
48. Ford, III, 1,216.
49. Catalina left Spain in 1585, when she married the duke of Savoy; she died in 1597, to the immense grief of her father.
50. Longlée to Henri III, 30 Apr. 1588, in Mousset, p. 366.
51. Lhermite, I, 94.
52. Roy Strong, *Art and Power. Renaissance Festivals 1450–1650*, Berkeley: 1984.
53. Yates, p. 125.
54. As we have noted in Chapter 6, a procession was held in Lisbon in 1581 after Philip succeeded to the throne of Portugal, but neither this nor the handful of Spanish royal celebrations during the reign seems to have had 'power' as a theme.
55. A Spanish film of the year 2008 bears the title 'The Conspiracy of the Escorial'. However, the 'conspiracy' it describes had in fact nothing whatever to do with the Escorial.
56. Karel Čapek, *Letters from Spain*, London 1931, p. 20.

SELECT BIBLIOGRAPHY

Alberi, Eugenio, *Relazioni degli ambasciatori veneti al Senato*, Florence 1839–40

Álvarez, Vicente, *Relation du beau voyage que fit aux Pays-Bas en 1548 le prince Philippe d'Espagne*, ed. M.-T. Dovillée, Brussels 1964

Álvarez Turienzo, Saturnino, OSA, *El Escorial en las letras españolas*, Madrid 1963

Antolin, Guillermo, 'La libreria de Felipe II', *Boletín de la Real Academia de la Historia*, 90 (1927)

Armitage, David, 'The Elizabethan Idea of Empire', *Transactions of the Royal Historical Society*, 14 (2004), pp. 269–77

Bouza, Fernando, *Imagen y Propaganda. Capítulos de historia cultural del reinado de Felipe II*, Madrid 1998

Braudel, Fernand, *The Mediterranean and the Mediterranean World in the Age of Philip II*. 2 vols. London 1973

Brown, Jonathan, 'Felipe II, coleccionista de pintura y escultura', *IV Centenario del Monasterio del Escorial. Las Colecciones del Rey*, Madrid 1986

Brown, Jonathan, 'Philip II as Art Collector and Patron', in *Spanish Cities of the Golden Age. The Views of Anton van den Wyngaerde*, ed. Richard L. Kagan, Berkeley 1989, chap. 1.

Bury, J.B., review of Cornelia von der Osten Sacken, *San Lorenzo el Real de El Escorial: Studien zur Baugeschichte und Ikonologie*, *Burlington Magazine*, vol. 123, no. 939 (June 1981), pp. 366–7

Bustamante García, Agustín, *La octava maravilla del mundo: estudio histórico sobre el Escorial de Felipe II*, Madrid 1994

Cable, Mary, *El Escorial*, New York 1971

Cabrera de Córdoba, Luis, *Filipe Segundo, rey de España*. 4 vols. Madrid 1876–7

Calvete de Estrella, Juan Cristóbal, *El Felicissimo Viaje del muy alto y muy poderoso Principe Don Phelippe*, Antwerp 1552

Capponi, Niccolò, *Victory of the West. The Story of the Battle of Lepanto*, London 2006

Checa, Fernando, *Felipe II, maecenas de las artes*, Madrid 1992

Delmarcel, Guy, 'Le roi Philippe II d'Espagne et la tapisserie. L'inventaire de Madrid de 1598', *Gazette des Beaux-Arts*, vol. 134 (Oct 1999)

Edouard-Laurent, Sylvene, 'Mystique et providentialisme dans la représentation de Philippe II', online article in the Bulletin annuel des centres de recherches en histoire religieuse, *Chrétiens et Sociétés. XVIe–XXe siècles*, no. 8, 2001, of the University of Lyon 3

Eire, Carlos M., *From Madrid to Purgatory. The art and craft of dying in sixteenth-century Spain*, Cambridge 1995

El Escorial 1563–1963, 2 vols. Madrid 1963

Felipe II y el arte de su tiempo, Madrid 1998

Ford, Richard, *A Hand-book for Travellers in Spain and Readers at Home*, ed. Ian Robertson, 3 vols. Repr., Carbondale, Ill. 1966

Forneron, Henri, *Histoire de Philippe II*, 4 vols. Paris 1881

Gachard, L.P., *Correspondance de Philippe II sur les affaires des Pays-Bas*, 6 vols. Brussels 1848–79

Gachard, L.P., *Don Carlos et Philippe II*, Paris 1867

Gachard, L.P., *Collection des Voyages des Souverains des Pays-Bas*, 4 vols. Brussels 1876–82

Gachard, L.P., *Carlos V y Felipe II a través de sus contemporáneos*, Madrid 1944

Gautier, Théophile, *A Romantic in Spain*, New York 2001

Gil Fernández, Luis, *Panorama social del humanismo español (1500–1800)*, Madrid 1981

Goodman, David C., *Power and Penury. Government, technology and science in Philip II's Spain*, Cambridge 1988

Hänsel, Sylvaine, *Der Spänische Humanist Benito Arias Montano (1527–1598) und die Kunst*, Münster 1991

Hillgarth, J.N., *The Mirror of Spain, 1500–1700*, Ann Arbor 2000

Howarth, David, *Images of Rule. Art and Politics in the English Renaissance, 1485–1649*, Berkeley 1997

Iñiguez Almech, Francisco, *Casas reales y jardines de Felipe II*, Madrid 1952

Jardín y Naturaleza en el reinado de Felipe II, Madrid 1998

Jardine, Lisa, and Jerry Brotton, *Global Interests: Renaissance Art between East and West*, Ithaca, NY 2000

Jorzick, Regine, *Herrschaftssymbolik und Staat. Die Vermittlung königlicher Herrschaft im Spanien der fruhen Neuzeit (1556–1598)*, Vienna and Munich 1998

Kamen, Henry, *The Phoenix and the Flame. Catalonia and the Counter-Reformation*, New Haven and London 1993

Kamen, Henry, *Philip of Spain*, New Haven and London 1997

Kamen, Henry, *Imagining Spain. Historical Myth and National Identity*, New Haven and London 2008

Kubler, George, *Building the Escorial*, Princeton 1982

Lazure, Guy, 'Possessing the Sacred: Monarchy and Identity in Philip II's Relic Collection at the Escorial', *Renaissance Quarterly*, 60:1 (2007)

Lhermite, Jehan, *Le Passetemps*, 2 vols. Antwerp 1890–6

Los Leoni (1509–1608): Escultores del Renacimiento italiano al servicio de la corte de España, Museo del Prado, Madrid 1994

Mariana, Juan de, 'Del rey y de la institución real', *Obras del padre Juan de Mariana*, 2 vols. Madrid 1854 (Biblioteca de Autores Españoles vols 30, 31)

Merriman, R.B., *The Rise of the Spanish Empire in the Old World and in the New*, 4 vols. New York 1918–34, repr. 1962. Vol. IV: *Philip the Prudent*

Morales, Ambrosio de, *Viaje por orden del Rey D. Felipe II a los Reinos de Castilla, León, Galicia y Principado de Asturias*, Oviedo 1866

Morán, J.M. and Fernando Checa, *El coleccionismo en España: De la cámara de maravillas a la galería de pinturas*, Madrid 1985

Mousset, Albert, *Dépêches diplomatiques de M de Longlée, resident de France en Espagne (1582–1590)*, Paris 1912

Mulcahy, Rosemarie, *Philip II of Spain, Patron of the Arts*, Dublin 2004

Muñoz, Andrés, *Viaje de Felipe Segundo a Inglaterra*. ed. P. Gayangos. Madrid 1877

Noone, Michael, *Music and Musicians in the Escorial Liturgy under the Habsburgs, 1563–1700*, Rochester, NY 1998

Paris, Louis, *Négociations, Lettres et Pièces relatives au règne de François II*. Paris 1841 (Collection des Documents Inédits sur l'Histoire de France, Ier série)

Parker, Geoffrey N., *The Grand Strategy of Philip II*, New Haven and London 1998

Prescott, William H., *History of the Reign of Philip the Second*, 3 vols. London 1855

Quevedo, José, *Historia del Real Monasterio de San Lorenzo del Escorial*, Madrid 1849

Real Monasterio-Palacio de El Escorial. Estudios inéditos en conmemoración del IV Centenario, Madrid 1987

Rivera, Javier, *Juan Bautista de Toledo y Felipe II*, Valladolid 1984

Rodríguez, Pedro and Rodríguez, Justina, *Don Francés de Alava y Beamonte. Correspondencia inédita de Felipe II con su embajador en Paris (1564–1570)*, San Sebastian 1991

San Gerónimo, Fray Juan de, *Memorias*, CODOIN, Madrid 1845, repr. Vaduz 1964

Santos, Fray Francisco de los, *Descripción breve del Monasterio de S. Lorenzo de El Real del Escorial*, Madrid 1657

Sepúlveda, Fray Jerónimo de, *Historia*, ed. J. Zarco Cuevas, *Documentos para la Historia del Monasterio de San Lorenzo el Real*, vol. IV. Madrid 1924

Sharpe, Kevin, 'Representations and Negotiations: Texts, Images, and Authority in Early Modern England', *Historical Journal*, vol. 42, no. 3 (Sep. 1999), pp. 853–81

Sigüenza, José de, *Historia de la Orden de San Gerónimo*, 2 vols. Madrid 1907–9 (Nueva Biblioteca de Autores Españoles vols 8, 12). (Citations in the present book come from vol. 12 of the NBAE edition, cited as vol. II of the two-volume edition)

Spanish Cities of the Golden Age. The Views of Anton van den Wyngaerde, ed. Richard L. Kagan, Berkeley 1989

Strada, Famiano, *Guerras de Flandes*, 7 vols. Antwerp 1748

Strong, Roy, *The Cult of Elizabeth. Elizabethan portraiture and pageantry*, Berkeley 1977

Strong, Roy, *The Tudor and Stuart Monarchy: pageantry, painting, iconography*, 3 vols. Woodbridge 1995

Taylor, René, 'Architecture and magic. Considerations on the idea of the Escorial', in *Essays in the History of Architecture Presented to Rudolf Wittkower*, 2 vols. London 1967, vol. 1

Varey, Simon, ed., *The Mexican Treasury. The Writings of Dr Francisco Hernández*, Stanford 2000

Varey, Simon, Rafael Chabrán and Dora B. Weiner, eds, *Searching for the Secrets of Nature. The life and works of Dr Francisco Hernández*, Stanford 2000

Vilá y Tomás, Lara, 'Epica e Imperio. Imitación virgiliana y propaganda política en la épica española del siglo XVI' (unpublished Ph.D. thesis of the Department of Philology, Autonomous University of Barcelona, 2001; available online)

Weiss, Charles, *Papiers d'Etat du Cardinal de Granvelle*, 9 vols. Paris 1841–52 (Documents Inédits pour l'Histoire de France)

Wilkinson Zerner, Catherine, *Juan de Herrera. Architect to Philip II of Spain*, New Haven and London 1993

Yates, Frances, *Astraea. The imperial theme in the sixteenth century*, London 1975

Zarco Cuevas, Fray Julián, ed., *Documentos para la Historia del Monasterio de San Lorenzo el Real*, 4 vols. Madrid 1924

INDEX